AF544866

DESIGNING A PHOTOGRAPHIC STUDIO

DESIGNING A PHOTOGRAPHIC STUDIO

Evelyn Roth

AMPHOTO
AN IMPRINT OF WATSON-GUPTILL PUBLICATIONS, INC./NEW YORK

Picture credits:
Chris Callis's Studio: All photographs © Chris Callis
David Langley's Studio: All in-studio photographs © Zander Lane
Cigar advertisement photograph © David Langley. Advertising agency: Fallon, McElligot, Rice. Art director: Mike Fazenda.
Car stereo system advertisement photograph © David Langley. Advertising agency: Ogilvy and Mather/Chicago. Art director: Rich Adkins.
Clint Clemens's Studio: All photographs © Clint Clemens
Eric Meola's Studio: All photographs © Eric Meola
Craig Stewart's Studio: All photographs © Craig Stewart
Michel Tcherevkoff's Studio: All photographs © Bill Schick and Jens Johnson
J. Barry O'Rourke and Robert Kligge's Studio: All photographs © J. Barry O'Rourke and Robert Kligge
Robert Wigington's Studio: All photographs © Robert Wigington
Jay Silverman's Studio: All photographs © Jay Silverman
Westside Studio: All photographs © Rich McKechnie
WFM Studio: All photographs © William F. Miller

First published 1988 in New York by AMPHOTO,
an imprint of Watson-Guptill Publications,
a division of Billboard Publications, Inc.,
1515 Broadway, New York, NY 10036

Library of Congress Cataloging in Publication Data
Roth, Evelyn.
Designing a photographic studio.
Includes index.
1. Photography—Studios and darkrooms—Design and construction. I. Title.
TR550.R67 1988 771′.1 88-16717
ISBN 0-8174-3786-X
ISBN 0-8174-3787-8 (pbk.)

Manufactured in Japan

1 2 3 4 5 6 7 8 9 / 96 95 94 93 92 91 90 89 88

Edited by Liz Harvey
Designed by Jay Anning
Graphic production by Hector Campbell

INTRODUCTION

Rarely, if ever, can it be argued that an interior setting comes about randomly. In contemporary Western society, there is a growing sensitivity to good design. The environment that a person chooses to live or work in speaks volumes about that individual's sense of self. And, our outer trappings are the best indicator of who we would really like to be.

For professional photographers—and the clients who seek them out—a studio's appearance is an important visual indicator through which the very nature of a business can be discerned and evaluated. A studio can be a photographer's premier showcase. On the simplest level, reception areas and client lounges often double as gallery space for the photographer's most exciting endeavors. Of course, the strongest signals are often the most subtle.

Chris Callis's pastel-colored enclave with its warm, nonstylized layout is extremely unusual in a profession populated by white, high-tech spaces. Its quirky furniture and profusion of unique knickknacks, many of them designed and built by the photographer himself, are a clear manifestation of Callis's highly creative side as well as his determined pursuit of an economical yet original solution.

Similarly, the space that photographers J. Barry O'Rourke and Robert Kligge share conveys much about the way the two conduct their business. Dividing start-up costs and rental expenses—in order to produce an ideal workplace without decimating individual cash flows—is a resourceful solution to a problem that both beginning and experienced photographers face continually. The astute client can be sure that this same enterprising sense is reflected in O'Rourke and Kligge's photographic solutions.

A studio's organizational structure is another indisputable indicator of professionalism and quality. It's important in understanding whether the photographer has a sense of his or her own, as well as the client's, needs. A well-stocked, thoughtfully run studio, complete with an efficient staff and a supply of amenities, can only reflect positively on the photographer.

By extension, a space that is well suited to the work done within it—such as large shooting areas for photographers who specialize in vehicular photography; a well-equipped kitchen for food photographers; or a smaller, brightly lit location for those who concentrate on tabletop shooting—is proof that the photographer has a realistic knowledge of the services he or she provides.

Of course, the most important indicator is the final product, the photograph itself. Even the most spectacular studio can't create stellar images; that job rests solely on the photographer's shoulders. And, outstanding images can, of course, be produced in almost any environment. Good photographs have far more to do with knowledge, talent, skill, and equipment than with individual facilities. But once a business is established, promotional pieces can't counteract the impression a poorly run, badly equipped, unsuitable studio will make.

All the photographers interviewed for this book emphatically agree that initial costs, as well as monthly outlay, can be prohibitive. But none of them regrets the expense involved. In a field as visually oriented as photography, with its emphasis on fine design and attention to detail, the well-conceived workplace can be a photographer's greatest asset. In the final analysis, a professional photographer presents his or her portfolio and studio to the world, and it is upon them that craft and professionalism are most often judged.

BUILDING A STUDIO

Born in Northern California near Sacramento, Chris Callis decided to become a photographer during a tour of duty in Vietnam. When he was discharged, he returned to California, settled in Los Angeles, and attended the Art Center College of Design. At the same time, he assisted fashion photographer Jean Pagliuso. But assisting didn't provide enough of a challenge, and after a while Callis set up shop in his living room, quit school, and went out on his own. Through friends in the record industry, he began getting work shooting album covers. But it seemed to Callis that the real challenges were available on the east coast; so, in 1974, he moved to New York City. **F**or the next three years, Callis worked out of a small studio in the Chelsea section of the city. His client list grew to include such magazines as *Viva*, *New York*, *Geo*, and *National Lampoon*. These assignments, coupled with a slow but steady stream of album covers from his California contacts, required him to look for larger quarters.

A bank of windows provides ambient light for the front portion of Callis's shooting stage. The table and chairs were constructed by the photographer and are perched on wheels, allowing Callis to move the furniture anywhere in the studio.

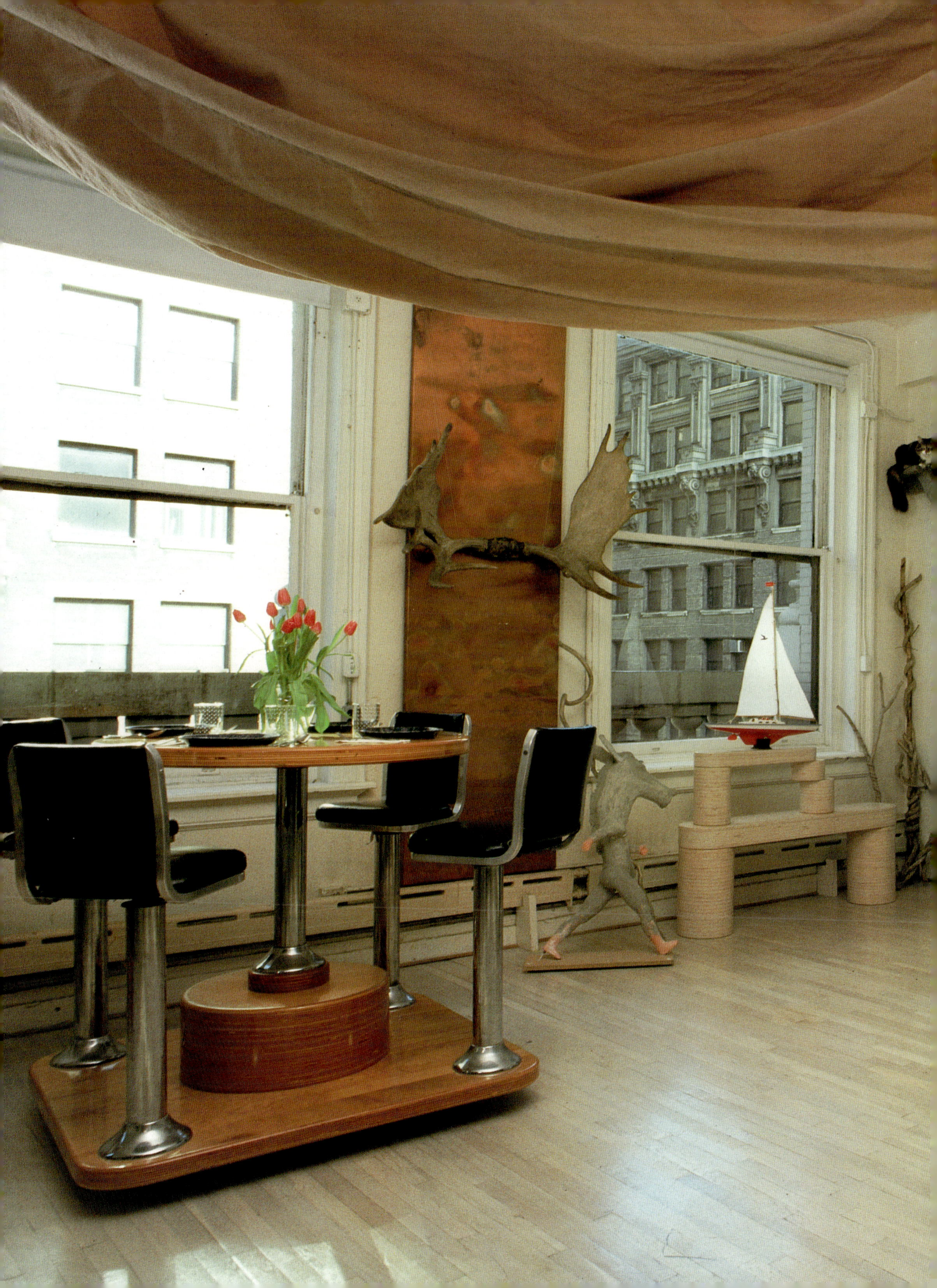

FINDING A SPACE

In 1977, Callis began to search for that eternally elusive Manhattan commodity: more room. He found a loft that offered 3,200 square feet of space in a neighborhood that was then known as the men's garment district and was considered predominantly commercial. However, because many of the lofts were empty, artists and photographers were moving in.

Although the transition took a few years, the neighborhood is currently known, informally, as the photo district because of the preponderance of shooters and the attendant support services that have sprung up nearby. At the time, though, "the space was really much bigger than I needed," recalls Callis; he decided to live in his studio as well as work in it.

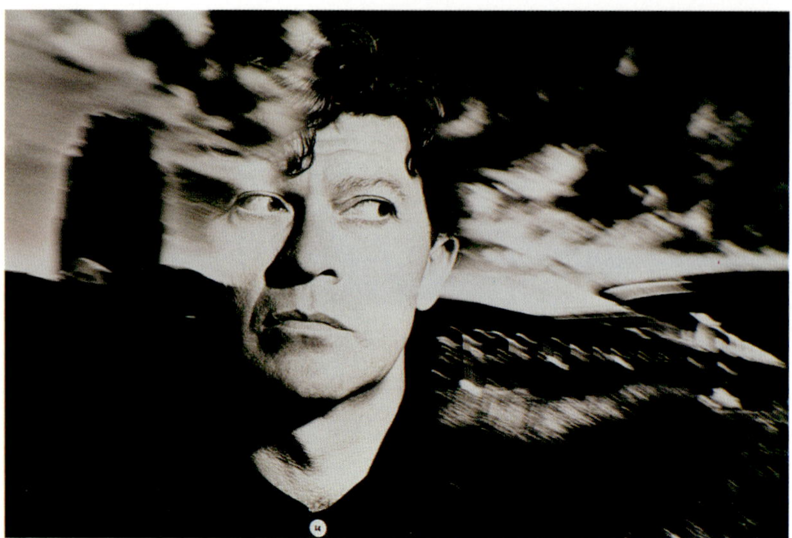

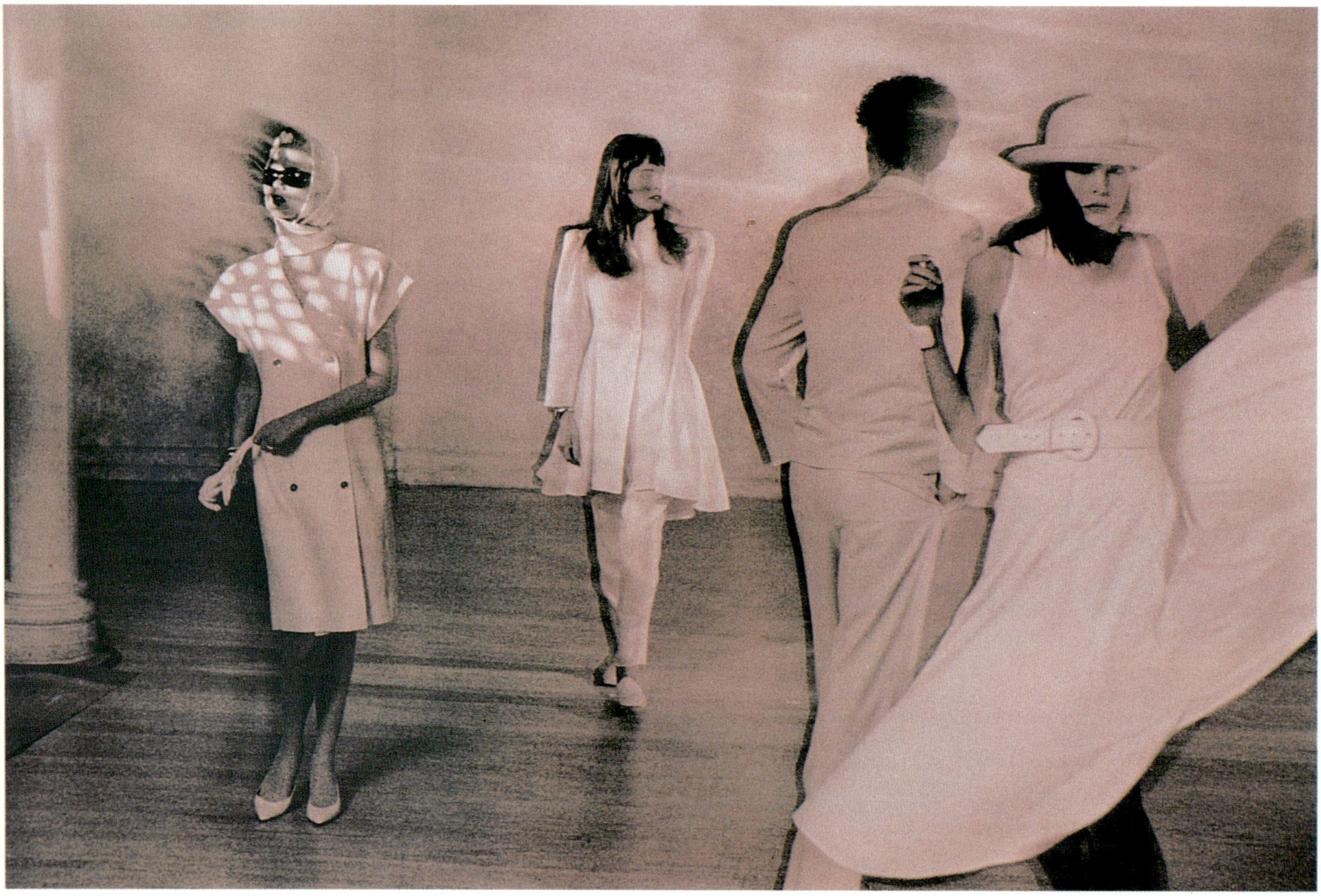

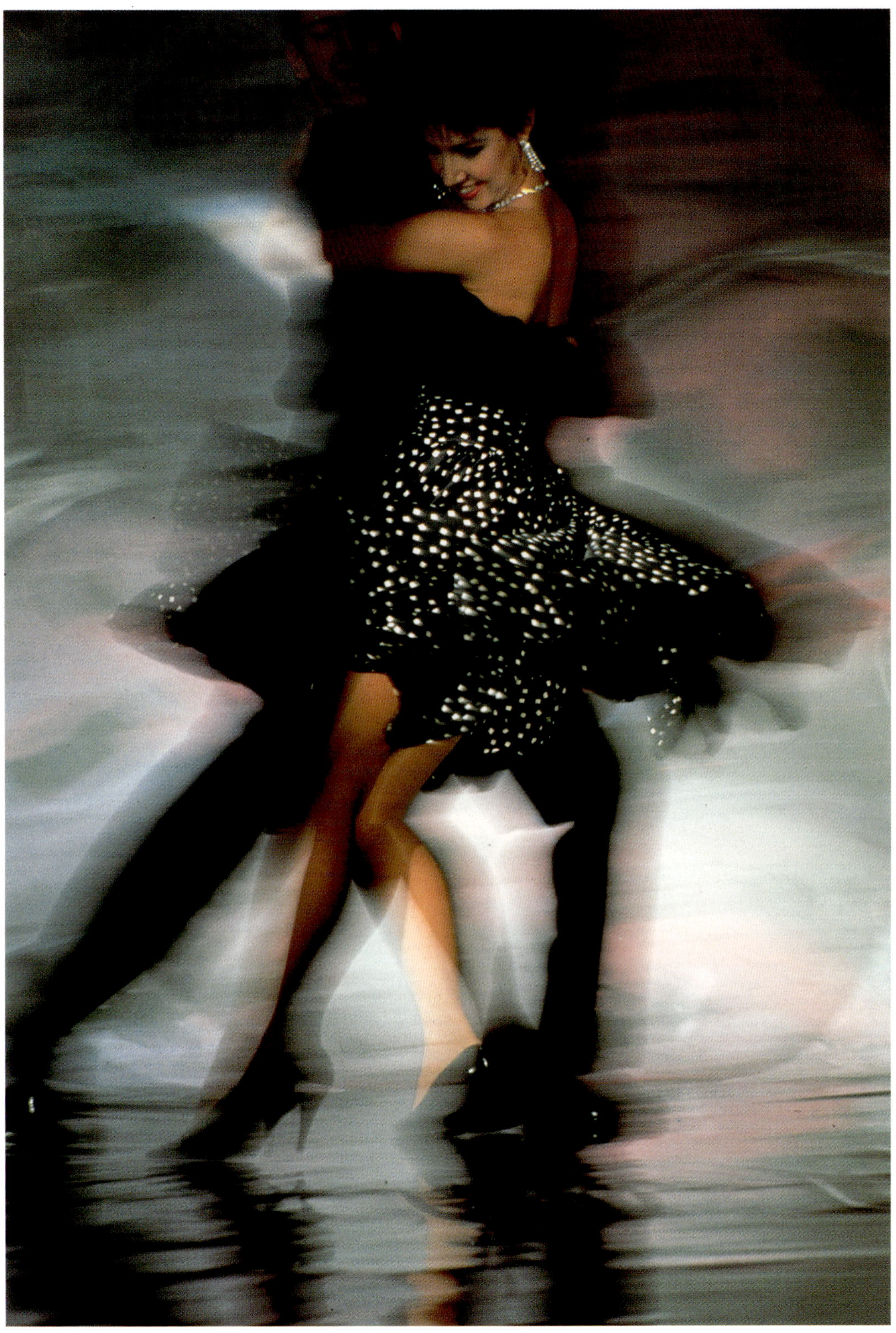

Chris Callis's adept handling of light and his skill with a wide range of subjects—from portraiture to fashion—have made him sought after by editorial and commercial accounts.

ACHIEVING A PERSONAL STYLE

Finding a satisfactory location is only a first small step in setting up a working studio. Equipping and designing it require more capital than the rent. A large sum of money was one thing Callis did *not* have. But he'd always designed and built props for himself, and he didn't lack initiative. And, given the vagaries of a beginning freelance business, he also had free time.

The first indication that Callis's New York City studio isn't a standard, slick photographer's enclave strikes visitors immediately after they step out of the elevator on the seventh floor of the lower Fifth Avenue building in which Callis lives and works. There, behind a pastel pink door that bears a plaque with the photographer's name, is a breezy, Southern California-like interior that says, "The man who owns this knows what he wants."

The comfortably idiosyncratic studio, painted in various pastel tones, bustles with activity. On this particular day, there are seven different setups, to be used for a variety of commercial and editorial shoots. The studio also contains props and trophies—many of them handmade by the photographer—from Callis's favorite shoots, and reveals as much about his distinctive, clever, and humorous work as it does about Callis himself. Relying on his ingenuity and his ability to create, Callis decided to build many of the studio's props and design features. The actual construction took a number of years and a great deal of effort.

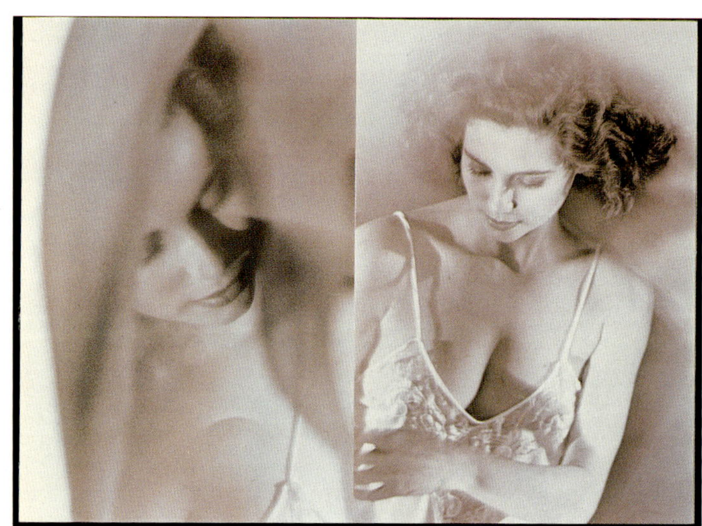

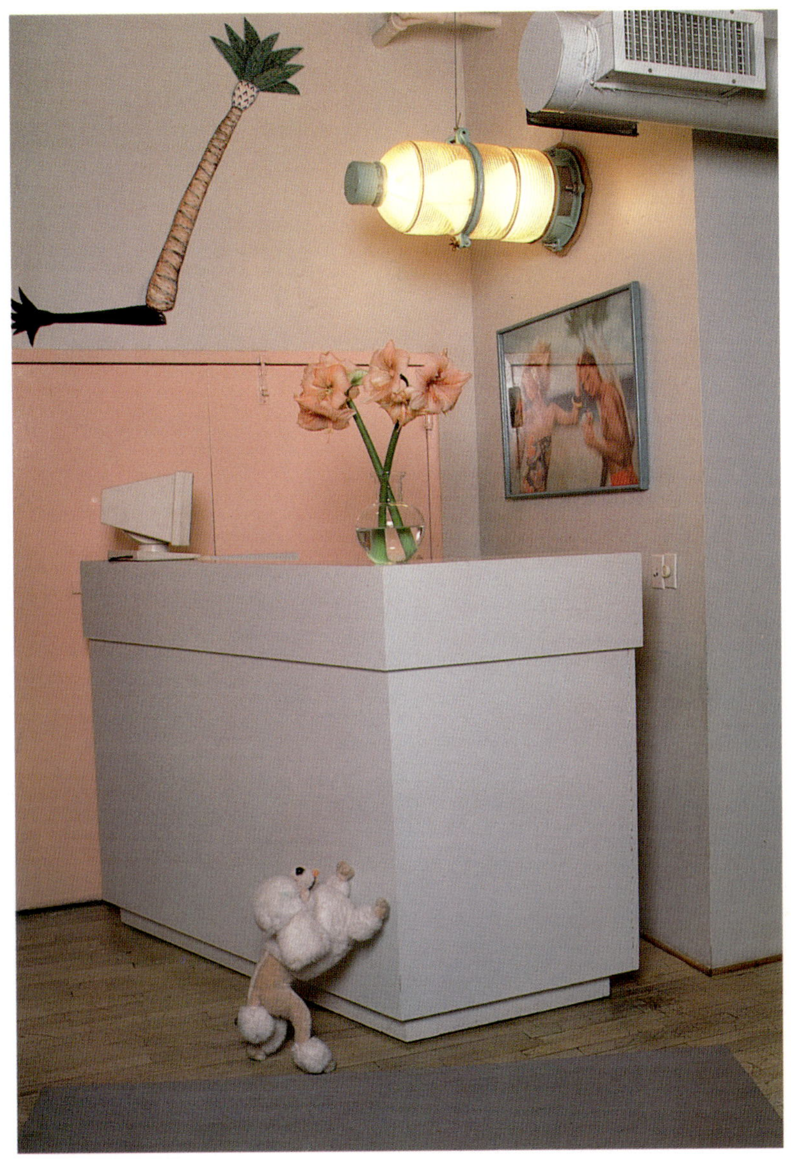

Chris Callis's reception area reflects the easygoing attitude of the entire studio's design. The poodle has become something of a studio mascot and often appears in the photographer's pictures.

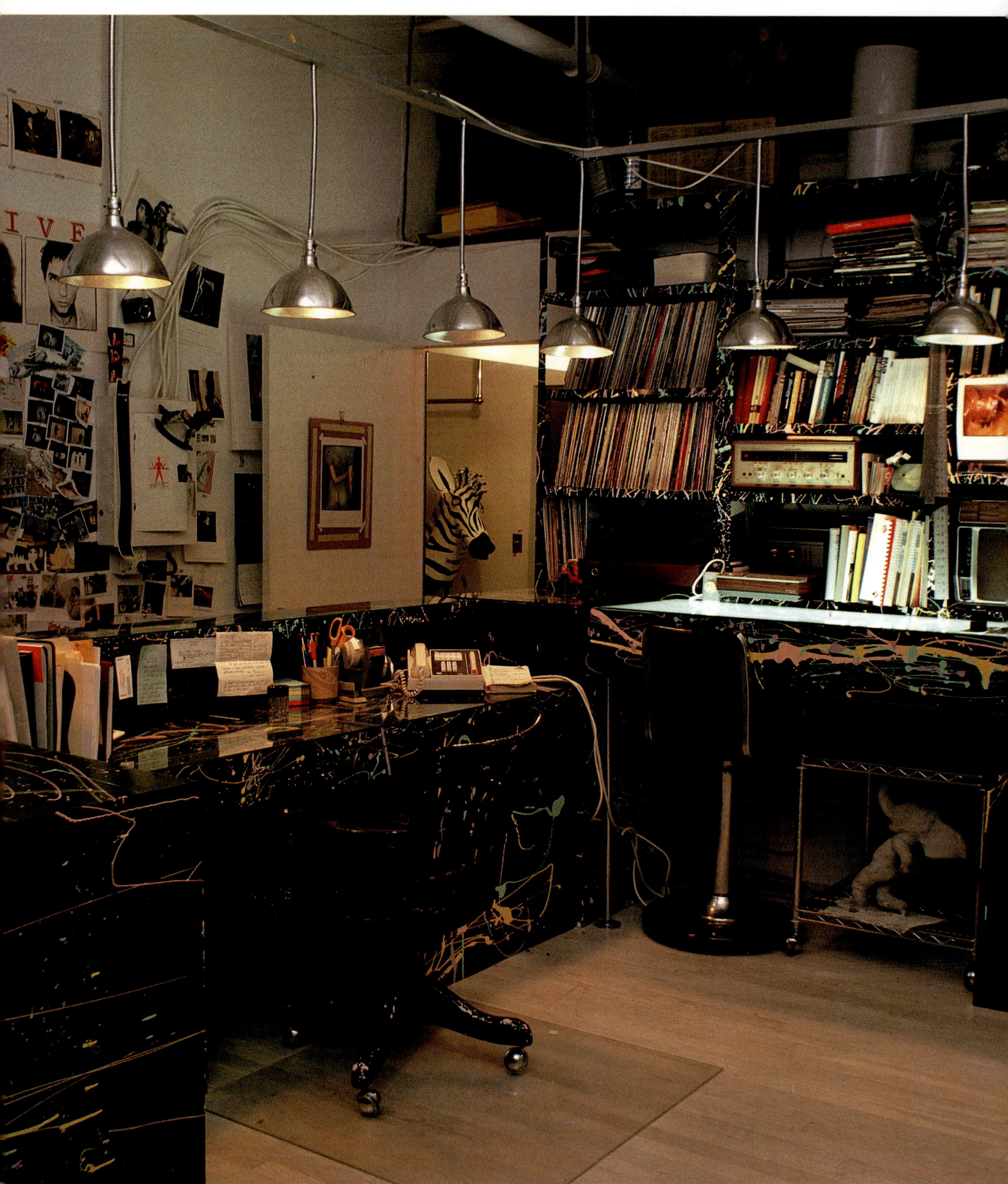

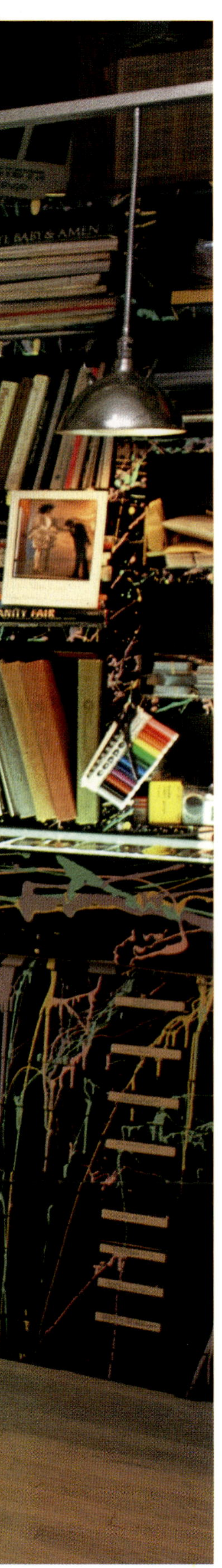

CREATING A RELAXED ENVIRONMENT

Callis's requirements were actually fairly simple. "I wanted to keep the space open and flexible," he says. "At first, all I really needed was an area to work in and a shop in which to construct my various projects. I knew I didn't have a chunk of cash," continues Callis. "So I found an engineering student who had completed his B.A. and was about to begin work on his M.A. For approximately $12,000, he did the plumbing, the wiring, and put up the walls." During his free time, Callis spackled and painted.

"Soon after that I got a $10,000 job," recalls the photographer. "I put that entire sum into the floor." And so, unlike many professional shooters who set up their own studios only after they have a complete master plan, Callis's space grew as his business needs grew.

When jobs came in, Callis took them. When things were slow, he worked on the studio's interior. During an extended free period, Callis built the darkroom—in which all of his black-and-white work could be processed—and a dressing room, so that models, stylists, hair and makeup people, and portrait subjects could have a comfortable workspace of their own.

"Initially, I hadn't included an office in the studio's design," he says. "That room was used for storage and as my shop. When I got busier, I hired an assistant to do mailings, billing, and other sorts of paperwork. He needed a place in which to work. So I moved the shop over to the opposite side of the studio."

"When I set up the office, I wanted it to have a big light table," says Callis. He had allocated a 2 × 8-foot space for the table. As a result, it required a custom-made unit, but, says the photographer, "I didn't have the money to buy something that fancy, so I built it myself." Callis's budget was so small that it didn't include buying a complete set of office furniture either. He purchased used metal shelving and a secondhand filing cabinet. "At the time, I had a lot of cheap plywood left over from a shoot, so I built the desks and work tables with it." But the wood was not high quality, and the surfaces, though more than adequate, were not visually appealing. Callis disguised the irregularities by painting the furniture black, then randomly splattering it all with a variety of colors, creating an upbeat, easygoing environment in the process.

The walls of the office were equally drab. With typical Callis ingenuity the photographer solved two problems at once. He took all his rolls of seamless, lined them up according to color, and carefully mounted them into sockets he had devised and meticulously attached along two of the office's four walls. This rainbow of hues echoes the splattered tones that adorn—and disguise—the office furniture and enhances the relaxed environment that makes Callis's studio such a pleasant place in which to work.

The photographer's studio was beginning to reflect Callis's personality. Like the man himself, it conveyed an attitude that was at once professional, yet comfortable and friendly. The studio was becoming the sort of place where clients, models, and staffers enjoyed spending time.

The main office in Callis's studio was furnished with used items that he'd purchased at deep discount. To jazz up the stark, often battered items, Callis splattered pastel-colored paint on the black surfaces.

Certain rooms in the studio began to serve in more than one capacity. Accordingly, the kitchen underwent an evolution. Designed at first for Callis's personal use, it was a tiny space that could barely contain the basic appliances—refrigerator, sink, and stove—the photographer had installed. But where there's a kitchen, there should be a table. So, after casting around for a likely spot, Callis devised a counter arrangement in a nearby alcove that would otherwise have been too cramped to be of much use. There, the photographer installed a table, soldering it diagonally into the juncture where two walls meet. Seven stools were attached, and an eat-in area that juts out of the corner was created. In this way, Callis overcame his space problem without infringing upon the more important work areas. At the same time, he managed to make use of what might otherwise have been a dead section of the studio. Finally, and perhaps most importantly, the photographer provided his studio with a pleasant enclave in which visitors and staffers could congregate, away from the office and the sets. "This rapidly became *the* area where people wanted to sit," Callis says with a grin. "I guess you could say it became the family room." And if the day were slow or if a shoot were finished, Callis would invariably cook lunch, with his most frequently requested recipe being pesto lasagna.

"We like to have real china at meals," the photographer acknowledges. "I don't mind, since I consider it a family time. The hard work and long hours we put in warrants it," Callis says. "Eventually, I realized we needed a dishwasher." The kitchen was redone, and new appliances were installed.

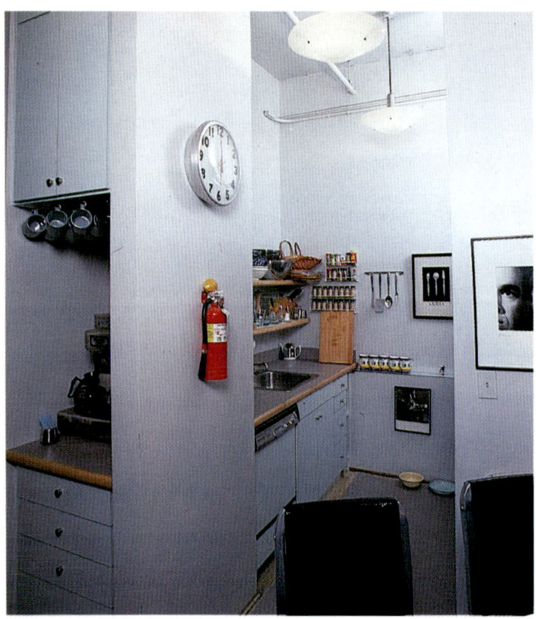

Though small in size, Callis's kitchen contains all the necessary appliances, including a newly installed dishwasher.

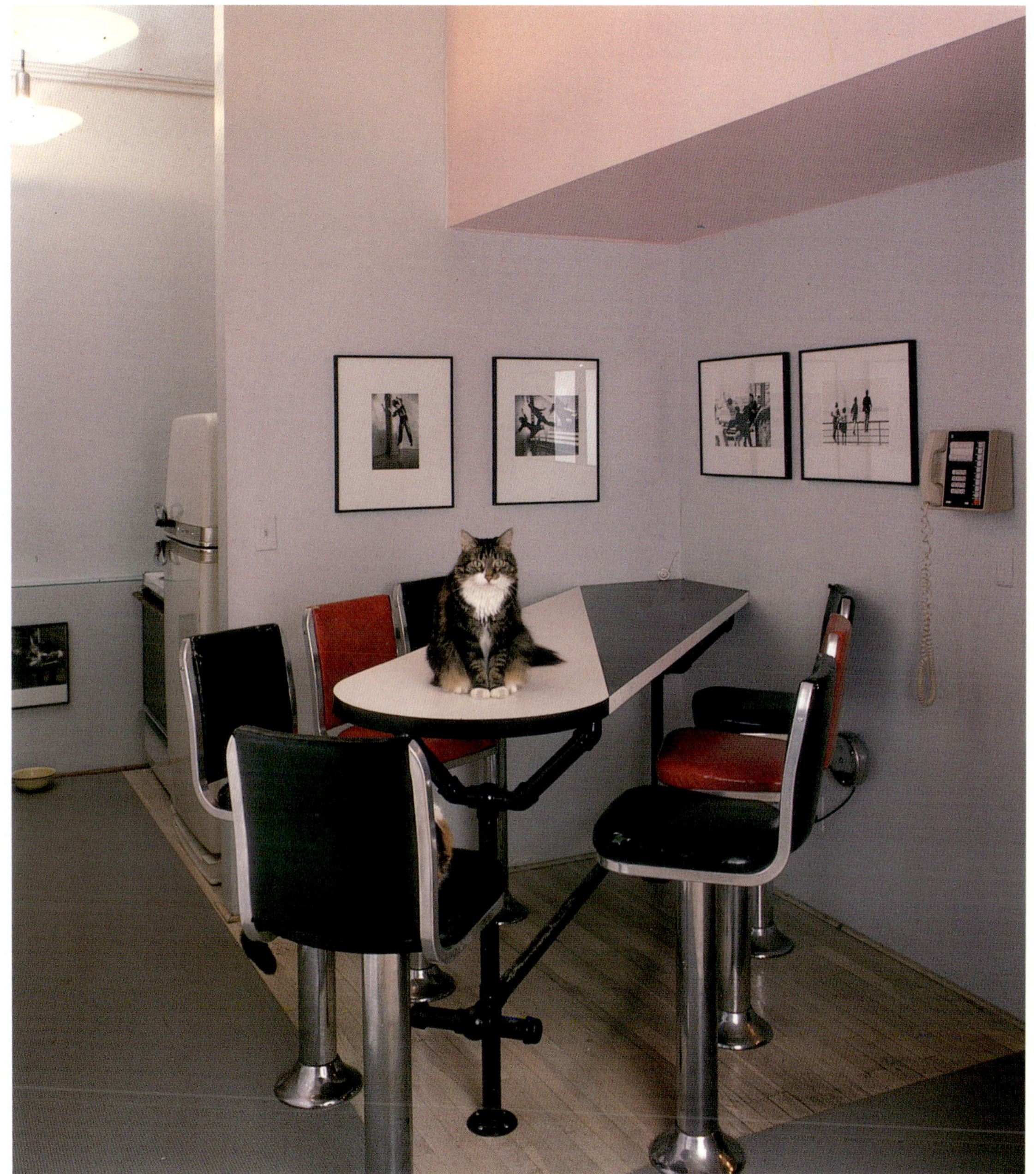

Callis realized that the small alcove next to his kitchen was too small for a regular table and chairs. Therefore, the photographer built a counter that juts out of a corner, utilizing the space to maximum effect. The counter seats six comfortably and is located immediately outside the kitchen.

Of all the well-used sections within Callis's studio, the room he considers most important is his workshop. As in the kitchen, the shelving is not enclosed, so that tools and utensils are part of the visual display. "I like things to be open, with everything I use right there," he explains. In keeping with his philosophy of "cluttered but organized," there's an assortment of hammers, pliers, screwdrivers, saws, T-squares, and wire occupying a pegboard along one wall. This same wall also contains a number of bins into which small hardware is neatly segmented. Along the room's work surfaces are drills, jigsaws, and various tools for doing specialized carpentry.

The number and variety of items that have been created within this room are a testament to Callis's ability to make something useful out of almost anything; he turned an old golf bag caddy into a moving tripod from which he can make photographs of shoes at ground level, while the model walks around unhindered. Callis has also built an overhead rail system with moving platform so that he can shoot scenes from above his studio. A full-sized rowboat, smoothly crafted and sleekly finished, has also emerged from the shop, as has a roving, in-studio lunch counter that consists of a round table and four barstools mounted to a small platform on wheels. Perhaps, though, it is the diversity of lighting equipment that is the most impressive element of Callis's workshop.

Beginning in 1982, Callis formulated what he calls, for lack of a better term, his "philosophy of light." Before that, he worked in any style requested by the client. But in developing this new way of approaching his work, the photographer has been able to imbue his images with distinctive results that have become trademark lighting techniques. In order to create "the look"—an amalgamation of projected light, strobes, movement, and mixed light sources—the photographer has often had to modify or alter his existing lighting equipment. His well-appointed shop allows him to make these changes at a moment's notice.

The shelves that line the outer wall of Callis's studio, as open as those in the kitchen and workshop, are filled with the results of his experiments, and various metal and wood strobe housings can be found next to assorted cameras, film backs, and modeling lights. Should a visitor assume that the items visible here are Callis's entire inventory, the photographer assures the individual that this is not the case. "I have a storage bin at another location that is filled with my least active equipment," he says.

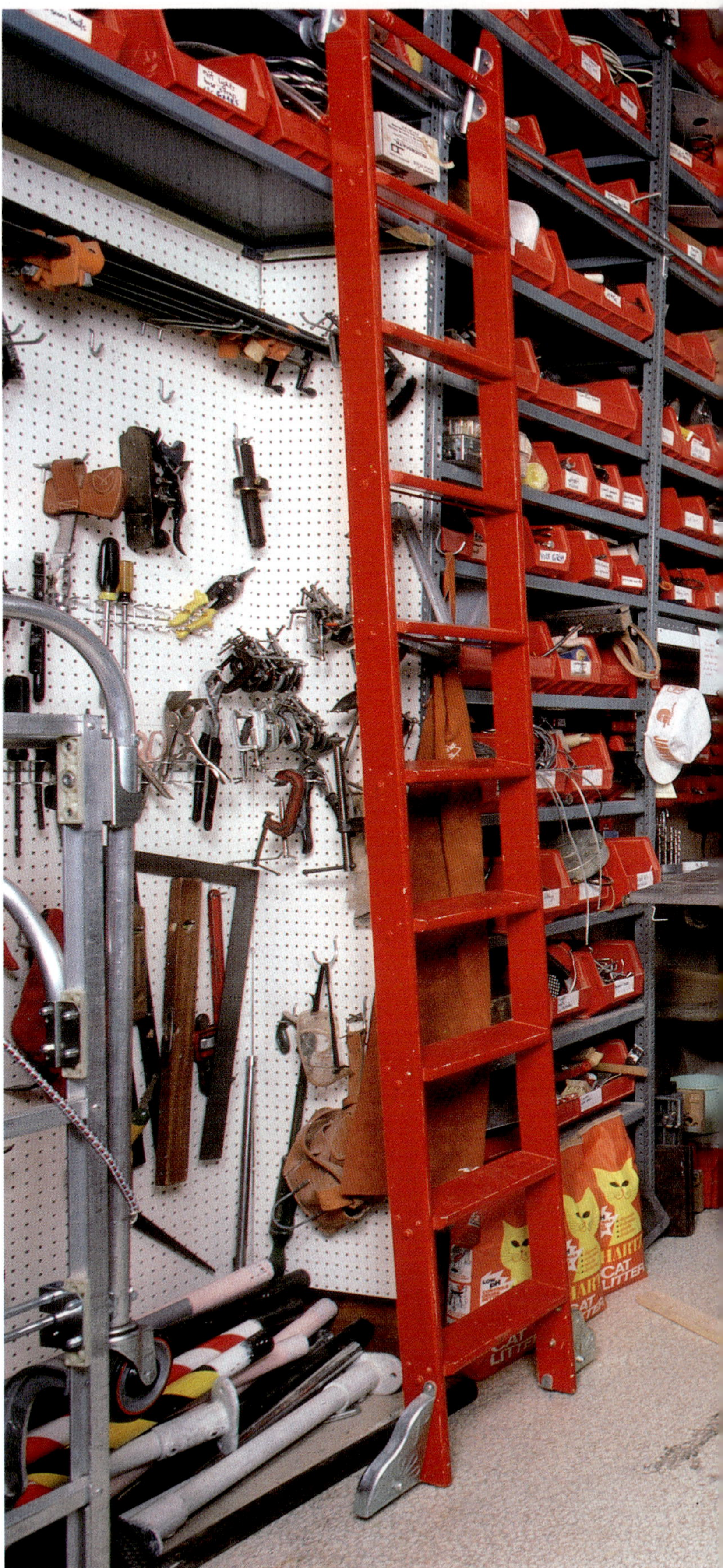

Perhaps the most important room in Callis's studio is his workshop.

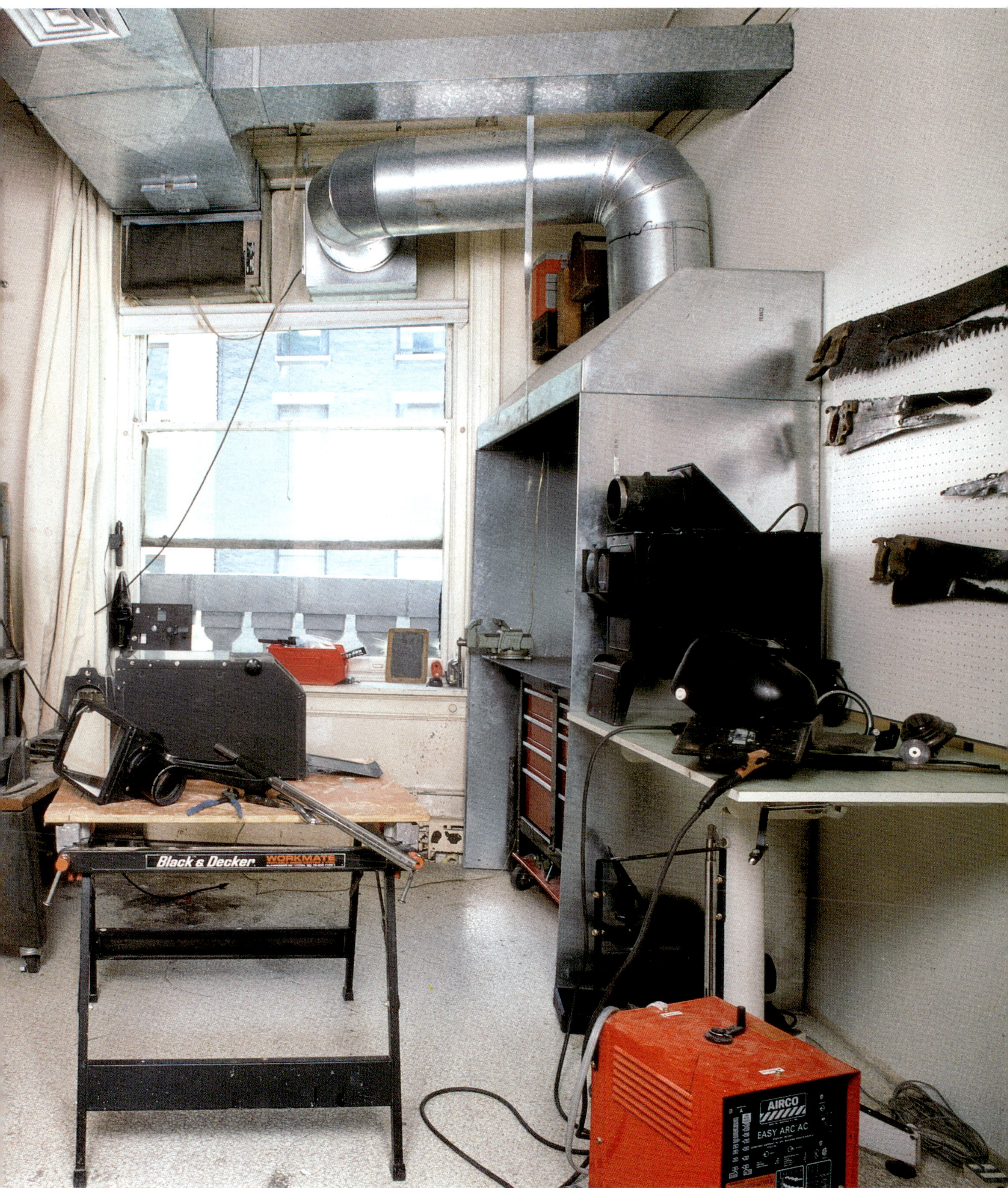
Black & Decker
WORKMATE
AIRCO
EASY ARC AC

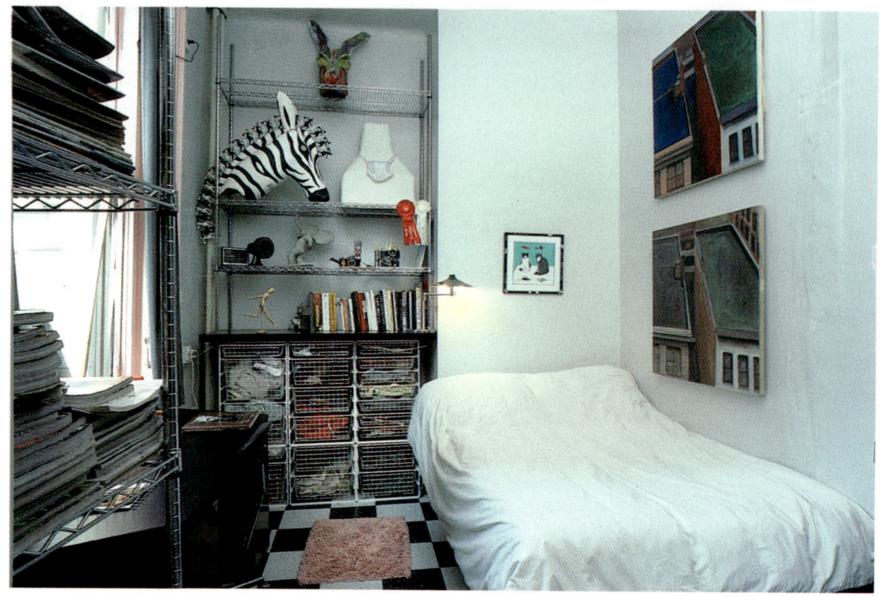

Callis's bedroom is small but unique. All of his equipment is carefully displayed on open shelving immediately off the shooting stage (opposite page).

The only room that has remained the same throughout the studio's evolution is Callis's bedroom. It appears to be the smallest area within the larger environment and contains nothing more than a bed, desk, and shelving, not only for clothing, but also for a collection of odd items that Callis has found, bought, or built over the past ten years. Many of these—including a toy poodle, three custom-made "gimmick" cameras (all built by Callis), and an oversized zebra head—have appeared as props and/or subjects in at least one of Callis's photographs.

In the ten years since he moved into his studio Callis estimates that he has spent only $50,000 in small increments to bring it to its current, work-efficient state. His first expenses went toward the physical design of the environment. Currently, he's either updating equipment or modernizing the office setup.

Within the last three years, Callis's volume of business has increased to such an extent that his in-house staff has grown sixfold. Where once there was just enough work for one assistant, Callis now employs a studio manager whose duties include the production and organization of shoots, the casting of those shoots, and the attendant paperwork; a first assistant who hires freelance help, oversees the construction of all sets, and maintains the film stock; a second assistant who sets up backgrounds, acts as a "gofer" and takes care of studio clean-up; and "the great luxury of my success," says Callis: a full-time darkroom person whose job involves processing all black-and-white negatives and prints from current assignments as well as a twenty-year inventory of negatives that has remained, until now, unprinted. This person might be called on to assist in the studio as well. A receptionist answers all phone calls and maintains Callis's growing mailing list.

The surest sign of the photographer's success might just be symbolized by the most recent addition to his studio: his rep's office. Callis's in-house agent formulates all Callis's promotional mailings, obtains and negotiates his assignments, maintains client contacts, and oversees the dissemination of the twenty-two portfolios that highlight a number of Callis's specialties, including fashion, portraits, commercial work, and black-and-white portraiture. Current commercial clients include DuPont, Redken hair products, Hanes hosiery, Valentino clothing, Avon, and Seagrams. A steady flow of editorial work continues to come from *Vogue*, *Rolling Stone*, *Parenting*, *Spy*, and *Manhattan, Inc.*

The office Callis once built to accommodate a single assistant now contains job and print files, accounting resource books, a copying machine and dry mount press, and assorted mail boxes. A bookkeeper will soon be hired to supplement Callis's staff, and the work that was once done by hand is now taken care of by five computers run on the BOSS system. Meals are no longer prepared by the photographer, but rather are brought in by an outside caterer.

By all accounts then, Chris Callis has definitely found and successfully met the professional challenges he was looking for when he left California. He's the first to acknowledge that he is indeed in an enviable position. Yet for him, a large measure of his success is embodied by the studio that he painstakingly built. "There's something wonderful to me about it, simply because I built it myself," Callis says. "I'm proud of this studio precisely because it came out of a time when I wasn't working and I didn't have much money." That, then, might be the secret behind his success: for Callis, the final two-dimensional result is nowhere nearly as exciting as the three-dimensional process of putting it all together.

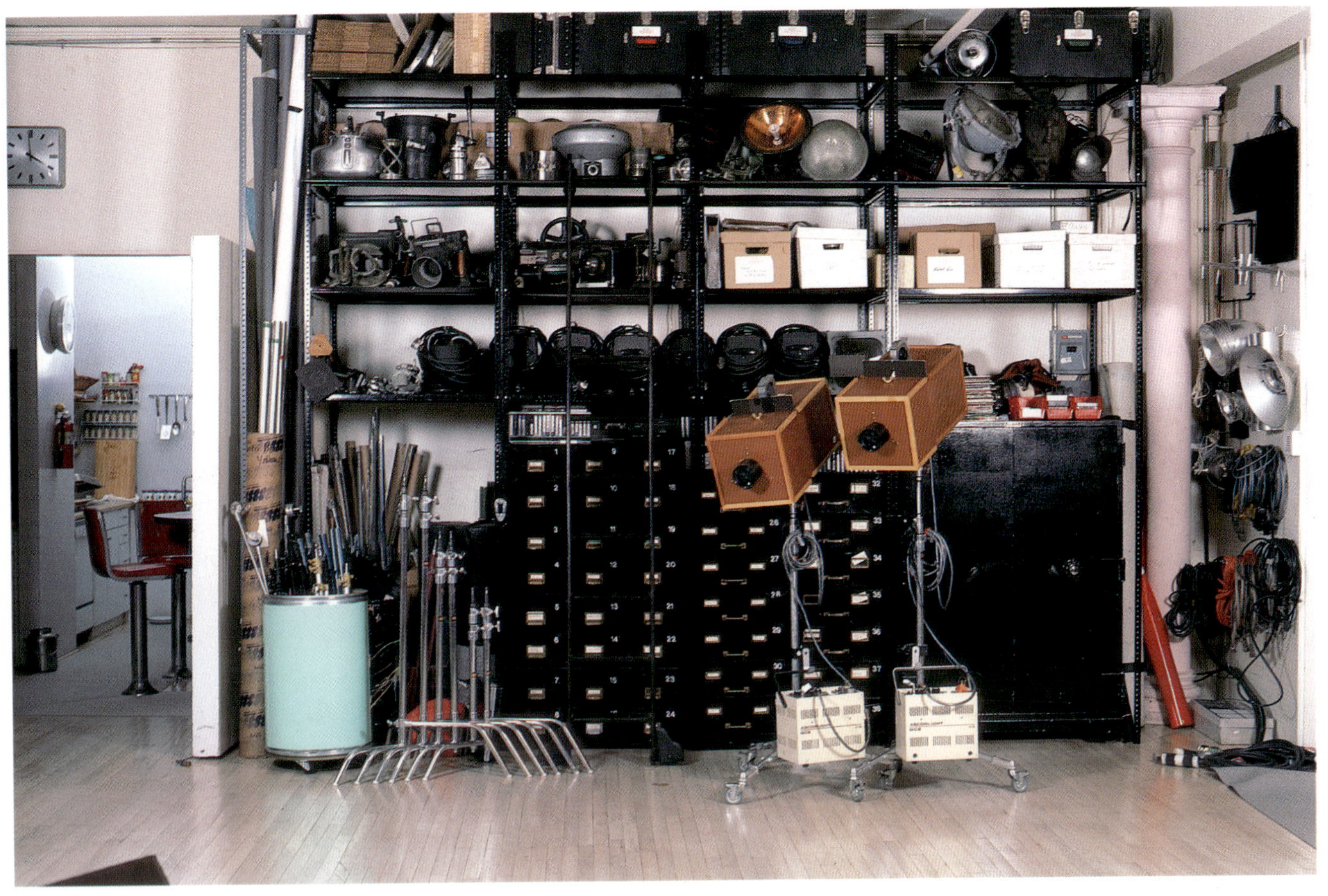

Callis has definitely found and successfully met the professional challenge he was looking for when he left California.

TRANSFORMING A MODEST STUDIO

Hell's Kitchen is a rough, undeveloped, lower-class neighborhood on New York City's West Side. It isn't chic, but it is within walking distance of midtown Manhattan. And, for photographer David Langley, whose imagination and extraordinary perseverance brought him to this neighborhood, it offered a large industrial space perfect for his type of commercial work. **L**angley has been a photographer since the 1940s. "I wormed my way into a photographer's job in the army because it seemed easier than carrying a gun, which I ended up having to do anyway," he says. The young private had studied horticulture at Cornell University, but found that he enjoyed photography more.

David Langley relaxes at the garage entrance of his upper West Side studio in Manhattan.

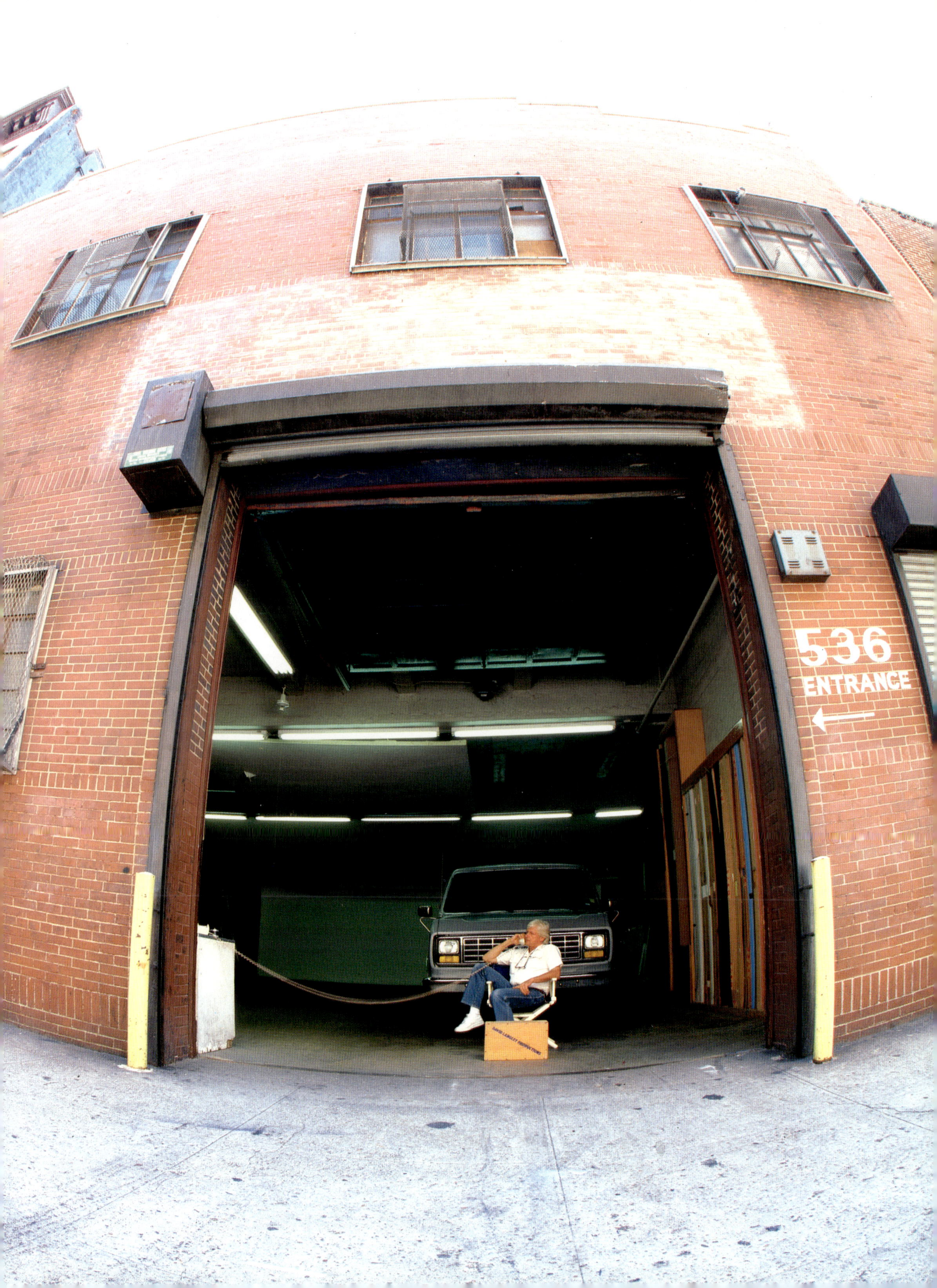
536
ENTRANCE

After Langley's discharge, he supported himself by assisting another photographer and taking wedding pictures. Langley also did a lot of street shooting in an effort to discover his photographic forte. "During this time, I became what I am today: a picture *maker*, not a picture taker," he explains. "I just couldn't relate to street shooting and the random discoveries that are at its core." Instead, Langley saw himself as a photographic problem solver. His strengths, he realized, lay in providing art directors with the images they wanted. "At first, because I was working from sketches made by others, I felt like an automaton," admits the photographer. "But I realized that if these people could take their ideas further, or if they understood how to work the photographic process, they'd do what I'm doing themselves." Langley was indeed providing a worthwhile service, thereby becoming a "hard-core picture maker."

At the same time, the photographer began honing his craft, both to better himself and to find a unique position within commercial photography. "I started to really look at advertising pictures," recalls Langley. "And I noticed that a strong aspect of the images done during this period (the late 1940s) was the element of contrivance, of a lack of spontaneity, that existed throughout commercial photography." Langley became aware that the imagery that featured models rarely reflected real life. "I wanted to imitate Norman Rockwell's ability to paint in the nuances of gesture that conveyed spontaneity," says Langley. The photographer—who for the past 3½ years had been assisting—finally found the niche he was looking for.

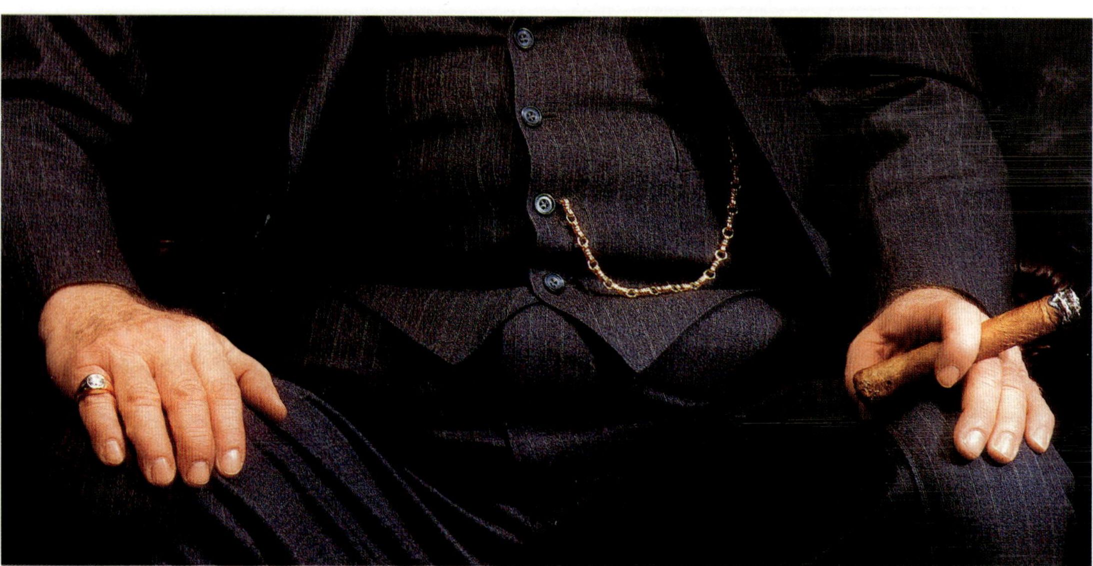

An eye for texture and fine detail is just one of the hallmarks of a Langley photograph.

IMPROVING THE INTERIOR

Langley left his job as a photographer's assistant in order to strike out on his own. He teamed up with Dick Stone, a New York City-based graphic designer. The pair worked out of midtown Manhattan in a two-room studio that had a total of 350 square feet. Langley built a tiny darkroom in the space and, with the small sum of money he had left, bought a minimal amount of equipment. The team's initial efforts resulted in a joint portfolio that brought in their first clients. When business got even better in the late 1950s, the two moved to a bigger space, renting 1,800 square feet in the more residential upper East Side.

Once again, Langley and Stone constructed the interior themselves. "Where the first studio had low ceilings and low amperage, this one had, by comparison, infinitely more space," notes Langley. And, he adds, "It was here that I made all of my interior design mistakes." One of the biggest problems with this larger studio was the profusion of structural columns built to support the ceiling. "I learned that pillars were the death knell of commercial shooters," Langley points out. "You must have a big, open space in which to effectively work." But, at the same time, the barnlike interior suited Langley's working methods. "Since the studio was spacious but not highly designed, I could drive nails into the floor without the slightest regrets, or paint the floor a different color if that's what a shot required," explains the photographer. "It was here that I developed a belief in abusing the space for the betterment of the final picture."

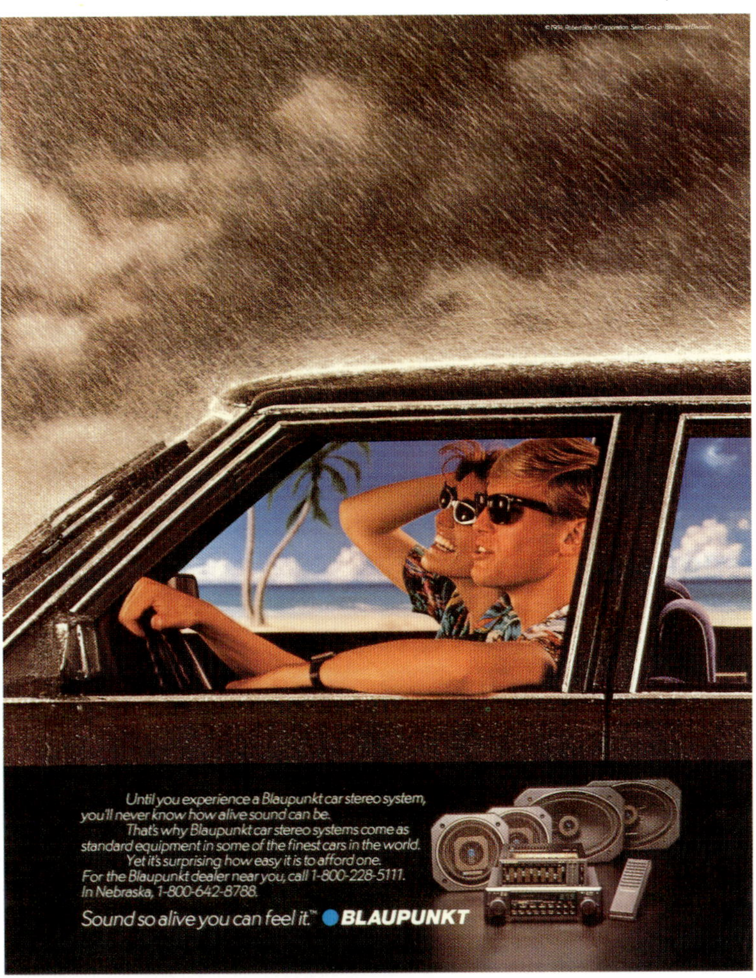

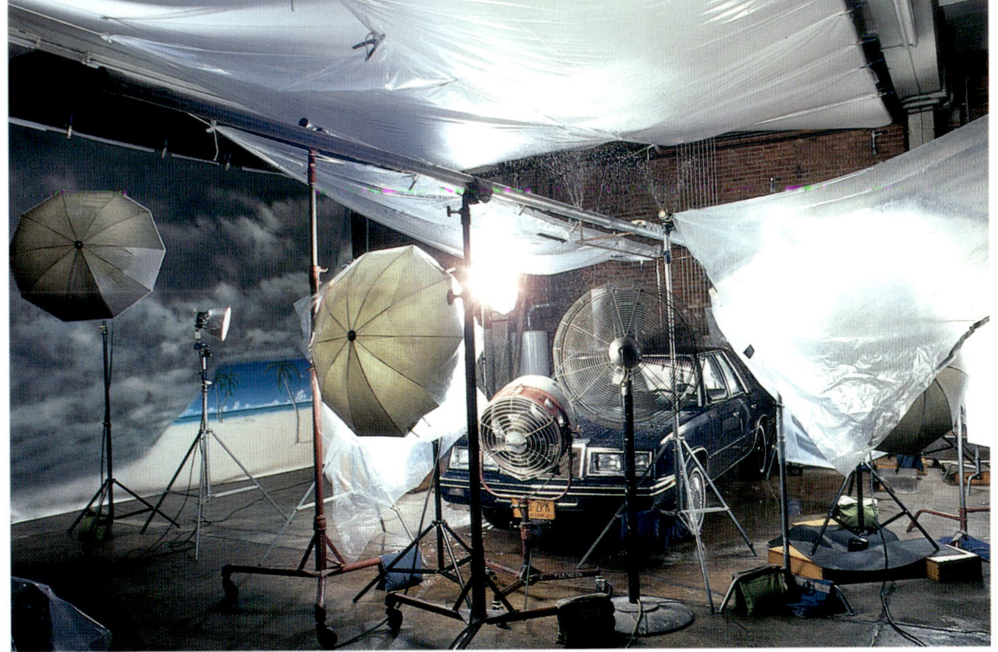

An "outdoor" ad was actually done entirely inside Langley's studio. His ground-floor shooting stage is large enough to accommodate the rigging for the setup plus hoses, fans, backdrops, models, staff, and photographer, not to mention the size and weight of an entire automobile.

For the next eight years, Langley and Stone shared a particular point of view and developed a reputation in film as well as stills. In 1966, however, the pair agreed to separate. "I was more involved in the film aspect," recalls Langley, "but I still wanted to make a statement in advertising photography." He rented 10,000 square feet of studio space in New York, set up his new business, and proceeded to shoot both stills and film. Yet, as much as he told himself that he could continue to work in both media, he began to concentrate on film. Over the next eight years, Langley made approximately 175 commercials. "The first seven years were fine," notes Langley. "By 1976, though, I had a gnawing desire to return to stills." But while he focused his energies on filmmaking, his photography business had foundered. His portfolio had become dated, and many of his clients had gone elsewhere. On top of this, Langley's landlord began to give him trouble, and the two ended up in court.

"Suddenly, I was forced to think about starting over," says the photographer. On New Year's Day 1977, on a rundown street in Hell's Kitchen, the beginnings of an opportunity presented itself. "I was just strolling around when I saw a 'For Rent' sign in front of this large, empty building," explains Langley. "I stood on a milk crate, peeked through the grimy window, and saw a raggedy space, but one which had large doors suitable for vehicles to drive through, high ceilings, and no columns—in short, a place that was dying for a photographer's studio. I set my heart on it."

This was an audacious wish, coming from a man who "didn't have a current portfolio, whose production company had died, and whose print business was moribund." Nevertheless, Langley met with the children of the elderly owner, who had constructed the space in 1947 out of two turn-of-the-century brownstones. Since then, the family had been using the space as a truck body shop. To make it viable for the repair business, the family had added a reinforced concrete floor, and a crane and track that expedited lifting. The location featured a shower and drain system. "The owner must have had me in mind when he built the space," Langley says, smiling. "It had everything I needed."

Unfortunately, Langley didn't have the necessary cash. He didn't lack determination, though. "I knew this was my shot at starting over," he says. "I proposed renting the building from them with an option to buy. They wanted only to sell." But his strong desire for their father's building impressed the sellers who, although eager to sell the property, were looking for someone who would love the building as much as their father had. In Langley they found the ideal buyer.

They worked out an agreement wherein Langley, by borrowing money, would make the down payment, and the sellers would take out the mortgage. "It was a dream come true," says the still incredulous Langley.

The first small, albeit significant step had been taken. Yet, in order to work in the studio, Langley needed to renovate it. The reconstruction would cost a substantial amount of money, however, and that could come only from work. "Therefore, my biggest priorities became increasing my income and revamping my portfolio," notes Langley. The photographer spent the next month locating back issues of magazines that featured his best advertising images. Then, he says, he "put together a super book" with the clippings. He took his new portfolio to the people he had worked with earlier, and many of them gave him assignments. The resulting fees went directly into his new studio.

"It cost me $20,000 just to clean the grease off the floors, sandblast the walls, and repair the heaters," Langley says. "In addition to that, I had to consider power needs, heating costs, darkroom expenses, plumbing repairs, workshop supplies, and an extensive security system." Operating costs for the first six months were close to $100,000. "And I arrived at that figure by carefully budgeting and really cutting corners," he says.

His modest studio grew as his business did. Langley altered his initial plan—to turn the second story of the building into a loft—in order to accommodate his increasing need for a larger work area. The ground floor, with its ability to sustain an unlimited load and its enormous drive-in entryway, features 4,000 square feet of shooting space. As Langley shows visitors this portion of his studio, he points out the cavernous atmosphere (enhanced by the 16-foot ceiling), the exposed brick walls, the concrete slab floors, and the lack of any design scheme. "A studio's interior design has everything to do with a photographer's personality," he says. "I like my space to be rough, so I can abuse it and know that it will always bounce back."

In an effort to keep the space as flexible as possible, Langley made sure that only one rod from which backdrops can be hung was suspended from the ceiling. When he needs a cyclorama, the photographer hangs a sheet of linoleum, the back of which has been painted white. "I size and angle it as needed," Langley explains. "I do the same with bank lights: I build them according to the shooting circumstances. In this way, I'm not restricted by my equipment, and I avoid having every shot look exactly the same."

To the left of the shooting area is a large workshop crammed with tools and hardware. Here, sets are created and bank lights are constructed. Next to the workshop are three film-handling rooms. The first and smallest is used for film loading and contains a refrigerator stocked with film; from this room, visitors can enter the film-processing room or the darkroom. Between these rooms and the shooting floor is a large open space in which Langley stores props, flats, and assorted pieces of equipment.

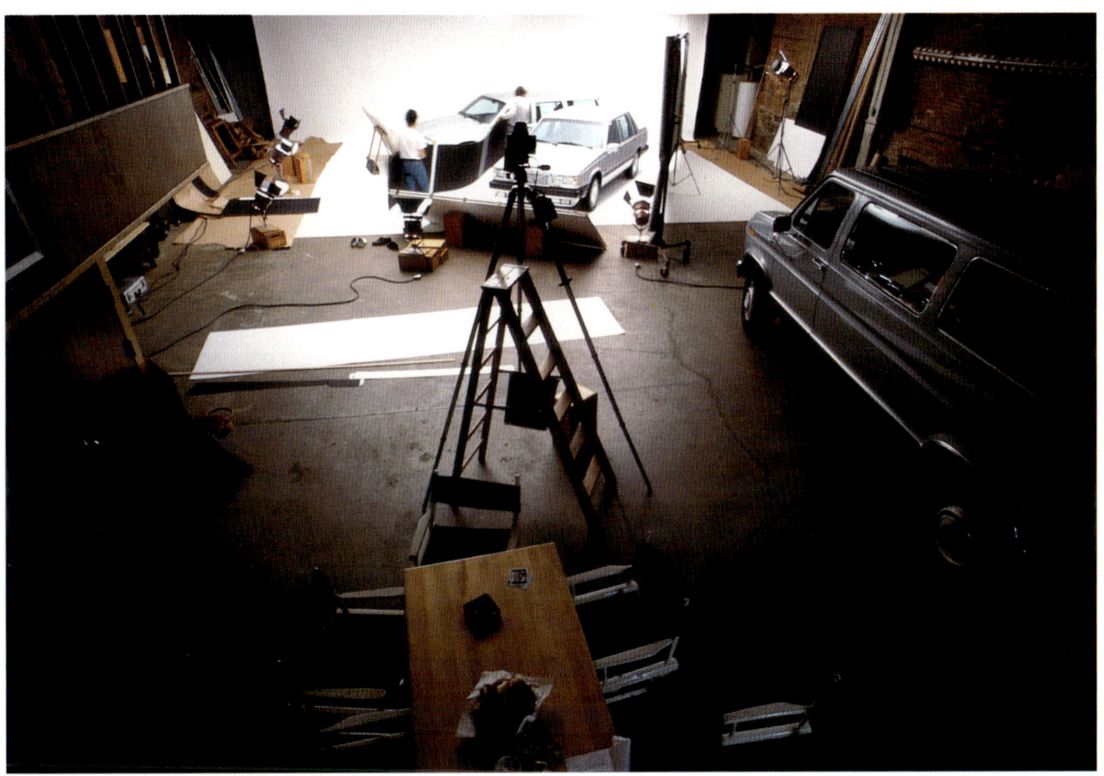

Langley's large shooting stage affords him great flexibility when he sets up shots.

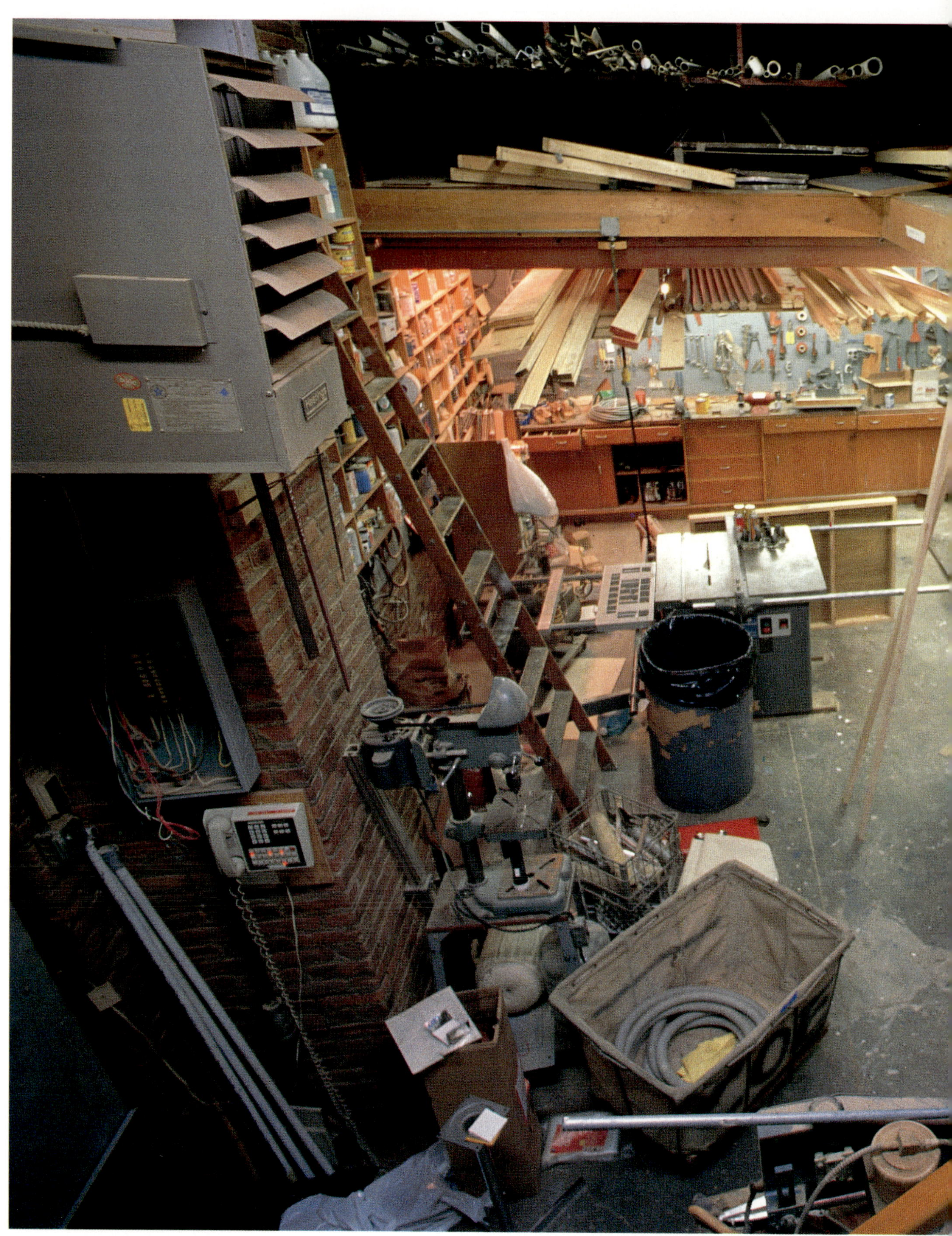

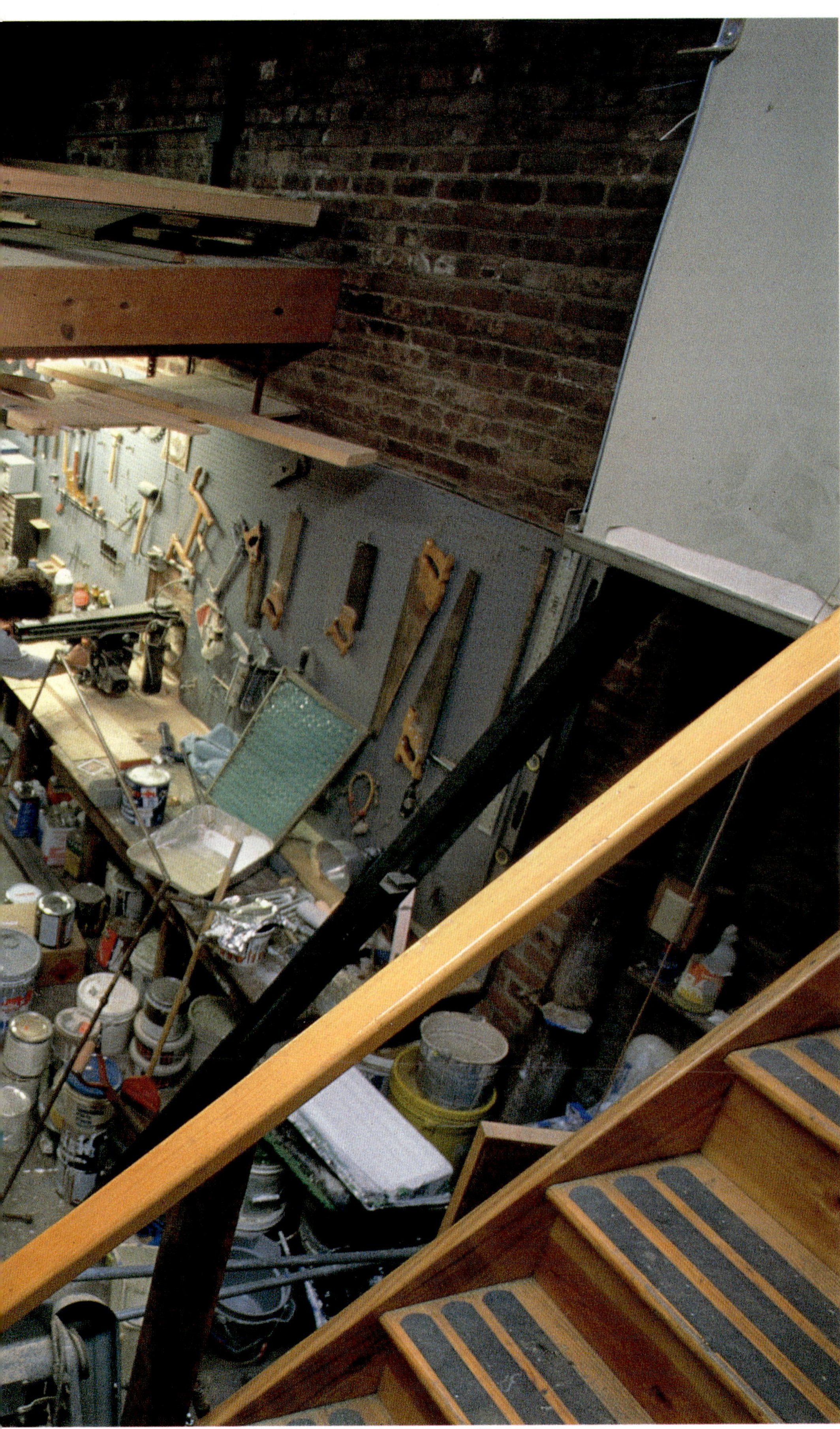

Langley's in-house workshop sees a variety of activities, including construction of backdrops and modification of props.

SPECIAL FEATURES

One of the most important parts of the studio is a sizable elevator shaft (located in the far left corner) that contains a crane. Langley makes good use of this feature, which had been an integral part of the building in its previous incarnation. The photographer hoists equipment and sets with the crane and moves oversized subjects, such as pianos, to the second floor. Opposite the shaft is a small room where Langley conceals his photographic equipment. In contrast to the randomly stored flats and props at the back of the studio, this space is orderly and well maintained, with each piece carefully stored and easily accessible.

The contrast between the first and second floors is immediately apparent. The ground floor is well lit and intentionally spartan; the second floor is dark and, although equally spacious, the 16-foot ceiling is riddled with tracks and cables that remind visitors of the studio's industrial origin. Without a doubt, though, the most striking feature is the well-cared-for, fully stocked bar that sits on a low platform running along the right wall. Langley, laughing a bit sheepishly, explains that he purchased it when he was still planning to live in the studio. The bar came from a tavern in Queens that was going out of business. "Although the purchase price was very cheap, I knew when I bought it that it was a white elephant," admits Langley. "But owning a bar had always been a dream of mine."

The photographer disassembled the counter, mirrors, cabinets, refrigerators, and taps, loaded all of this into his truck, and hauled them back to his Manhattan studio. He stripped and refinished everything, purchased bar stools and turn-of-the-century light fixtures, and lovingly duplicated the original saloon. "I realized that I was spending too much money on refurbishing it," says Langley, "but it's been fantastic for clients." Indeed, while in most studios staff members and visitors tend to congregate around the kitchen or lounge area, Langley's assistants and guests find the bar to be the undisputed focal point of his studio. As an accessory, the bar is an original within the photography business. According to Langley, the circumstances surrounding a shoot may be quickly forgotten, but "Dave's Bar" is remembered.

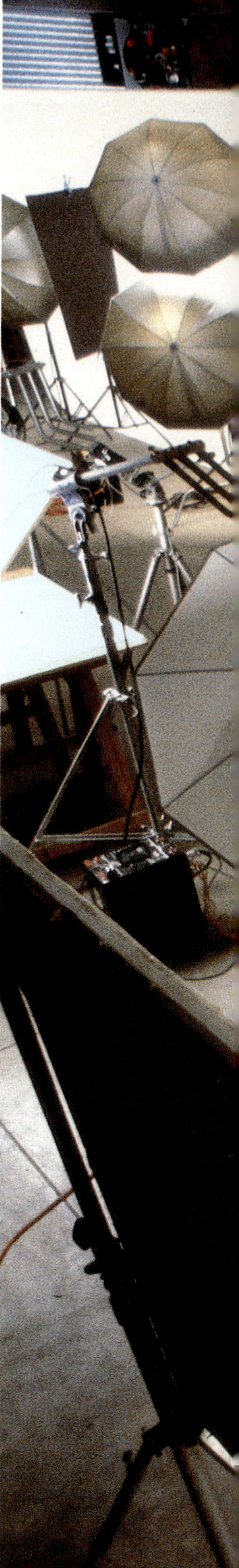

The second-story studio is often used to accommodate more than one shoot at a time. Three different setups can easily be worked on: a portrait session, a tabletop shoot, and a small print piece. Notice Langley's bar in the upper right.

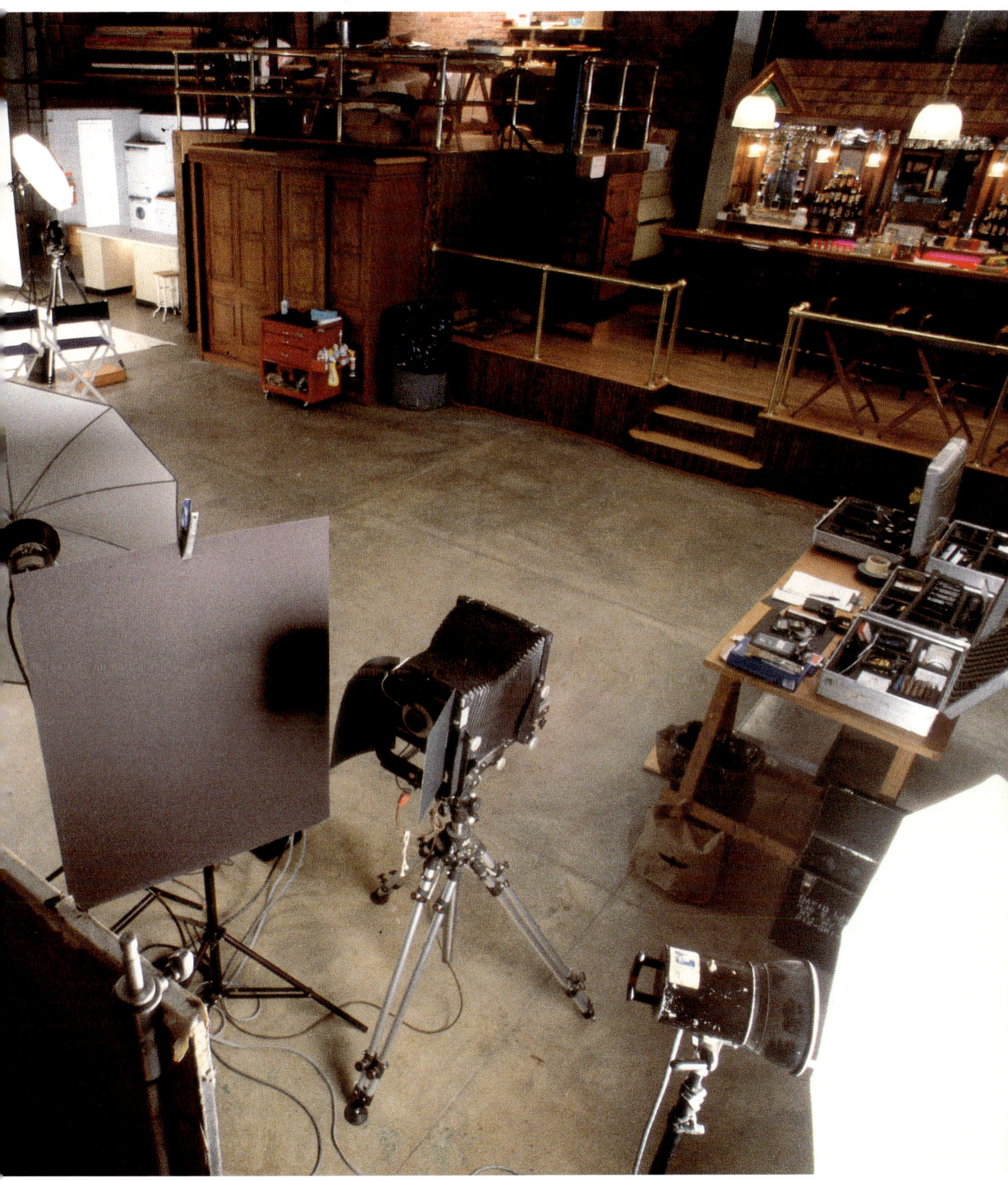

Langley and his staff make efficient use of the production area to accomplish a number of administrative tasks.

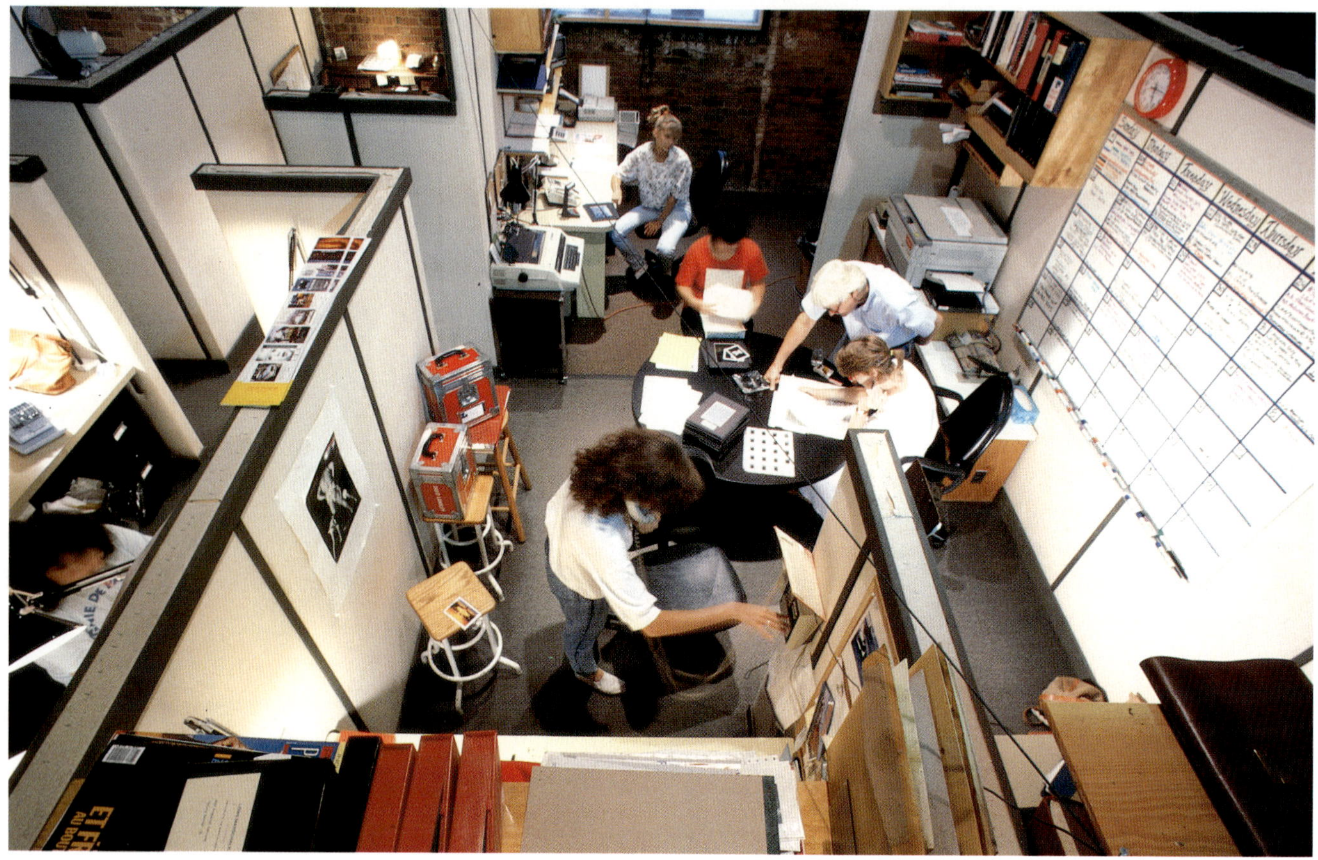

The bar offers an unobstructed view of 5,000 square feet of shooting space. A spiral staircase at one end leads up to a production loft where portfolios and promotion pieces are put together. Beneath the loft is Langley's office (which at one time doubled as his bedroom) and a kitchen complete with washer and dryer. The front section of the space contains the staff members' cubicles. The reception area is also located here, along with the copying machine, computers, and a large bulletin board on which a month's worth of jobs and appointments are carefully penciled in.

"Obviously, size is important to me," notes the photographer as he takes in the enormity of his space. "I can have work going on up here while the next shoot is being set up downstairs." He says that he can run up to eight jobs at one time: five smaller sets on the second floor and three larger ones downstairs. His studio has accommodated cars for such clients as Ford, Subaru, Toyota, and Porsche + Audi. Langley has also shot an elephant, a 29-ton swimming pool, and, for IBM, 400 prolific rabbits. And the bar became the set for an ad touting WCBS-TV's local New York City news program and for a series of proposed Miller beer advertisements.

Today, ten years after he acquired the building, Langley has a staff of eight, including a studio manager, a full-time assistant, a production coordinator with two assistants, a receptionist, a full-time maid, and a bookkeeper. The photographer also has a thriving business, an exemplary commercial venture, and an enviable studio setup.

As Langley moves through his studio, overseeing preparations, commenting on lighting, or consulting with his production coordinator, he is visibly proud of his "big, crude space." Not only is this his ideal working environment—the result of years of trial and error—it is the tangible representation of the rebirth of his extraordinary career.

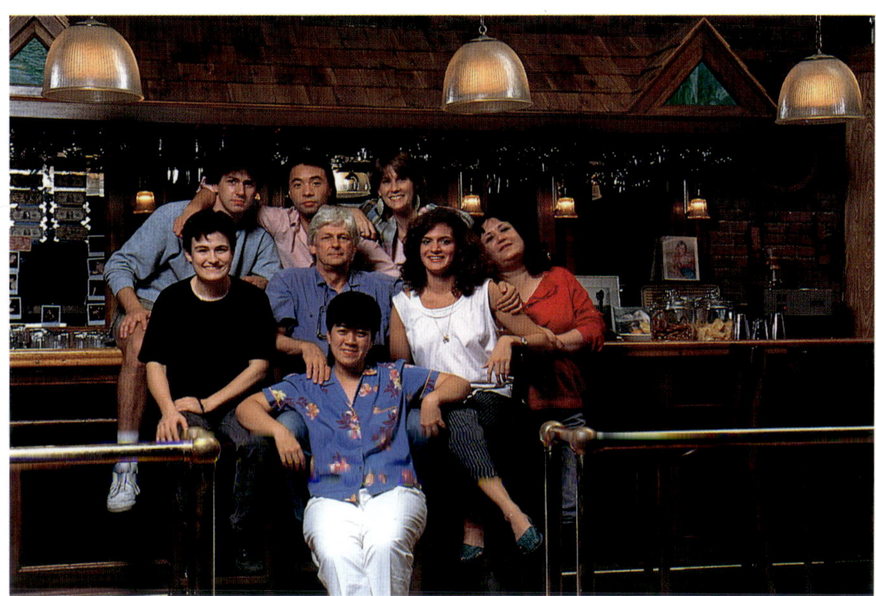

As Langley walks through his studio, he is visibly proud of his "big, crude space" his ideal working environment.

RENOVATING A STUDIO EXTENSIVELY

In Boston, Massachusetts, Newbury Street is synonymous with high rents, elegant boutiques, trendy restaurants, and influential art galleries. This graceful, treelined thoroughfare with its sought-after addresses is hardly the type of location where you would expect to find a large, active photographer's studio—yet this is exactly where Clint Clemens established his studio. **C**lemens grew up in Providence, Rhode Island, and "always wanted to be a photographer." After Clemens graduated with a degree in photojournalism from Syracuse University, he did what many ambitious young shooters dream of: he came to New York City to look for work. Unfortunately, a concentration in photojournalism isn't necessarily helpful in securing a job as a studio assistant. In 1972, Clemens finally decided to return to his native New England, choosing the Boston area as his destination.

The entryway of Clint Clemens's Boston studio is elegant yet unobtrusive.

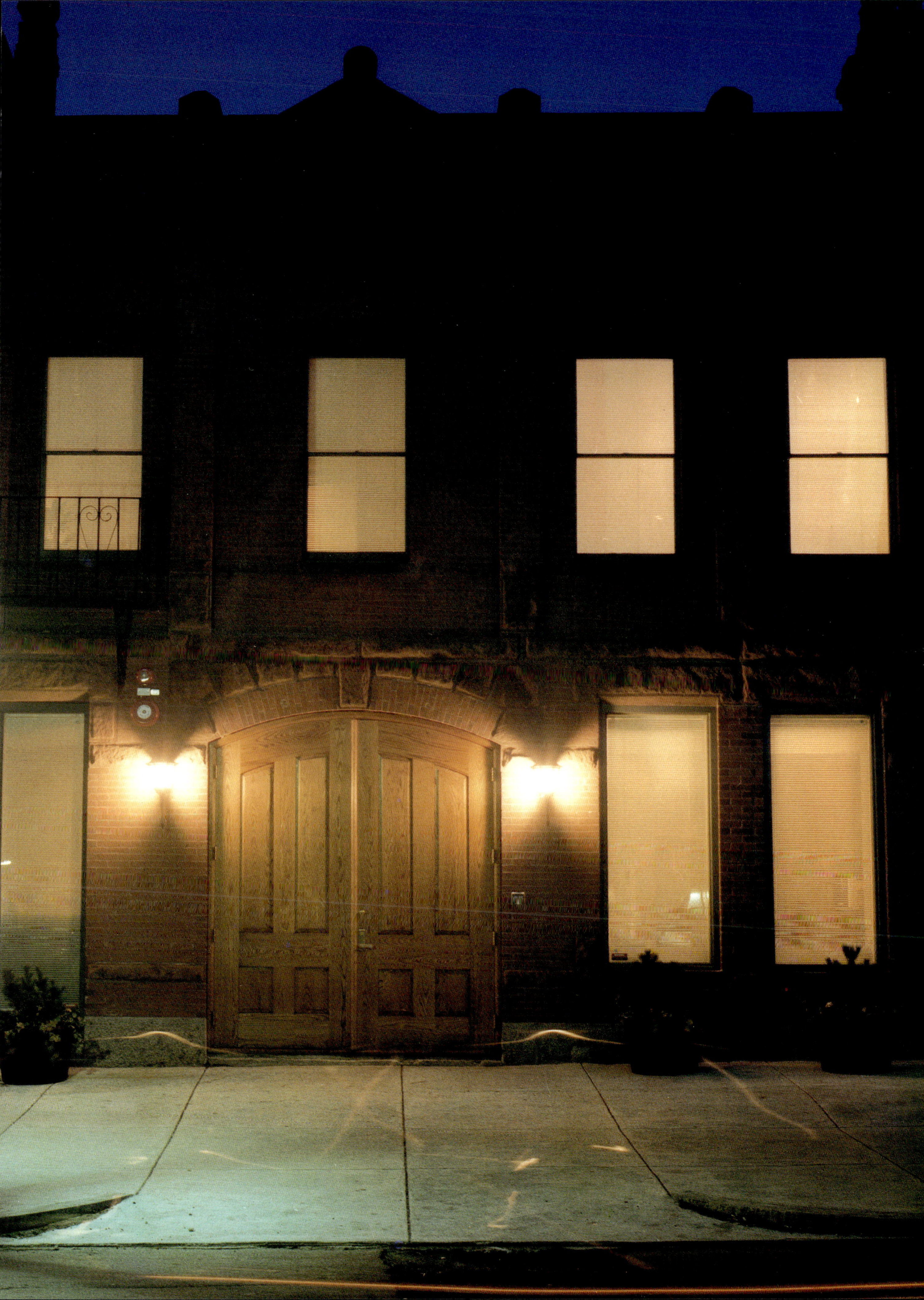

Clemens set up a tiny studio in the kitchen of his Brighton, Massachusetts, apartment and began taking on assignments. "At that time, it was a very small-town photo community," says the photographer. "And the accounts were generally minor." When he needed to process and print film, he rented darkroom space at another location. After a while, the volume of work increased as did his need for more studio space. Clemens moved to a second—but still relatively small—location on Newbury Street and stayed there for a few years.

The business was modest but prosperous and would have continued to grow at a slow, steady pace had it not been for the fortuitous increase in the Boston area of such high-tech industries as computer hardware and software, supplanting the manufacturing that had once been a staple of the industrial Northeast. "The change has propelled the area as well as the local agencies. The amount of work generated has increased fifty fold," says Clemens. Suddenly, the photographer found himself acquiring the large accounts he had always hoped for. He also had a serious need for more studio space. "Around the same time, I had decided that, in addition to my other jobs, I wanted to be able to shoot cars for no other reason than that I thought it would be fun," notes Clemens. "But to do this I needed a building that would be able to accommodate that kind of traffic."

At this point, Clemens realized that he had numerous and very specific requirements. He weighed his options and decided that he would rather buy a building and renovate it than rent a space and pour money into the reconstruction of someone else's property. Clemens's most pressing need was finding a location that was structurally sound enough to support the weight of a heavy vehicle and offered a large, unobstructed shooting area at the same time. This left the photographer with only one architectural option. He needed a building that was cross-spanned: here, the rods that maintain the flooring are laid horizontally, running through the floor, rather than vertically, in the form of pillars or columns. In addition, Clemens wanted a building that was at least 30 feet wide, and one that he alone would occupy.

The photographer looked at 150 sites before deciding to buy a three-story carriage house that had been constructed in the early part of this century. The building was located on lower Newbury Street in the Back Bay section, which was not very stylish in the 1970s. Historically, upper Newbury Street had always been home to blue bloods; the lower portion had sheltered their horses and coaches. By 1978, however, the area was a low-income, semi-industrial neighborhood. Despite this, Clemens knew that he could transform the building into the photographic studio he wanted.

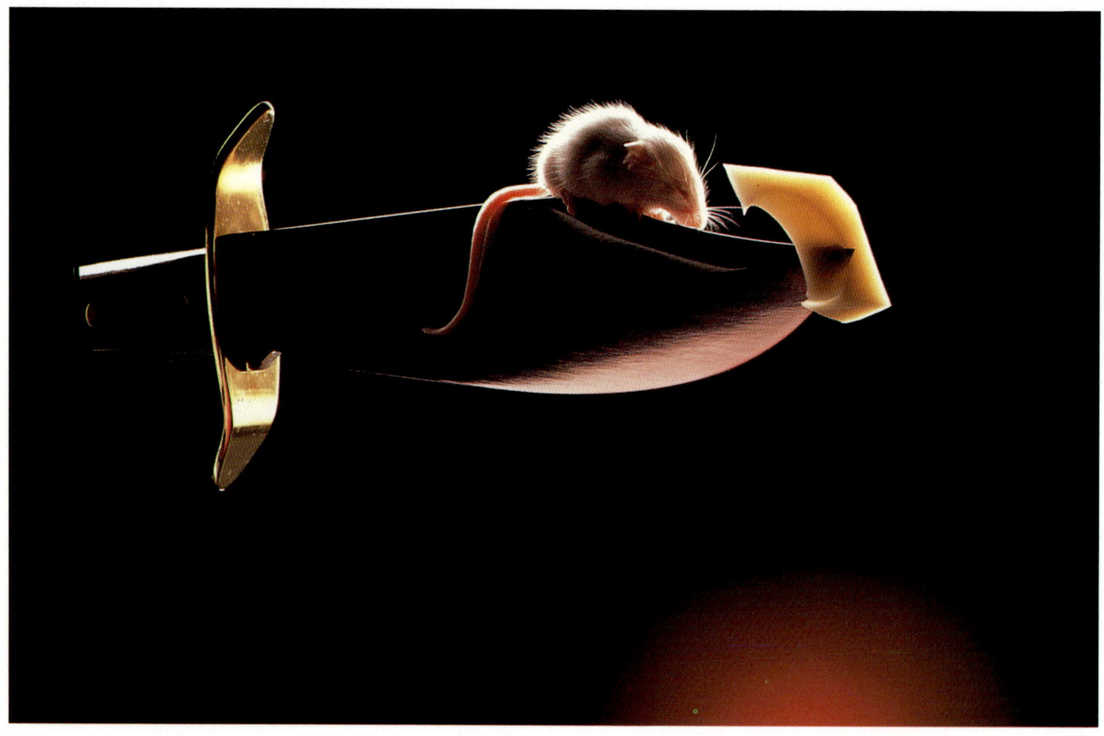

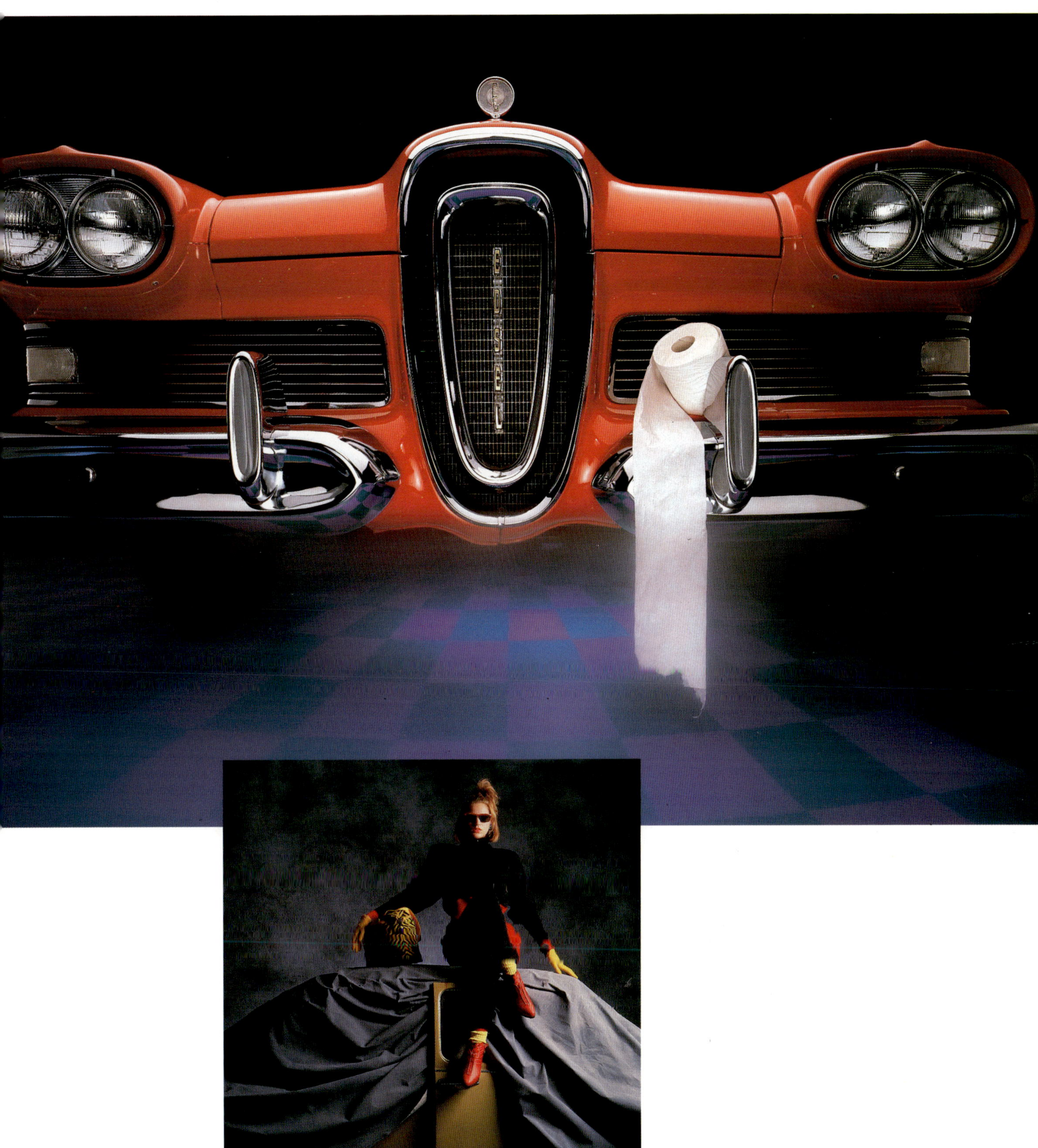

To begin, Clemens had the interior of the building gutted and a structural steel pad inserted under the main floor so that he "could be sure that it remained rock steady." Next, he and the architect worked out the floor plan for the studio on paper. "We went over everything extensively before construction began," says Clemens. "It's infinitely better to make your mistakes on paper, rather than with more expensive materials."

The space the two created reflects the amount of thought Clemens puts into his images and the careful way he treats them. The exterior of the building was cleaned up in order to bring out the burnished brick tones that had been obliterated by years of neglect. Also, heavy wooden doors, complete with brass handles reminiscent of the era during which the carriage house was built, were installed.

The entire structure is fireproof, and smoke detectors and heat sensors are found throughout all three floors. For security reasons, the entryway of the studio has an arched window in the reception area, which enables staff members to see into the waiting room. To the left of the reception window, a door—which must be buzzed open by the receptionist—permits access to the office and the studio space. A special switch, connected to the studio's electrical system, allows the person who locks up at night to turn off the lights all over the building while standing at the front entrance.

Most of the 30 × 80-foot ground floor is used solely for shooting. A small hallway leads to the studio's well-appointed kitchen (which has at times been used as a set) and to the main shooting area beyond it. To the left of the kitchen is a doorway that leads back into the entrance hall. These doors, however, are usually opened only to admit oversized subjects, such as cars, swimming pools, and, on one occasion, a forklift. For this reason, the entryway was made large enough so that a car could be driven through it without the problem of furniture getting in the way. And, a drain was built into the floor here so that rainwater or street dirt can be removed from the vehicle before it is moved into the all-white studio space beyond.

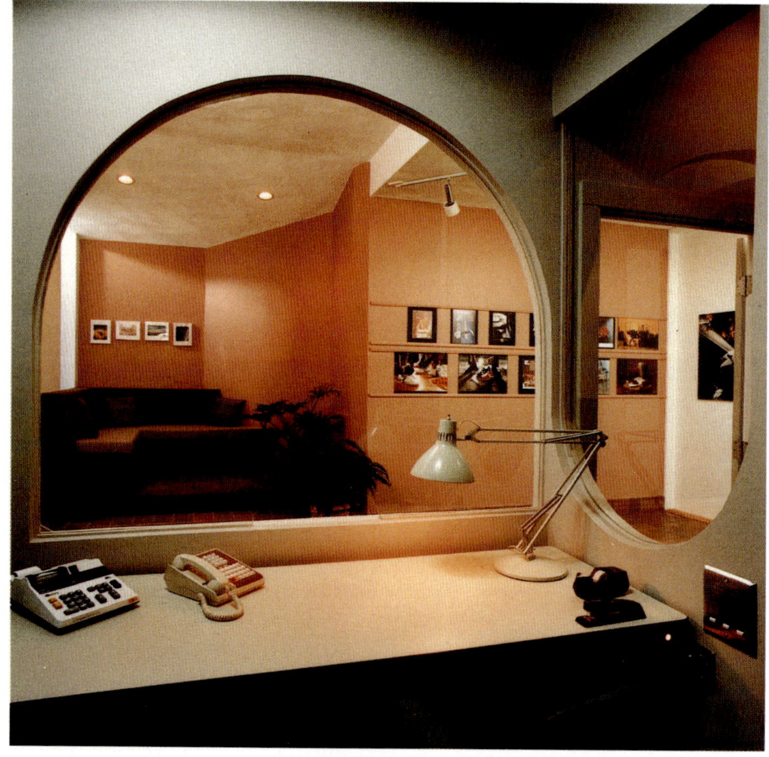

The arched window of the reception area serves as a dramatic introduction to Clemens's space and acts as a security device allowing staffers to see into the waiting room.

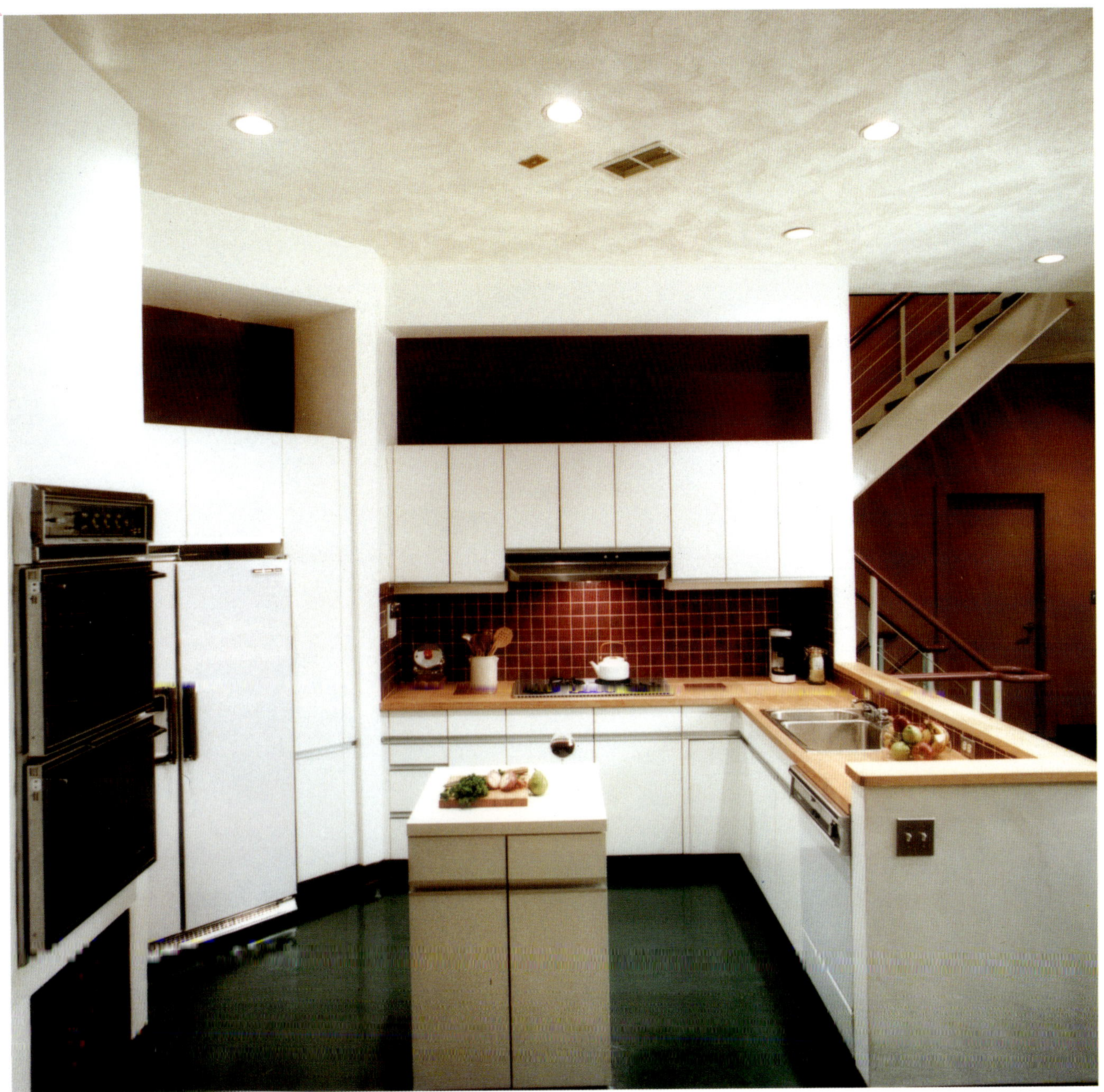

The kitchen in Clemens's studio was designed to be used as a set or as a catering facility.

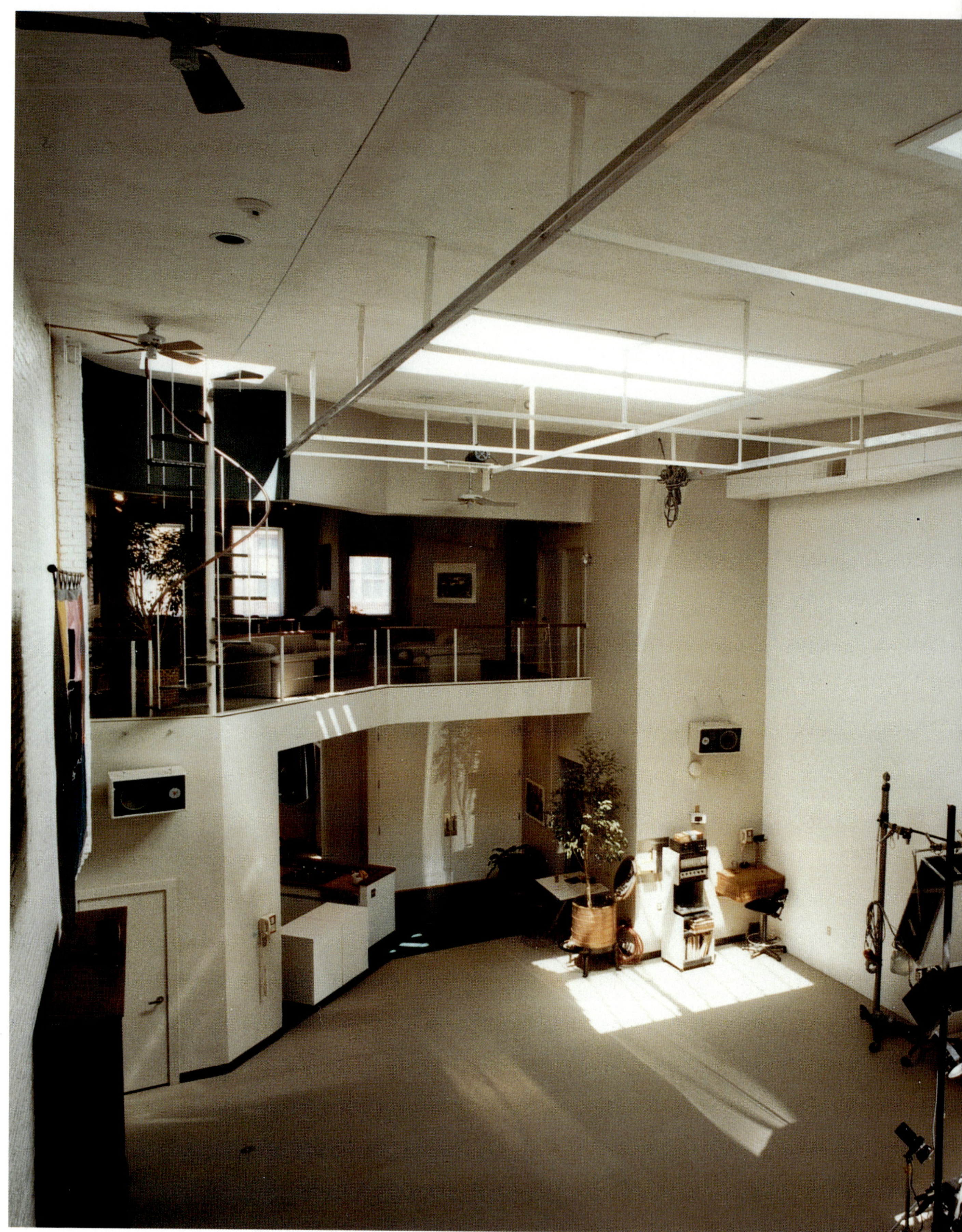

SPECIAL FEATURES

The rear wall of the studio is a cyclorama that spans almost its entire width. The cyclorama does not extend to the ceiling: Clemens had a balcony erected above (and behind) it from which he sometimes shoots. The photographer found the proper angle for the cyclorama by bending a small piece of paper until a floodlight aimed at it produced absolutely no shadows. The width of the cyclorama was decided when Clemens stood at the front door of his studio, looked through the viewfinder of a Hasselblad positioned at shooting level, and determined how much of the rear wall was visible. In this way, the photographer ensured that he had unlimited sight lines for shooting. The cyclorama was covered with 1,800 coats of white paint to guarantee consistently even light in every shot. In addition, the entire wall is freestanding, so it won't settle and, as a result, change the crucial angling.

To the right of the cyclorama, two barely noticeable doors provide access to the rear portion of the building; they were fitted with heat locks so that the air conditioning and heating systems can work at peak efficiency. This back section has a storage area for large flats and props as well as a driveway (for Clemens's car and various automobiles he might be shooting). In addition, because the front of the studio is on a busy street, deliveries are made through the rear entrance; to facilitate them, the photographer had a pulley system installed for raising objects out of and lowering them into the basement.

Other special features involve lighting. The studio's two skylights fill the room with a pleasing wash of natural light. But, when Clemens wants to regulate the illumination in the studio, he can quickly and effortlessly manipulate electric louvered blinds via floor-level controls. And a 6 × 20-foot custom-built light bank is suspended along a track that is fixed to the ceiling. By flipping a switch, Clemens can move the bank to the left or the right, or up or down; he can also tilt or rotate it. Furthermore, he can make the entire apparatus descend to the floor, which renders it effective for even the smallest jobs. For big jobs, the bank offers up to 54,000 watt/seconds of power.

The shooting stage includes the client area, seen here in the middle left of the image. It looks out over the shoot, yet keeps visitors away from the activity. The kitchen is visible underneath the lounge

Jobs that require lower wattage are no problem either: Clemens has a specially designed "light cart" that can be wheeled anywhere in the studio. It holds fourteen Norman 2000D powerpacks, provides up to 40,000 watt/seconds of power, and requires only one 150-amp plug. As a result, Clemens can keep the floor free of long, unwieldy, and possibly dangerous electrical cords.

Clemens's floor plan included other convenient design features as well. The ceiling contains a series of color-coded ropes that stretch across its length and width. These cables are anchored to a board on the wall on the left side of the space. Clemens can hang backdrops along these lines or "fly" various props as desired. He makes (or modifies) props and flats in his small but well-stocked workshop, where he also stores a large assortment of tools.

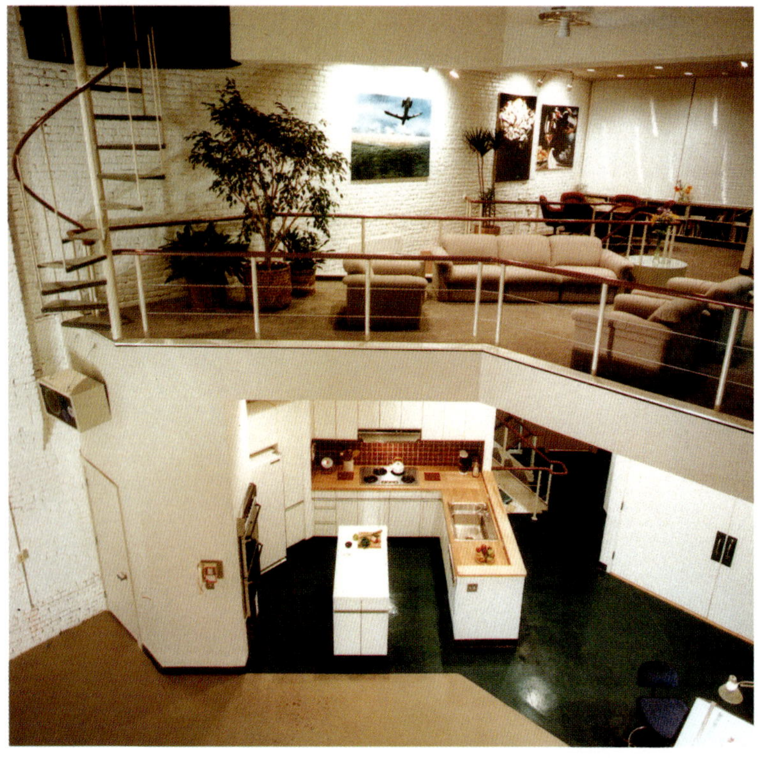

As is apparent in this more complete view of the lounge and kitchen area, the double doors at the bottom right can be used to admit cars and other oversized subjects.

Clearly, the photographer intended to make his studio as self-sufficient as possible. In keeping with this, Clemens has a complete laundry and full bathroom directly behind the workshop, as well as more storage space for props and flats. Furthermore, preparatory work for a shoot is done in the studio's basement. The front section is a large editing "room" filled with light tables, desks, and files containing Clemens's voluminous inventory of transparencies and prints. Directly behind this open area is a revolving, light-tight door that provides access to what used to be the studio darkroom. This space, which once housed enlargers, sinks, dryers, and storage racks, has been redone; today, it contains files with office and accounting information, as well as drawers filled with more of Clemens's inventory. Self-sufficiency gave way to a more practical concern. "At a certain point, the darkroom stopped being cost effective," explains Clemens. "Too much valuable time was being spent working in here, when there were other things that needed to be done." The revolving entryway—which is still light-tight—is now used for loading film.

The care with which Clemens determined his work needs is also reflected in the attention he gave to details of the studio's environment. At his suggestion, the heating ducts were installed in the ceiling, and vents were inserted in the walls so that the air would forcibly circulate rather than stagnate. "It's much easier to work this way," he explains. Drains were inserted in the studio's floor—which is tilted ever so slightly—so that dirt and water can quickly and easily be swept out of the studio (as in the entryway). A central compressor system puts out approximately fifty to sixty pounds of pressure, thereby rapidly blowing dust out of the shooting area. Another benefit: the compressor can draw out steam and smoke in one quick motion.

When Clemens discussed the design of the studio with the architect, he gave careful thought to the needs of his staff and clients, too. Overlooking the entire set is a balcony that doubles as a meeting area for the photographer and his clients. The balcony is located on the level that used to be the building's third floor (the architect ripped out his floor in order to give the shooting area extremely high ceilings). Plushly carpeted and comfortably equipped with couches, tables, and a full bar, the area is also a place where a client can watch a shoot without getting in the way or interfering with the often frenzied activity. Clemens provides other amenities as well. To the left of the main shooting area are a dressing room for models and a bathroom equipped with a shower for both models and staff members. Also, a circular iron staircase that leads up to the roof enables the staff to enjoy the sun and put together impromptu picnics.

Clemens's staff has increased in number. Once able to work alone, the photographer now has three assistants, an office manager, a receptionist, a full-time accountant, and a part-time bookkeeper. The first assistant, the studio manager, and the accountant have individual offices in which to work; these are opposite the editing "room." Clemens's own office, located behind the staircase, is a private retreat decorated with memorabilia from various trips and assignments.

Clemens is justifiably proud of his studio. The $250,000 he spent renovating the space has paid off in many ways. The main shooting floor has supported a 10-ton forklift and a 30-ton swimming pool without buckling or shifting. Once a run-down neighborhood, the Back Bay area—which Clemens refers to as a "former low-rent district"—has become gentrified and very upscale. As a result, the studio's location now lends an increased appeal to his business. "Certainly, clients are more and more willing to come down here," acknowledges Clemens. During the past eight years, the escalating glamor of the neighborhood has driven property values upward. Clemens estimates that the building is now worth twenty times what he paid for it, making the purchase an unusually smart investment.

Clemens admits that his reality is what other photographers' dreams are made of. But, he cautions, "Remember, the quality of your work has to support what you have. Unless you are really good, a studio is nothing but a large overhead."

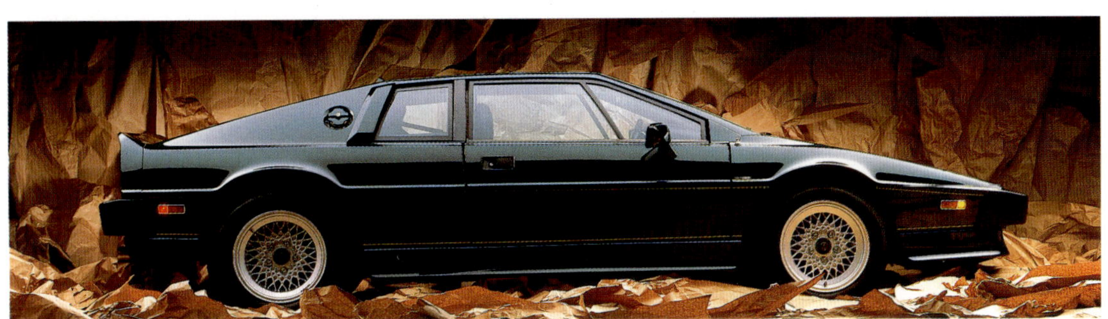

"The quality of your work has to support what you have. Unless you are really good, a studio is nothing but a large overhead."

COMBINING HOME AND STUDIO

Tucked in amidst the graying warehouses and bustling truck garages on Manhattan's lower West Side is a three-story building whose ashy façade is as unprepossessing as its interior studio is attractive. Eric Meola's spacious photo studio and his home on the floor above it are an example of how perseverance and insightful planning can produce an ideal situation. **"I**'d wanted to be a photographer since I was twelve-years-old," says Meola, but the dream didn't really take shape until 1970, when he was twenty-six and came to New York to assist Pete Turner. After a year and a half, Meola went out on his own and got editorial assignments from *Esquire*, *Time*, *Travel and Leisure*, and *Life* magazines.

Eric Meola's three-storied studio is easy to find because of its graphic, distinctive entryway.

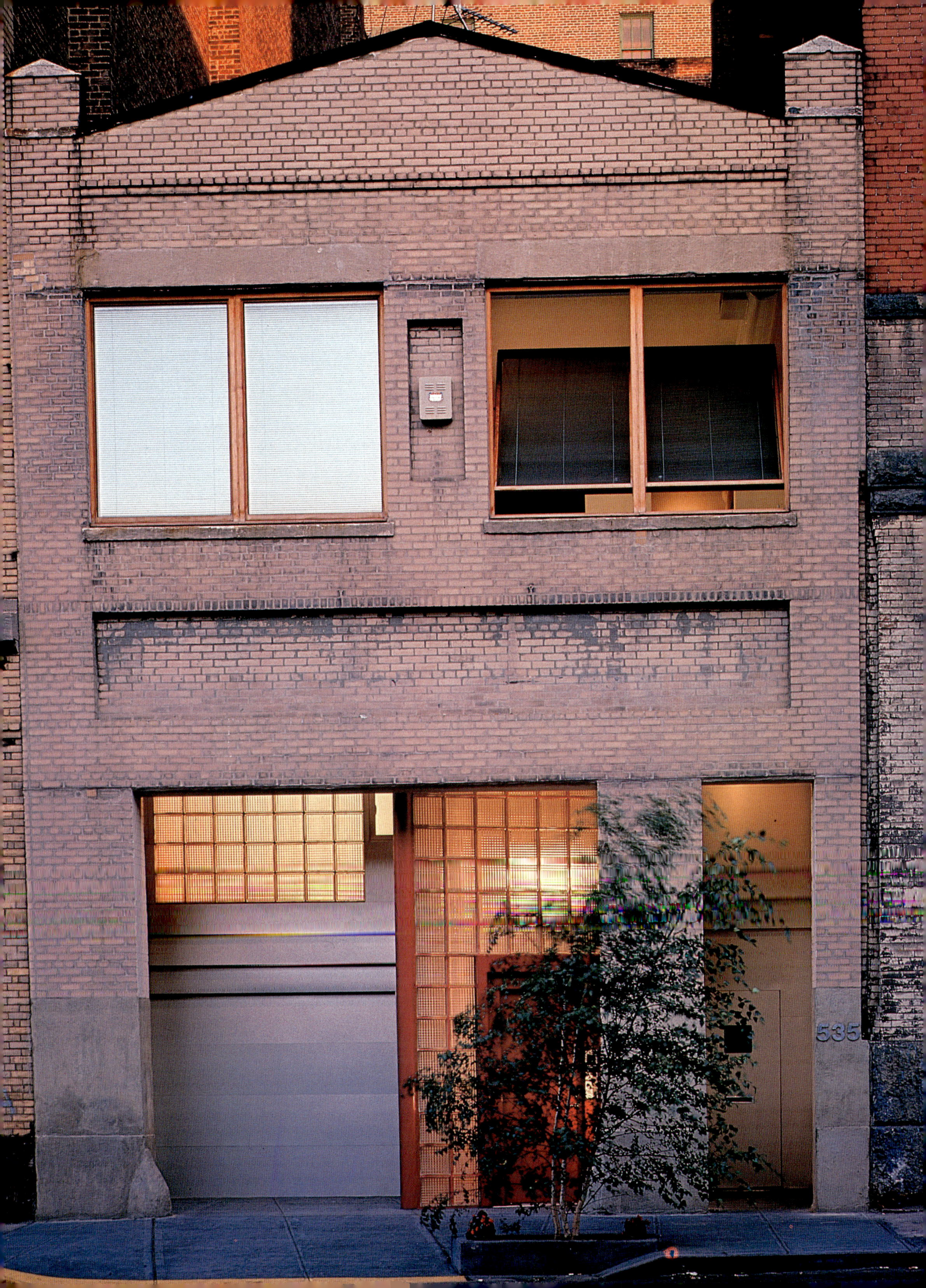
535

RECOGNIZING CLIENTS' NEEDS

In 1975, Meola's volume of advertising work increased to the point where a studio became a necessity. He found a place on Fifth Avenue and 19th Street—a location that, in the early 1980s, was to become known as "the photo district."

The 2,500-foot studio was functional, but the caliber of his clientele was improving. The commercial jobs he was acquiring included subject matter that varied in size from tabletop work to large items, such as cars and motorcycles, making it more and more obvious that his studio facilities were old and somewhat cumbersome. "I was on the third floor," recalls Meola, "and the elevator service was absolutely miserable. There were days when clients had to walk up the stairs. It was extraordinarily inconvenient, not to mention embarrassing." Meola was also tired of paying rent and felt that his money could be better spent. "I realized that rental prices had gone, and were continuing to go, way, way up. And I wanted more control over things," he says. "That's when I started dreaming about owning my own building."

Whether in a promotion piece (right) or an advertising account (far right), Eric Meola's bold use of color and light is his trademark.

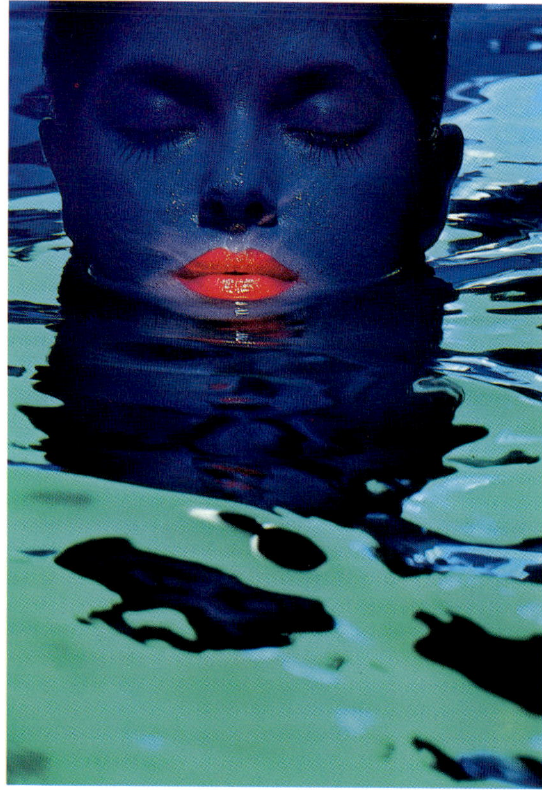

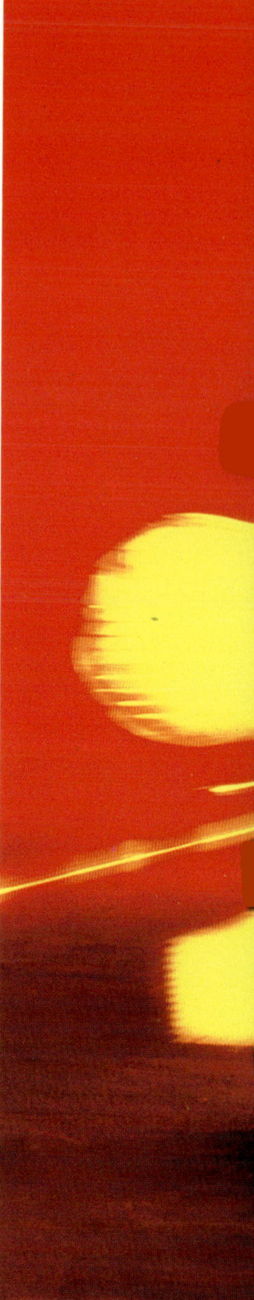

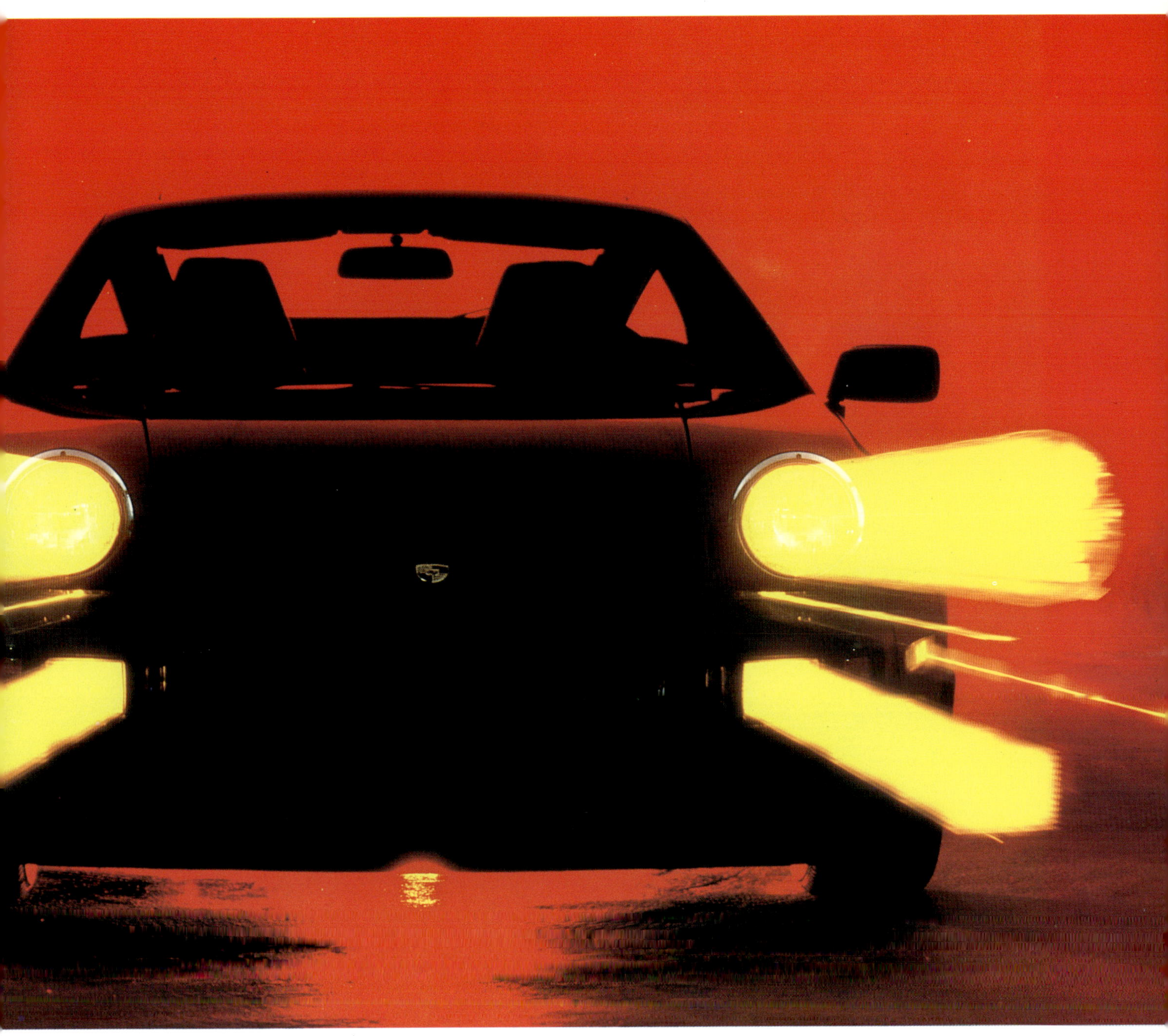

But the Manhattan real estate market was—even in 1979, when he set out—one of the most difficult in the country: it was volatile, availability tight, the demand for space great, and prices escalating at a rapid clip. Meola recalls one prospect that had a price tag of between $200,000 and $300,000. "In the short time it took me to decide whether I wanted to take it or not, the price had more than doubled to $600,000, which was far more than I cared to spend."

Meola's search was helped by the presence of the architect he had hired to eventually do the renovation, Ralph Gillis of Gillis Associates in New York City. "Ralph spent two to three years with me, looking at all those spaces," says Meola. "We had to find something that was workable for my business and my budget."

The photographer estimates that he looked at approximately three places a week. "I contacted brokers, scoured the *New York Times* and the *Village Voice*, went to city auctions, and even briefly considered living and working in Brooklyn," notes Meola. By April 1982, Meola's spirits were sagging, and the dream of owning a building seemed as elusive as ever.

Although Meola considered himself flexible, he did have certain requirements. "I wanted a location close to midtown, where most of the advertising agencies were situated. And, of course, it had to be a building that wasn't too big or too expensive to renovate. Unfortunately, the closer the building was to midtown, the more prohibitive" its price became. The photographer was basing his choice of studio on another criterion as well: "It had to have really high ceilings to accommodate the large-scale products I sometimes shoot, and a street-level entrance so cars and motorcycles could be driven directly into the studio."

One day, a broker suggested an empty warehouse in a commercial/industrial district of Manhattan occupied primarily by printers and their workshops. "I rejected it at first," says Meola. "The neighborhood was a bit too far west, and though the building was the right size, I kept thinking, 'God, it's a shambles.'" Meola continues, "Ralph would try to educate us, but I just kept thinking, 'If we're going to put this kind of money into a place like this, it will *have* to work.' But my wife, Joanna, felt very strongly that we could live here and make it work in terms of the business. I couldn't see it at all," he admits. A month later though, the Meolas decided that, given the instability of the market, it was now or never. Since the building was on the outer fringes of Greenwich Village and SoHo, it carried a relatively low price; Meola put in a bid and won.

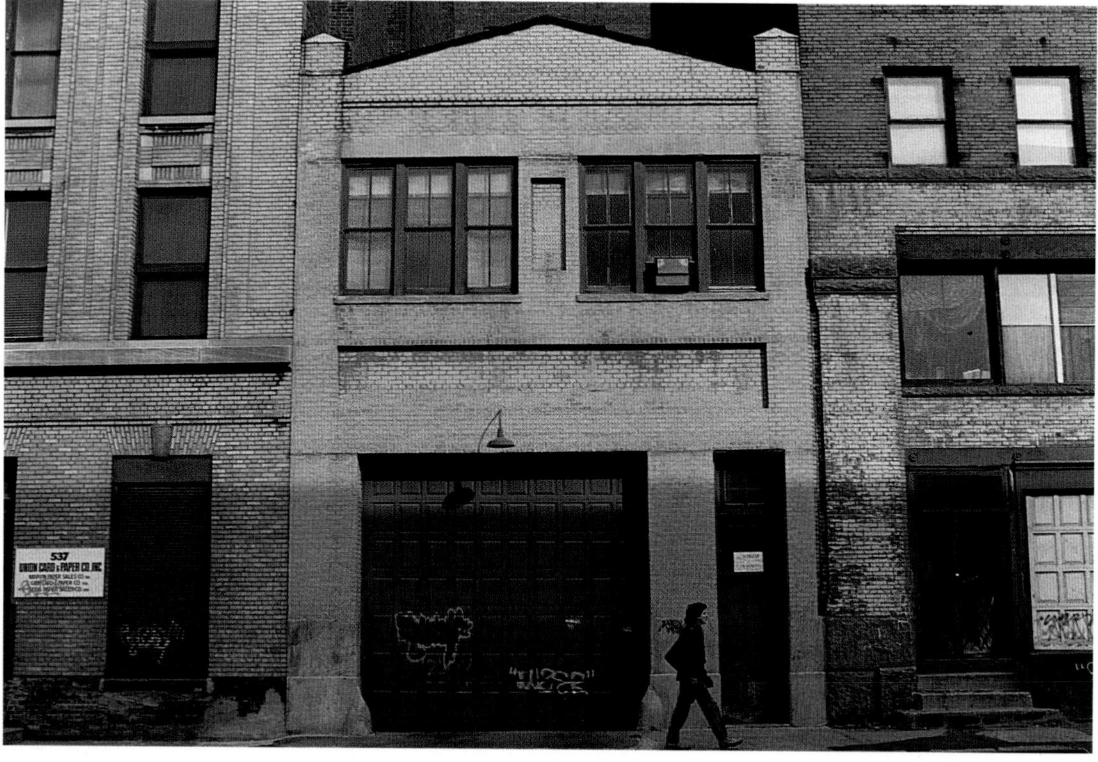

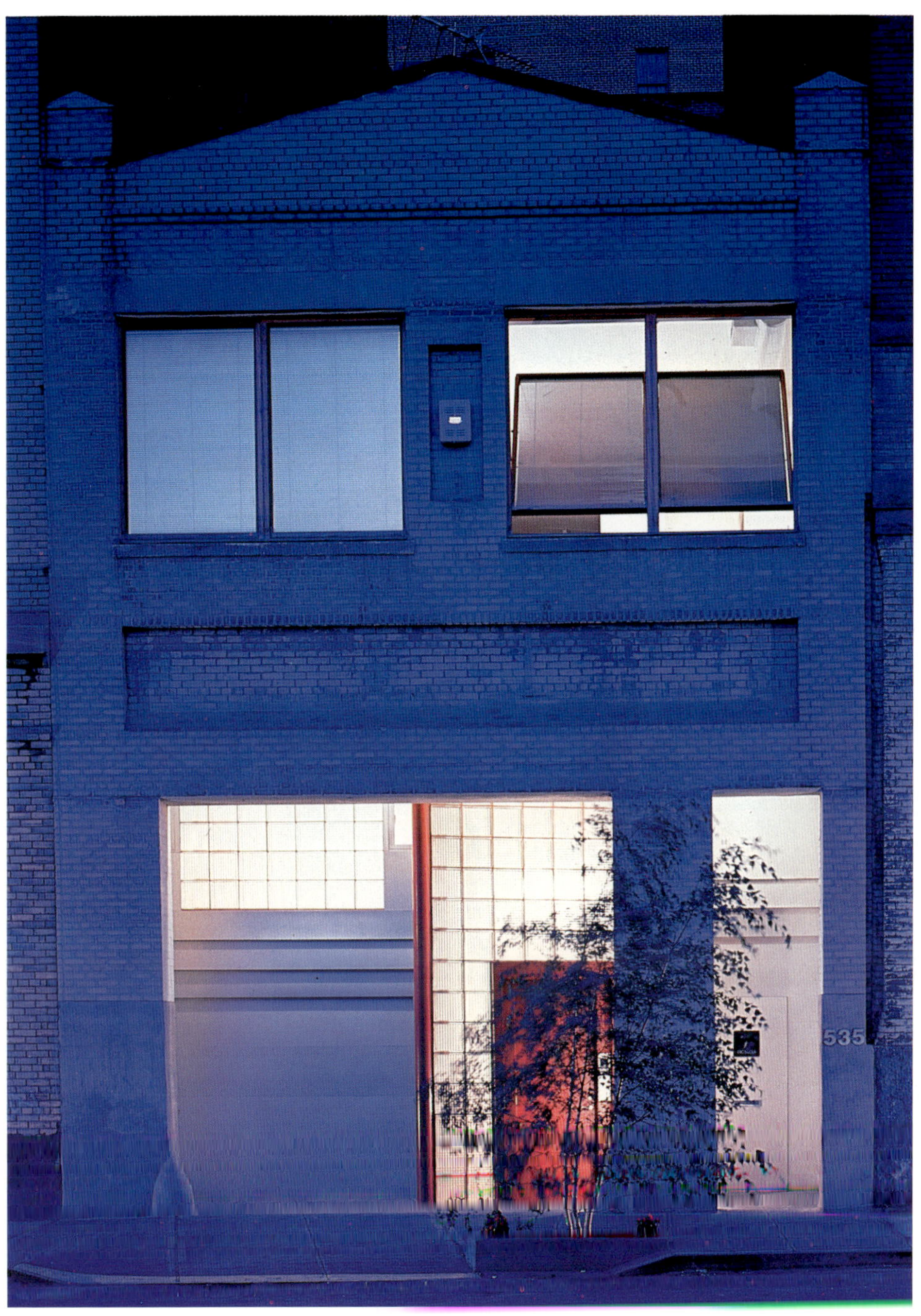

Meola's imagination enabled him
to envision a modern
photographic studio in a
nondescript truck garage.

REALIZING THE DREAM

After all the papers were signed, the photographer made an important discovery. "I came to realize that finding the space was only the beginning," says Meola. "Now I had to worry about what I could afford to do with it. It was a real education." Cash outlay was only one of the problems Meola was about to face. The location he had just chosen was zoned for businesses, and the printers who primarily worked there, fearful that artists looking for workable studio space would price the print shops out of their traditional neighborhood, had petitioned the mayor not to allow variances that would accommodate live-in loft spaces. For the next three months, Meola was blocked from constructing his studio. Finally, while city officials and the photographer's lawyers began working out the legal angles, Meola and his architect hired a contractor and work began in earnest. But it took a full year for a variance—called a caretaker's arrangement—that would allow Meola to live and work in his newly built studio.

The building had once been a truck garage, and the cavernous interior offered a 20-foot ceiling. The height of the garage required knocking out the second floor, but the third floor, which had once housed a messenger service, still existed. Because the structure of the building was in good shape although there had been a bit of dry rot, Gillis suggested maintaining the basic façade and interior and incorporating them into his overall design. The architect left the gray outer walls as they were, so that, at first glance, the studio blends perfectly with the other buildings on the block.

But directly behind the wall dividing the studio and the garage is a second, recessed façade that echoes the modernization within. It features a wall of glass tiles that encases three entryways: a steel garage door leading into a garage and behind it, a folding wall that allows access to the studio floor; a salmon-colored, unmarked doorway that opens onto a staircase leading directly up to the Meolas' third-floor living quarters; and a more deeply recessed entrance that has a white door and a plaque bearing the studio name. This entrance leads into the studio vestibule where clients, models, and other business visitors are received.

The white walls and bleached wood floors of the studio's interior are a major reason for the airy, immaculate feeling that permeates the space. Gillis's plans were unfolding. The architect designed a series of suspended storage cabinets that zigzagged back toward the rear wall of the studio, opening the room and increasing the sense of movement and space within. Meola refers to the design as "visually clean."

The cabinets contain storage space for prints, tearsheets, and transparencies; an area for props; a safe for cameras; and an assortment of cupboards for pieces of equipment that the photographer does not need to have immediately at hand. More important items, such as ladders, tripods, clamps, electrician's wire, and gaffer tape, are carefully arranged on pegboards that run along the opposite wall.

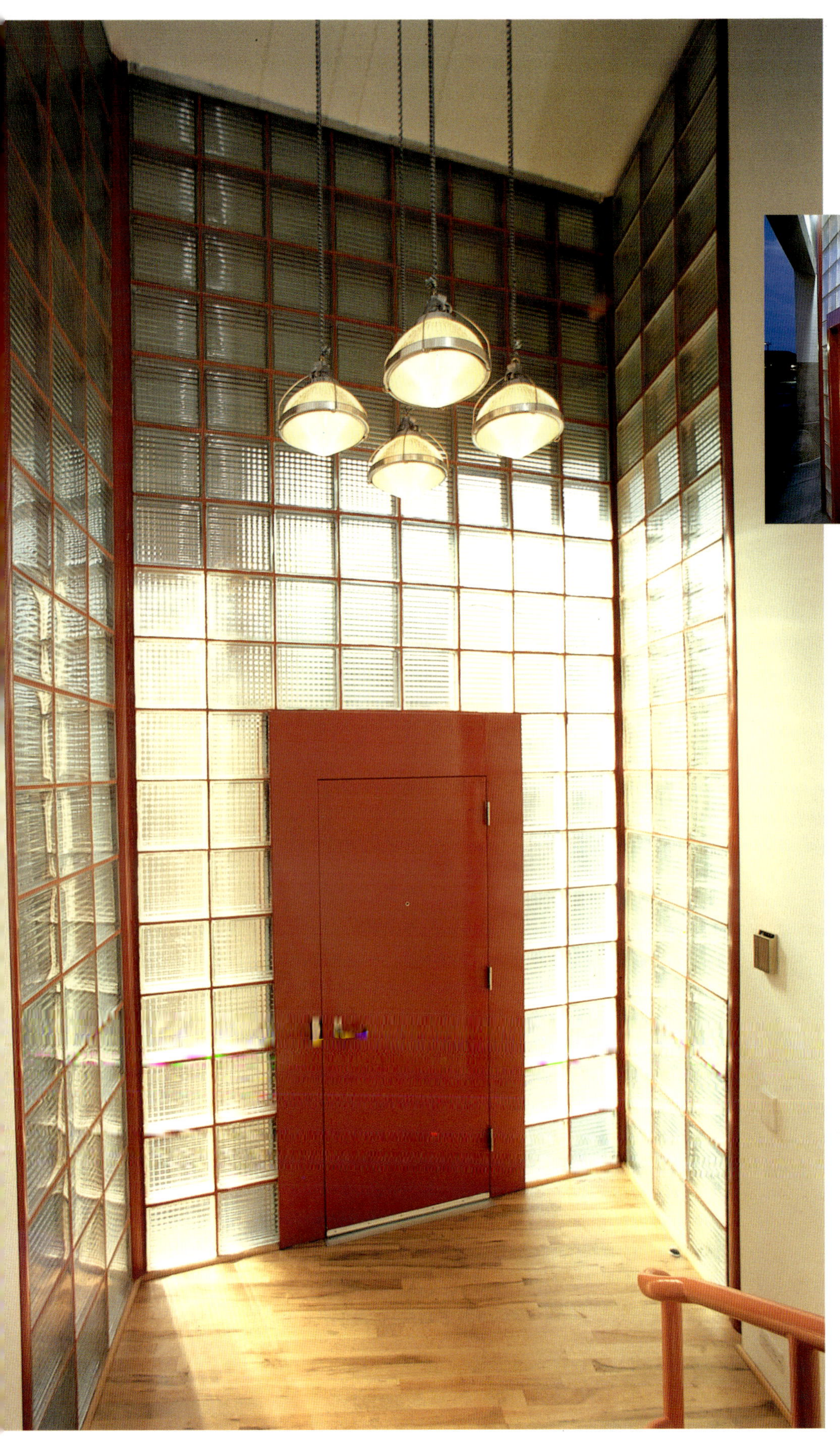

Careful attention to details, including such amenities as glass-brick walls, helps separate Meola's living environment from his workspace.

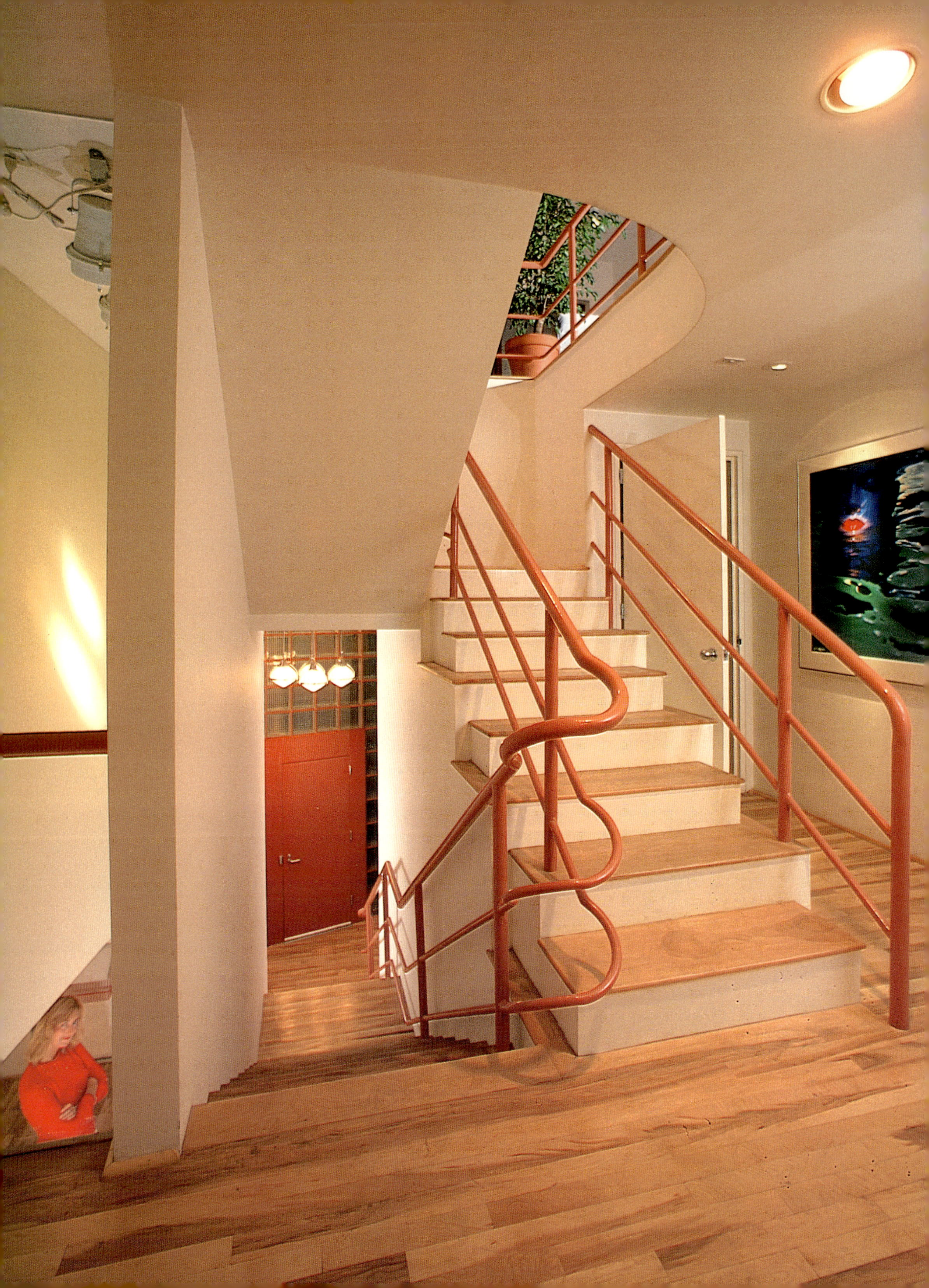

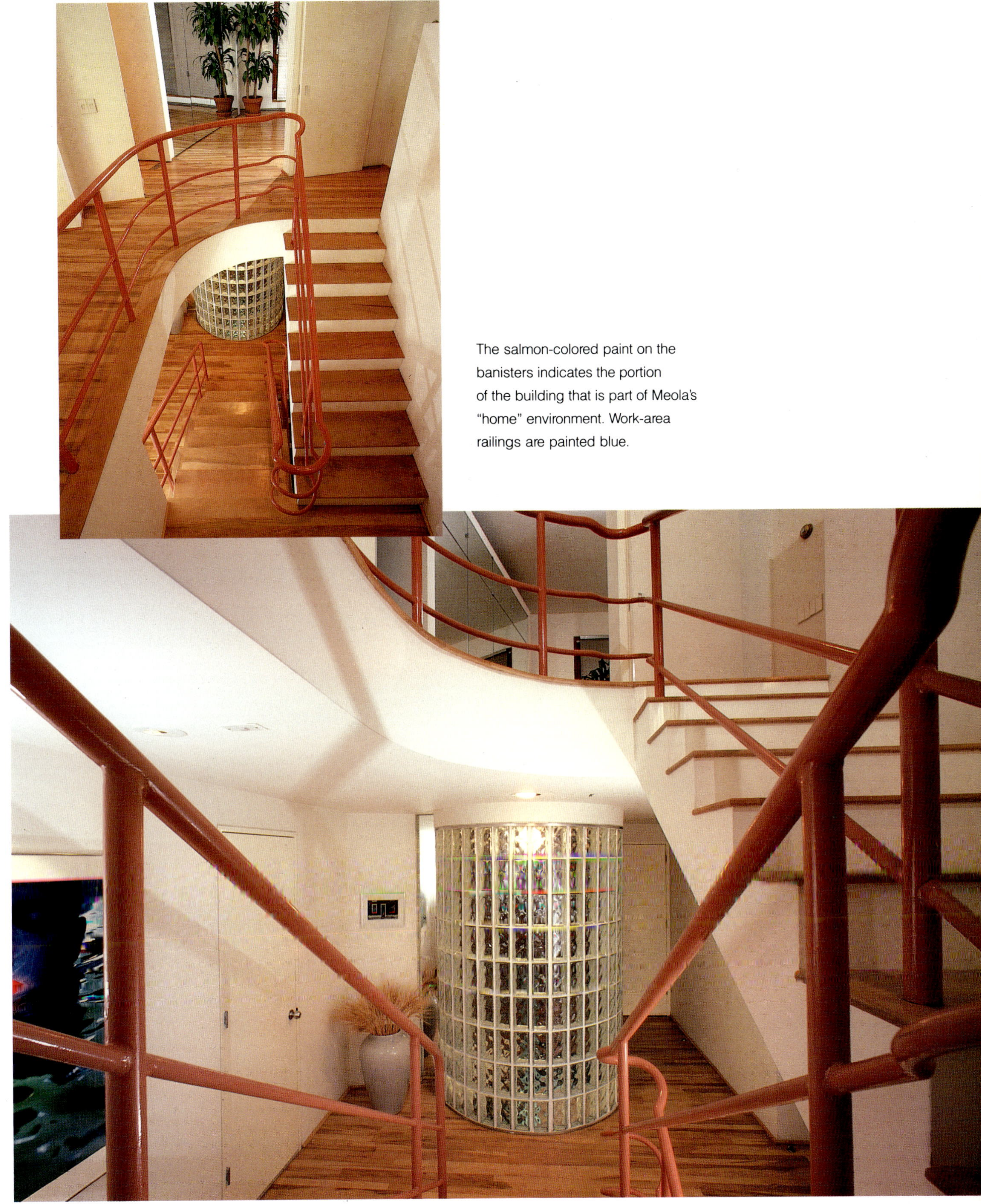

The salmon-colored paint on the banisters indicates the portion of the building that is part of Meola's "home" environment. Work-area railings are painted blue.

To the right of the main shooting area is a maze of rooms, including a kitchenette, a changing room for models, and a small darkroom. Most of Meola's work is in color and, therefore, is sent out for commercial processing. But he has both black-and-white and color setups available for emergency processing.

In front of the changing room and to the right of the reception area, a blue staircase winds its way up to the mezzanine level, where Meola's home and business areas meet. Gillis used color to differentiate between the living and working quarters. All the architectural trimmings on the business side are painted blue, whereas those on the "home" side are salmon-colored.

At the front of the mezzanine's overhang is Meola's office, which has a balcony that looks directly over the shooting area. A lightbox for viewing slides and a slide projector are built into a unit behind Meola's desk. The house lights and skylights can also be controlled from a panel in this office. For privacy or simply for darkening the area when the projector is on, a thick curtain can be drawn across the balcony. On the other side of the office wall are a guest room, a laundry room, and a salmon-colored staircase leading up to the Meolas' apartment.

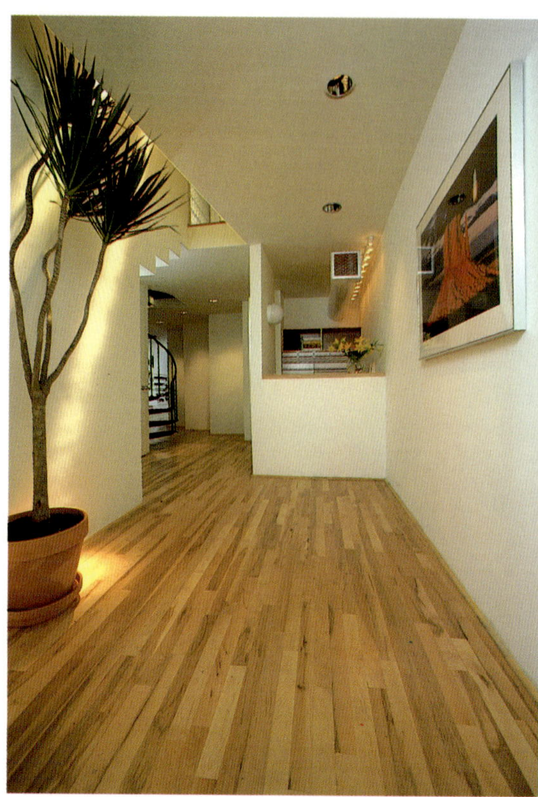

Both the reception area of Meola's studio (left) and his mezzanine-level office (below) add to the appeal of the workplace.

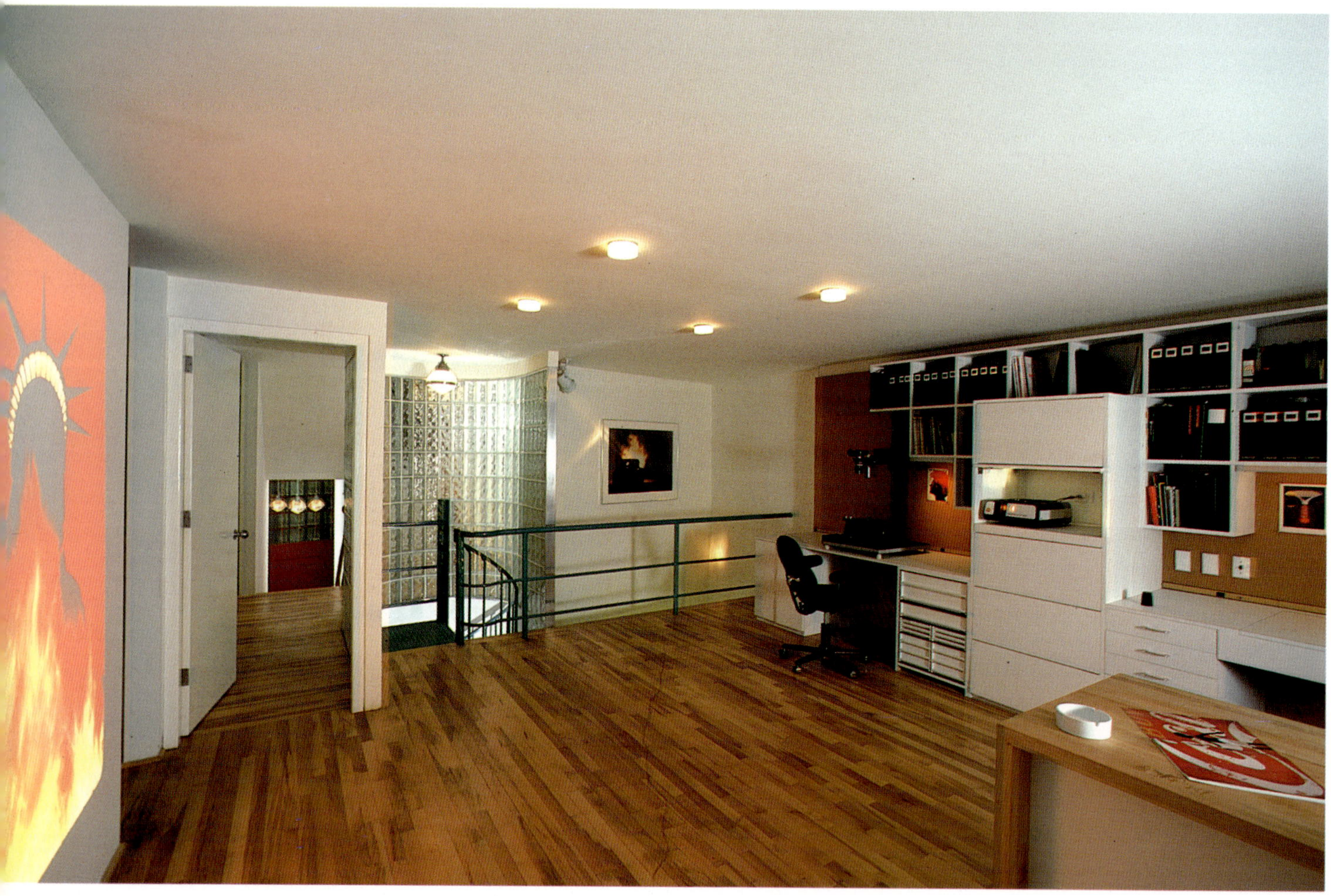

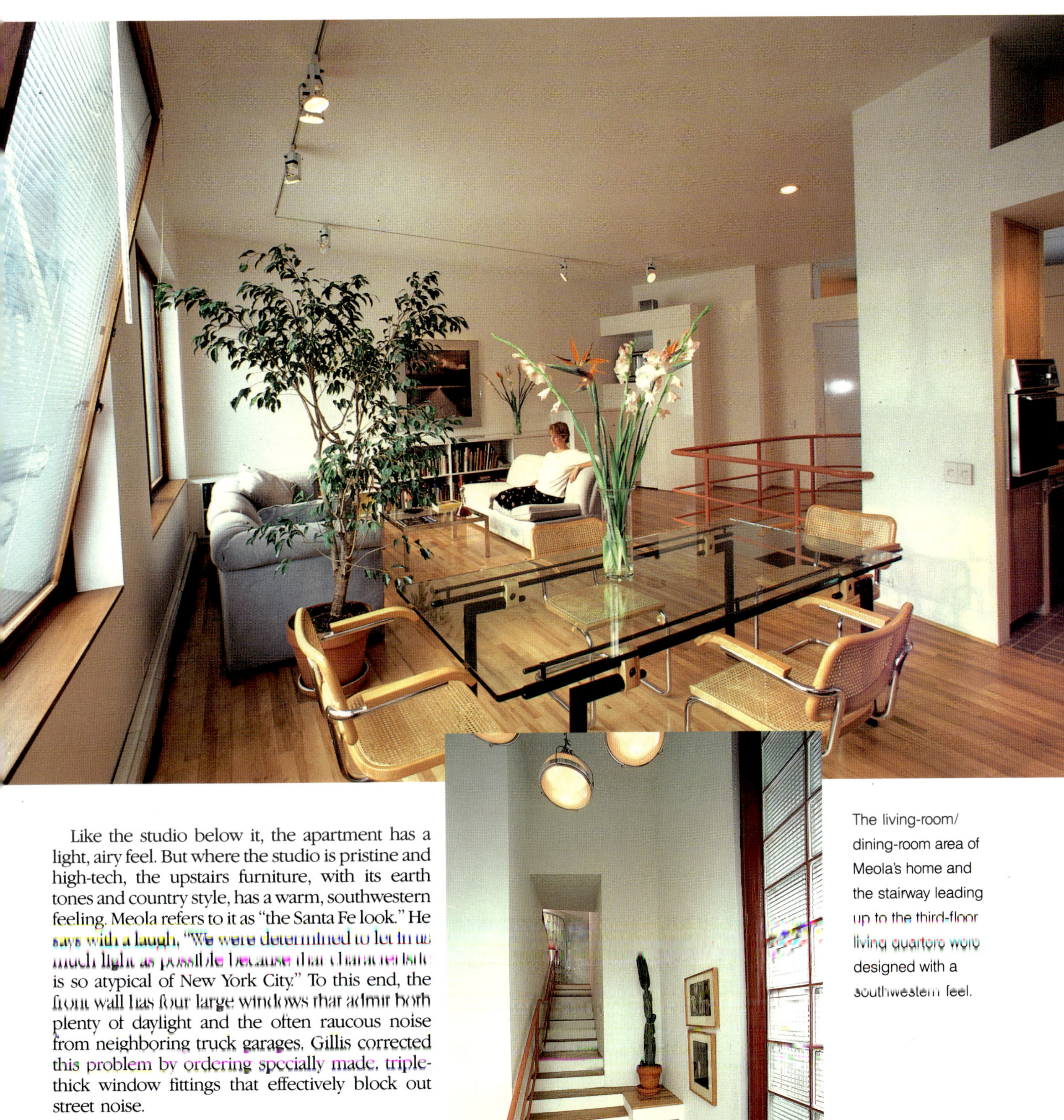

The living-room/dining-room area of Meola's home and the stairway leading up to the third-floor living quarters were designed with a southwestern feel.

Like the studio below it, the apartment has a light, airy feel. But where the studio is pristine and high-tech, the upstairs furniture, with its earth tones and country style, has a warm, southwestern feeling. Meola refers to it as "the Santa Fe look." He says with a laugh, "We were determined to let in as much light as possible because that characteristic is so atypical of New York City." To this end, the front wall has four large windows that admit both plenty of daylight and the often raucous noise from neighboring truck garages. Gillis corrected this problem by ordering specially made, triple-thick window fittings that effectively block out street noise.

The ceiling has three skylights that admit a steady stream of natural light. But on occasion, "all that daylight would affect the film," says Meola. Electric blinds, which cover the skylights but are powered by a remote control on the shooting floor, were installed to alleviate that problem. In addition, the skylight ports are removable so that the photographer can, if he chooses to, climb onto the roof and shoot down into the studio.

Strobe packs are housed in cradles anchored to the ceiling, as are two bank lights. One is 6 square feet, the other, 3½ square feet. The banks, which are electrically manipulated by a switch on the shooting floor, are specially designed to move up and down as well as to tilt.

The studio's 400 amps of electricity necessitated special wiring. Consequently, the entire electrical service had to be moved from the south side of the building to the north side. Although it cost an extra $10,000 to accomplish, the effort and expense allowed Gillis to incorporate electrical outlets into the floor and ceiling of the space. In this way, the clutter and attendant hazards of cords and wire snaking across the studio have been eliminated. The well-thought-out system also includes central heat and air conditioning, allowing the photographer to quickly and efficiently vent the space. As a result, smoke or dust can be quickly and completely sucked out.

The studio's far wall is entirely dominated by a freestanding, custom-made cyclorama. This panel acts as a shadowless backdrop, which is particularly useful when Meola shoots oversized products. The angle of the cyclorama's curve causes it to appear as unlimited space when photographed. It stands independently, so that when the building shifts, as all structures inevitably do, the cyclorama will not lose its crucial angle or crack. The wall separating the garage from the studio has also been expressly designed, so that it folds back to admit vehicles directly into the studio. In this way, almost anything can be driven in from the street through the garage and onto the set.

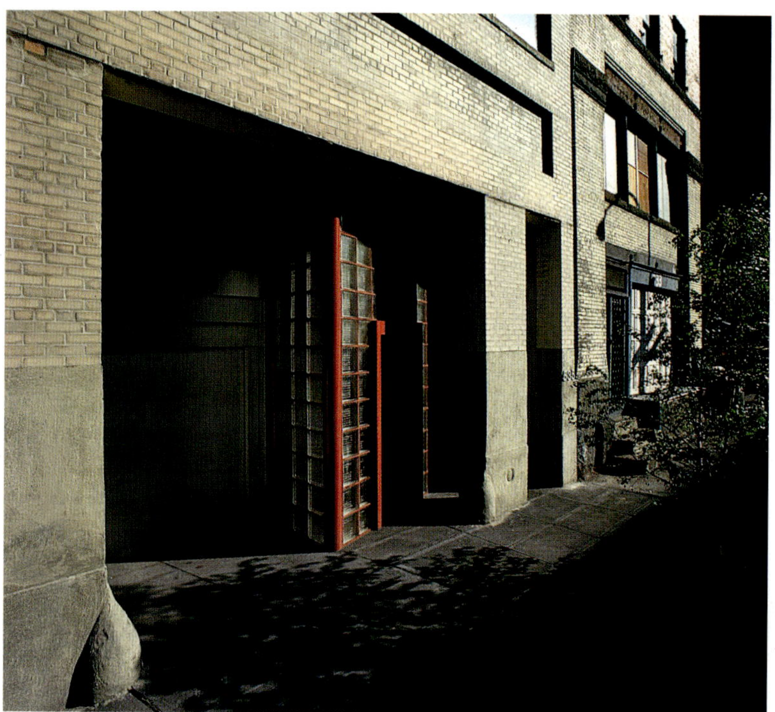

In another view of the entryway to Meola's studio (above), the garage door, which also opens to admit vehicles directly into the studio, is visible behind the recessed wall. The shooting stage (right) features a cyclorama.

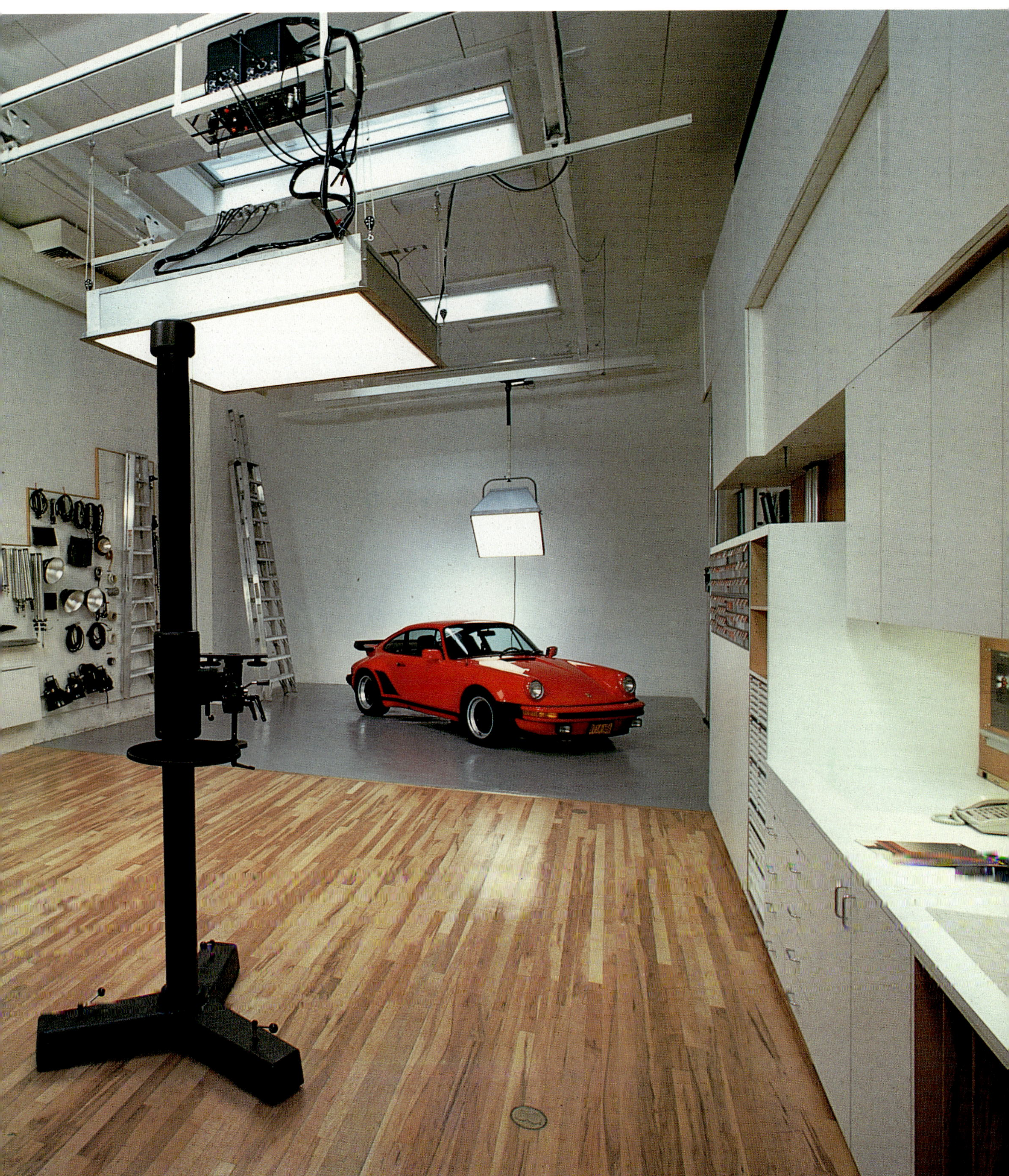

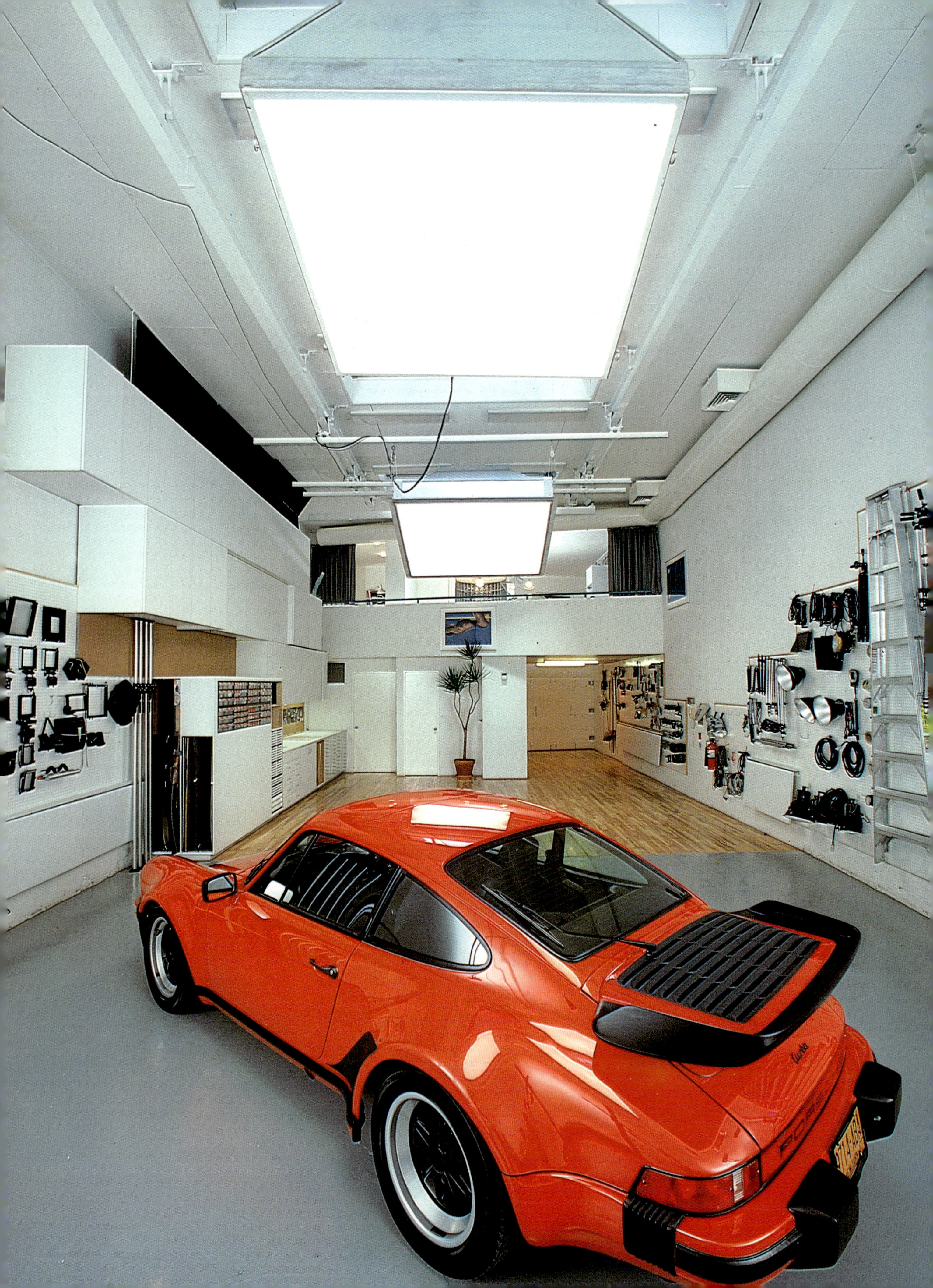

When the Meolas moved into their new home in 1982, the neighborhood was considered to be on the fringe, but now, a number of well-known advertising agencies have taken space here. Restaurants, coops, and supermarkets have followed. Other photographers and artists are moving in as well.

Meola estimates that he has between 45,000 and 50,000 square feet of working space. He declines to say how much the venture cost him, only that it took two full years to complete all the work on the studio, and two-and-a-half years before the living quarters were ready for occupancy. He is pleased that his desire to "look toward the future" has been successful. "This has given me a tremendous sense of peacefulness," Meola admits. "I know that everything I want and need is here. Best of all, it's mine, it's been done to my specifications, and I don't have to worry about a lease running out." But, he continues, "a great studio doesn't guarantee good pictures." It certainly makes it easier to get the best out of any assignment, though.

"I know that everything
I want and need is here.
Best of all, it's mine;
it's been done
to my specifications."

All items are carefully hung on pegs or stored in the recessed cabinetry along the left-hand wall of Meola's studio.

ESTABLISHING A LOCAL COMMERCIAL STUDIO

Houston, Texas, with its oil-related, currently depressed state, hardly seems the place for a high-tech photography studio. Though the number of clients to be found here might in no way rival the photographic prospects of New York City and Los Angeles, native son Craig Stewart has managed to carve out a viable niche in this less-than-rosy economic climate. **T**he son of a successful commercial photographer who spent his entire career in Houston, Stewart says, "I've been interested, and active, in the field since eighth grade." Throughout elementary and high school, the budding photographer won many paying assignments. Upon graduation, he attended the Art Center College of Design in Los Angeles, with the intention of going into business with his father. But the lure of Los Angeles was strong, and, after obtaining his degree, he opened a small commercial studio there, which he maintained for three years. Both Houston and his father beckoned, though, and Stewart finally relented and returned south. Although he worked at first with his father, Stewart had grown used to being independent, and the two parted amicably.

The dramatic exterior of Craig Stewart's Houston studio echoes the space's highly designed interior.

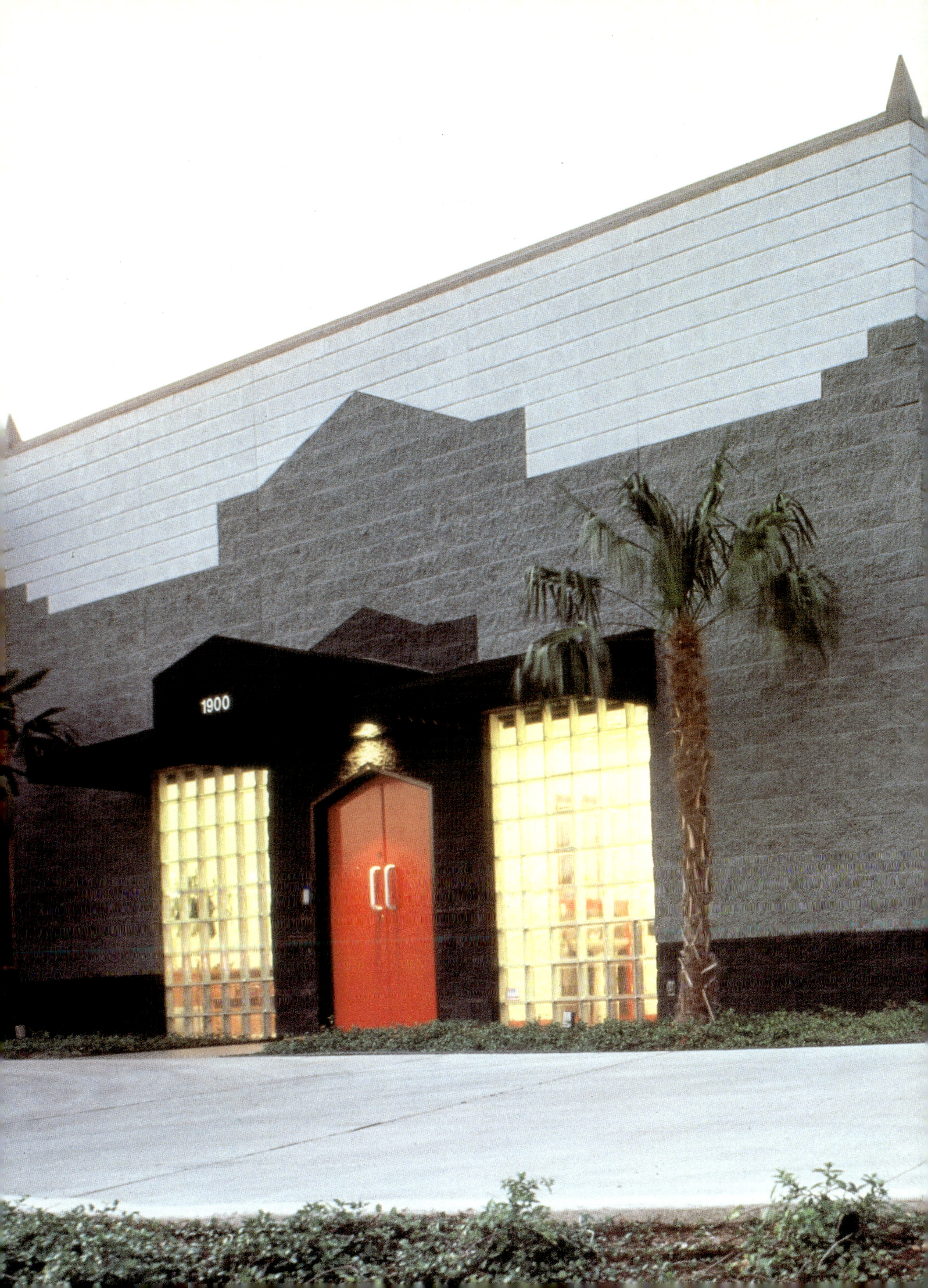
1900

The young photographer found a small commercial warehouse space in which to work. It had low ceilings, but offered 1,800 square feet of space. Were it not for an argument with his landlord, Stewart might yet be working in the same location. After signing a lease that gave the photographer permission to renovate his work area, the landlord changed his mind and refused to let the remodeling take place; he claimed that the alterations would make the space unrentable to future tenants. Stewart already had a design in hand, created by Tracy & Tracy, a husband-and-wife architectural team based in Houston. He was determined to stick with their plans and decided to relocate rather than change the interior design.

Literally overnight, Stewart was forced to go out and find a new work space. "I just wanted another lease," he explains. "I preferred not to be tied down, so that I could easily walk away from it all." He found a prime piece of real estate—then an automobile graveyard—in Montrose, an upwardly mobile residential neighborhood in Houston proper. "I did a study of where the major agencies were located, and that's how I chose this location. I'm in the center of the action," says the photographer. Stewart knew that the 7,000-square-foot lot could easily accommodate the 4,500-square-foot studio he envisioned.

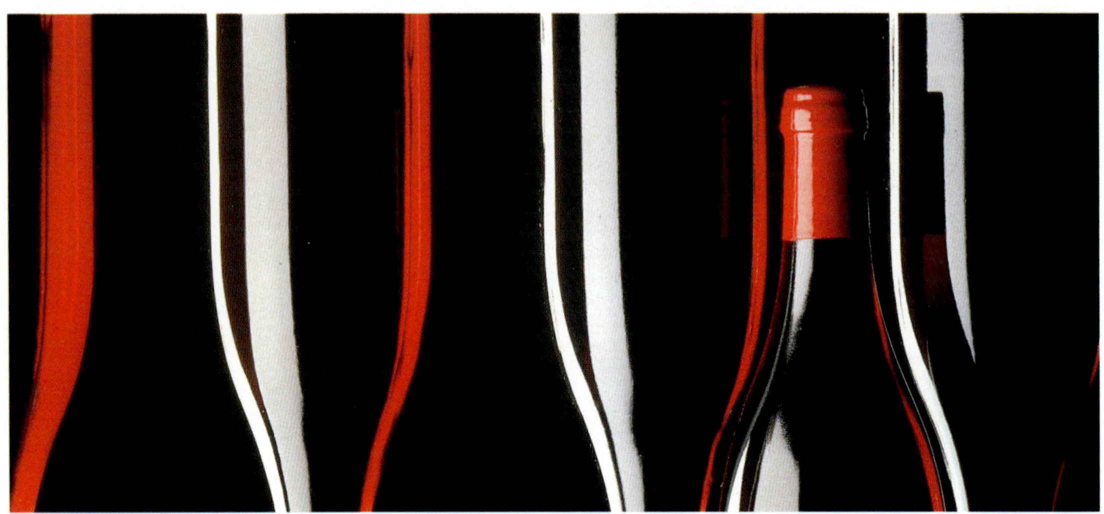

Within Houston's limited market, Stewart manages to do a lot of product work that is as up-to-date as anything being done in larger, less economically depressed locations.

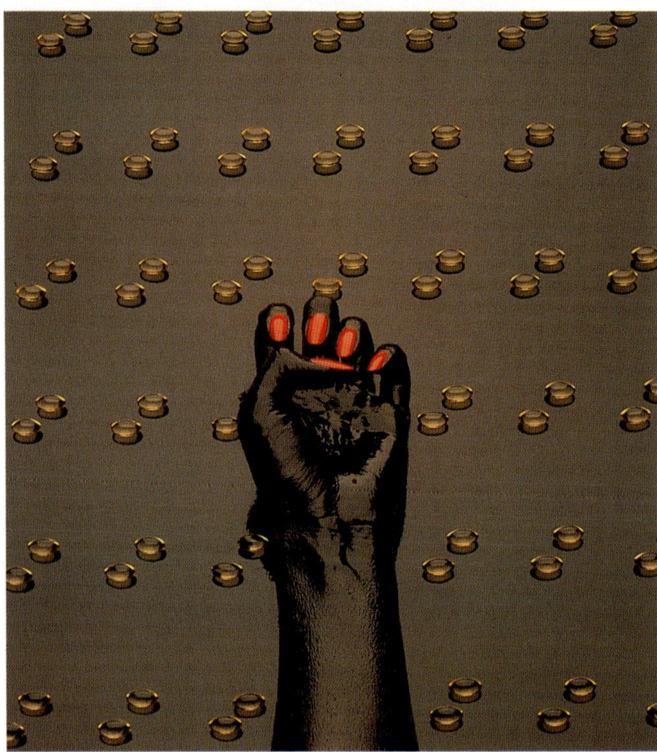

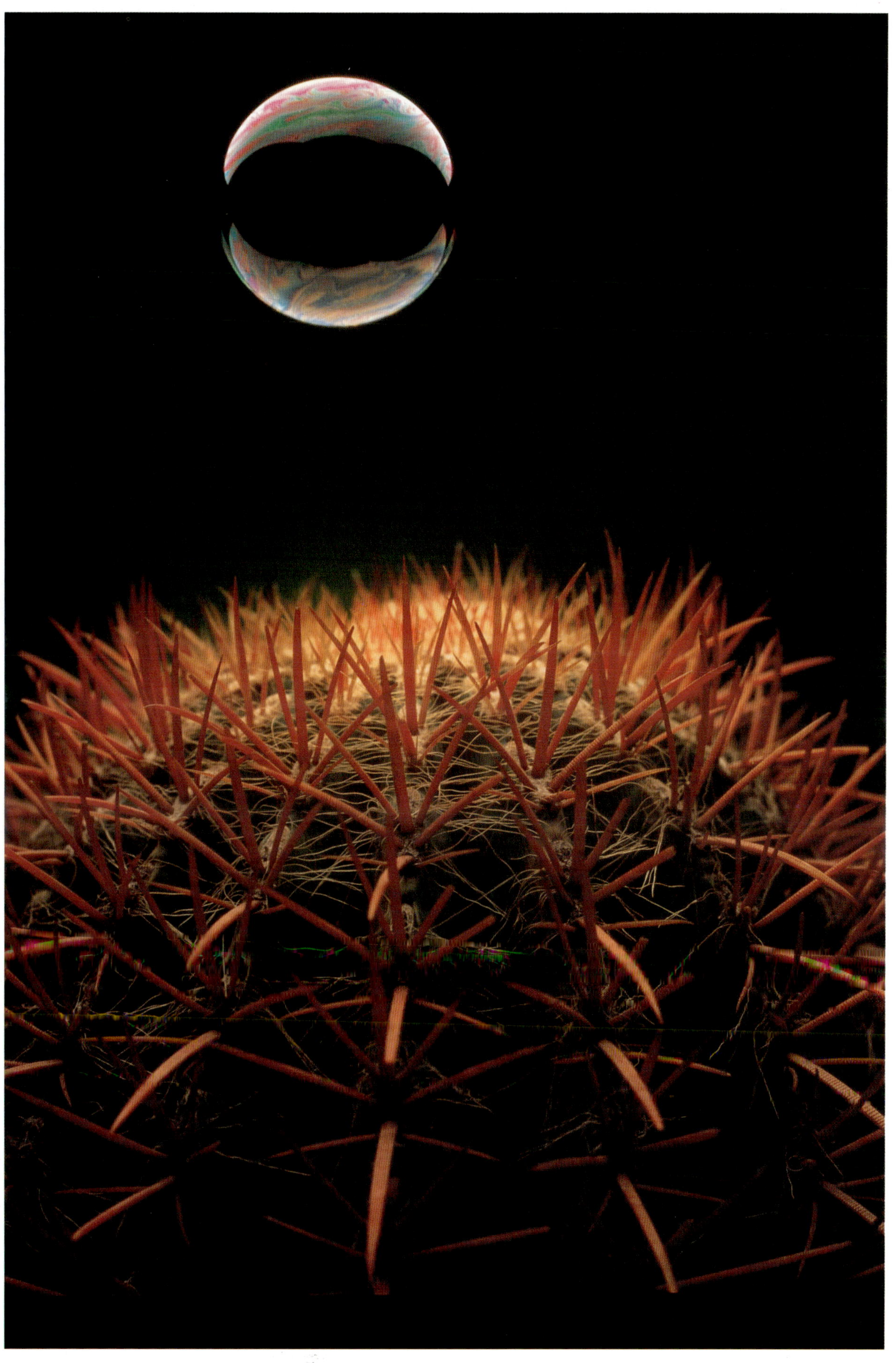

ENHANCING THE ORIGINAL PLAN

Since Stewart no longer had to consider a landlord's sensibilities, he was free to have the architects design the exact work environment he wanted. The photographer asked the design team to alter and improve their original plan. "Photo studio design was new to the Tracys," Stewart points out. "To give them an idea of my expanded needs, I wrote an outline of how my business operates and described the approximate size of everything I required. Then I explained how the flow of traffic and people might affect the space and noted which areas should be near other areas. Finally, I described how it all related to the shooting stage." The Tracys then submitted six different concepts to the photographer. "All had merit," reveals Stewart, "but the most original idea, that which was most different from the normal, was what we went with."

The studio's entryway has a series of arches that lead onto the shooting floor. In front of and to the left of the first arch is Stewart's office, which he uses for conferences. It contains a small sitting area with a couch and chairs, as well as a filing cabinet and a Macintosh Plus computer. "This is where I talk to clients," he explains. "It's a good atmosphere in which to discuss the job, pricing, bids, and the like." Opposite Stewart's office is a dressing room with a full-sized shower, makeup mirrors, and other amenities for models. To the right of the dressing room is the client office. Stewart had it installed so that while the shoot takes place in another portion of the studio, the client can find a private area in which to work. This office is equipped with a telephone, a bookshelf stocked with resource books, an assortment of art supplies, and a table and chairs.

Next to the shooting stage is a strikingly slick reception area. Maria Tracy coordinated the studio's color scheme, which is most apparent in this portion of the space. White leather chairs sit comfortably on dark gray carpet that, in turn, sits firmly on light gray tile. A red tile border surrounds the entire section. This detail is echoed on the stairs that lead into the studio, as well as on the final arch. Black design elements complete the dramatic effect. The three most notable design elements can be found immediately behind the reception area. A reproduction of a black Fortuny lamp is flanked on each side by a male and female mannequin. The lifesize statues are solid black as well. The photographer freely admits that the mannequins are uncommon additions, but he explains their presence by saying, "It's too hard to keep plants alive. I never have to water the mannequins, nor do I have to worry about their being plagued by bugs."

The entryway (right) to Stewart's spacious studio (far right) is lined with some of his best work.

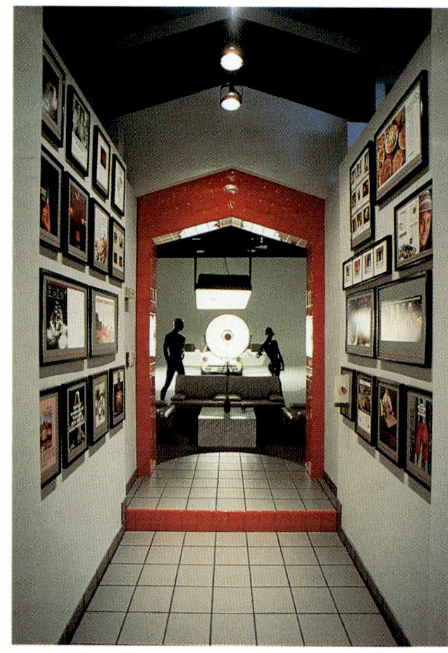

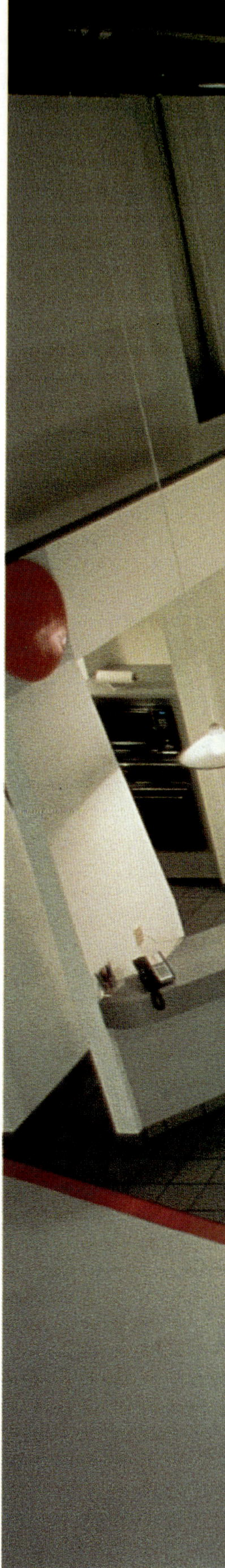

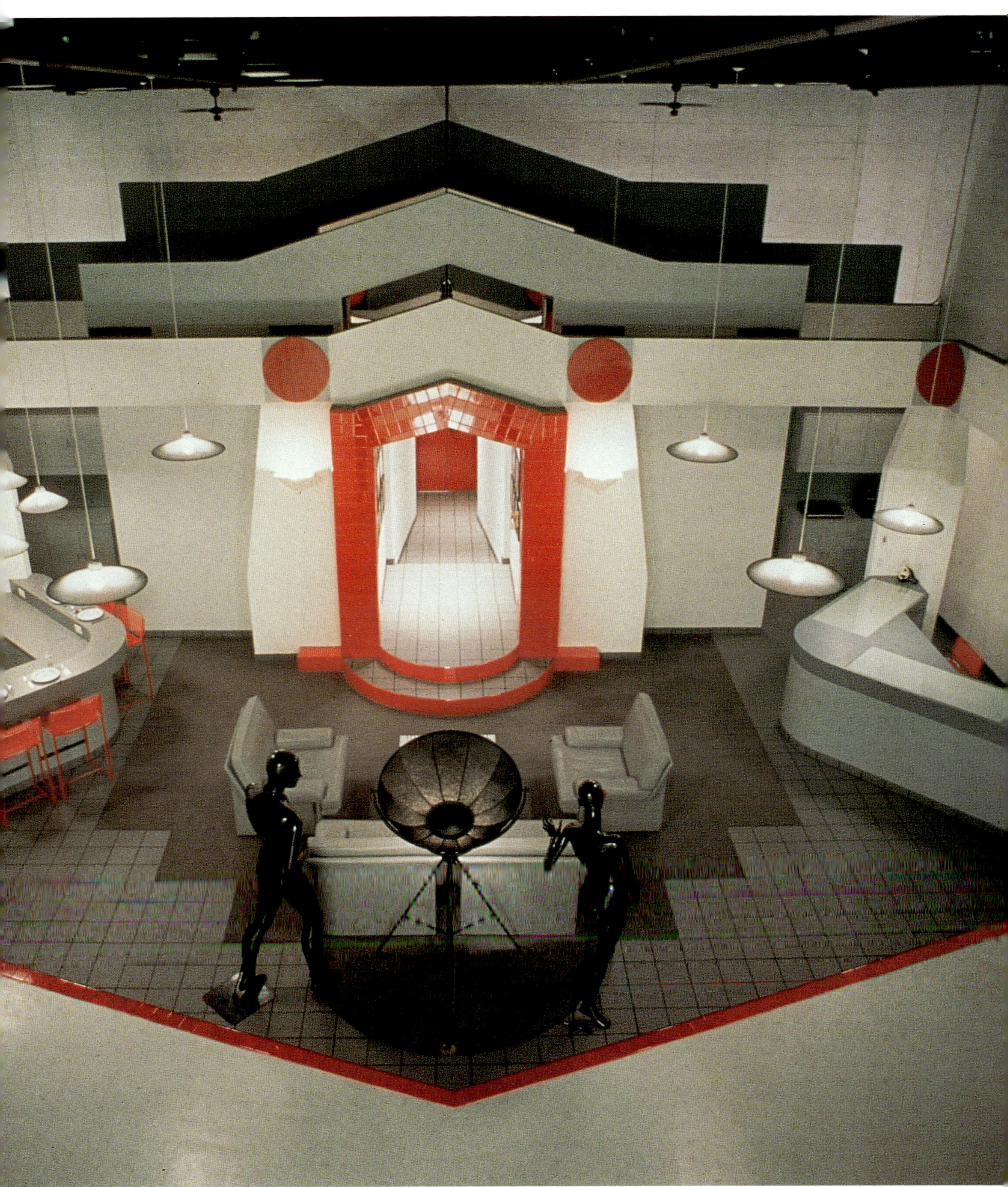

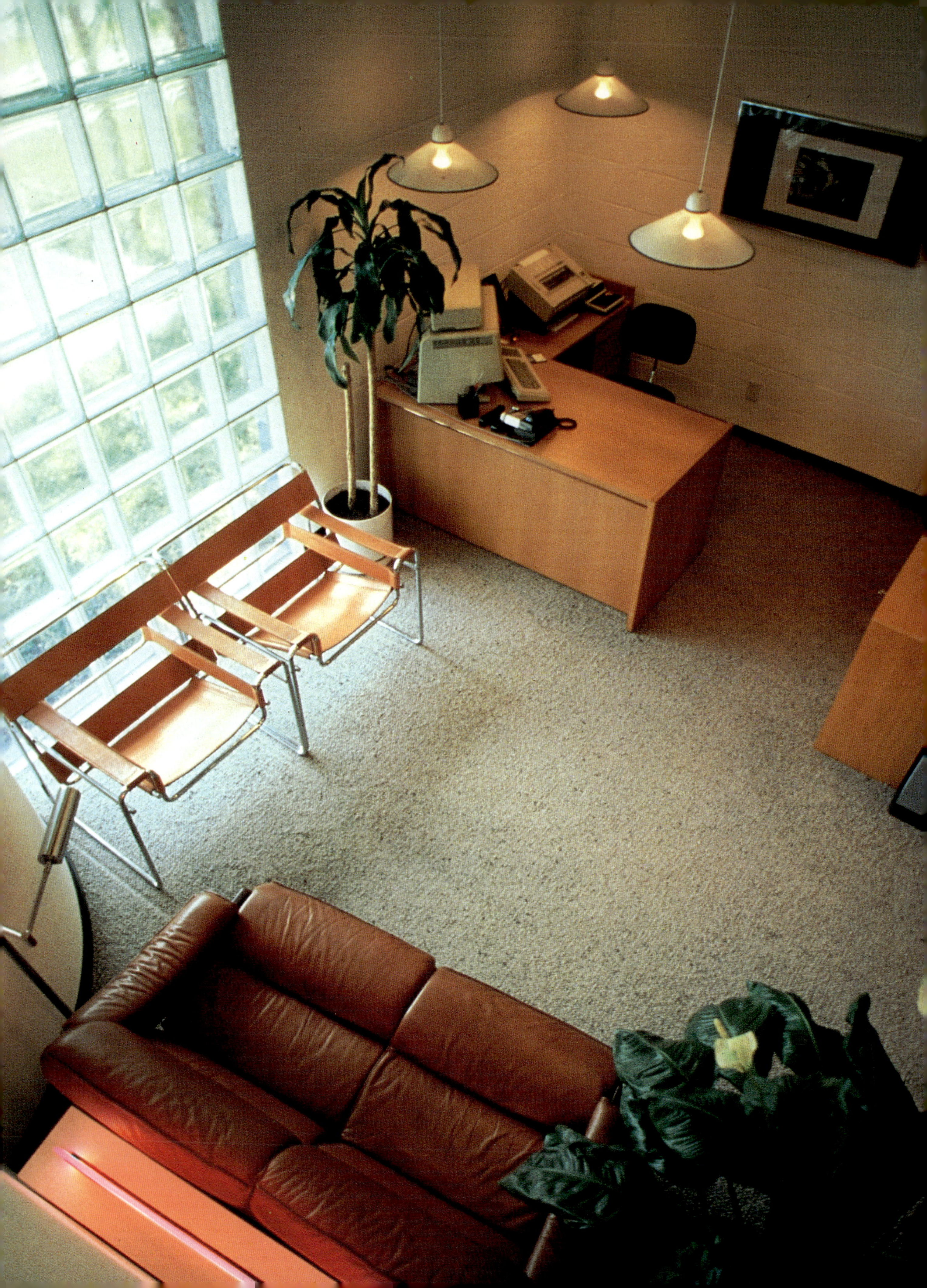

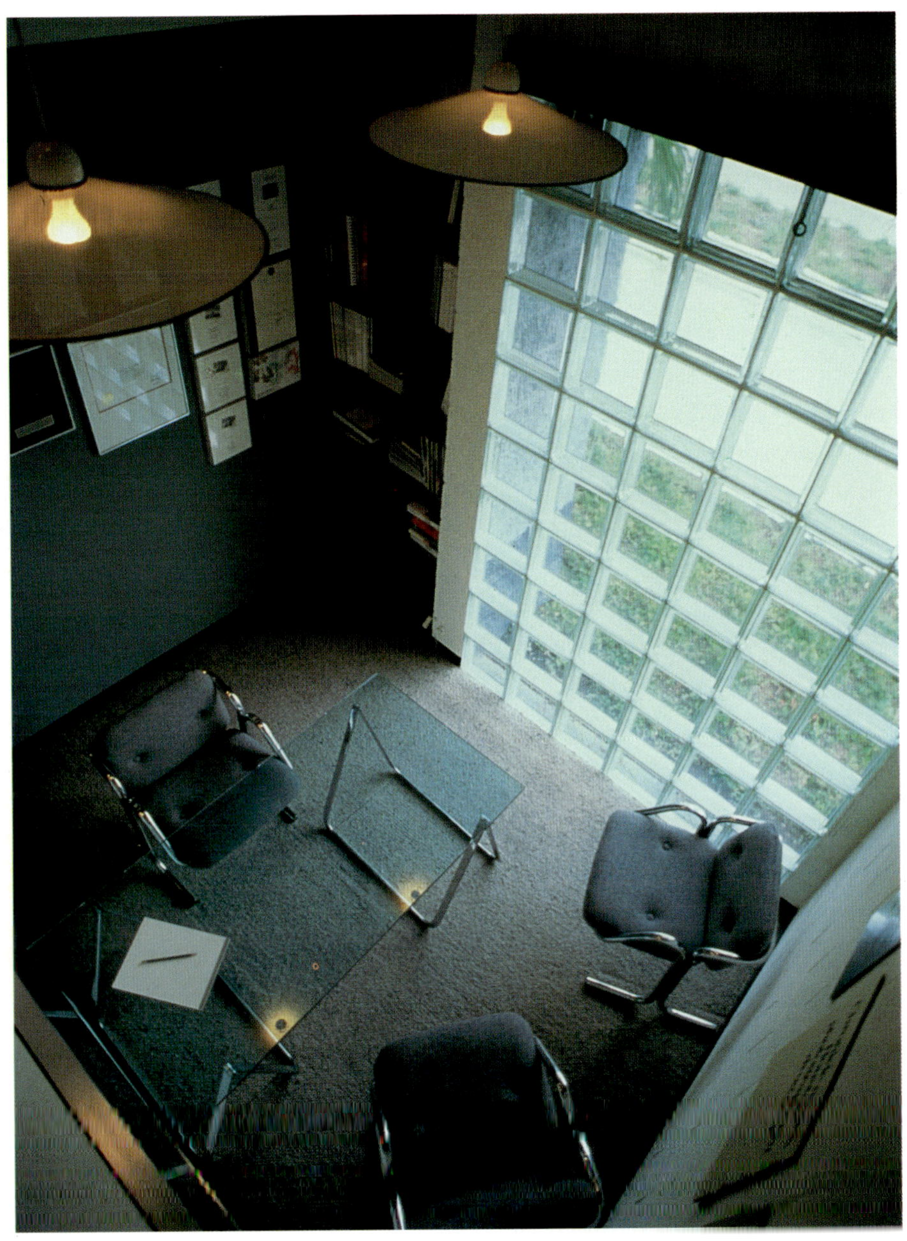

The understated designs of Stewart's private office (left) and the client meeting room (above) are in direct contrast to the boldness of the shooting stage and reception area.

Alongside and perpendicular to the reception area is a counter. Four red chairs flank the counter, which acts as a room divider. The studio's kitchen is situated directly behind this barrier, visible to visitors but not immediately accessible. The kitchen itself is fully equipped with the standard appliances as well as a dishwasher, microwave, and garbage disposal. As Stewart says, "Any sort of photographic food assignments can be prepared in this room." Nevertheless, primarily client lunches are arranged here. Facing the kitchen counter, positioned at the same angle and flanking the opposite side of the reception area, is a second counter that serves as a work table for both client and photographer. Like the reception area it borders, and the kitchen counter it echoes, a full view of the shooting stage is one of its main features.

Another special design element of Stewart's studio is the shooting stage with its 33-foot-wide cyclorama—the width of the entire studio—and its 20-foot-high shooting cove. Stewart admits that he would have preferred a 40-foot-wide shooting cove, but the studio's design was limited by the size of the property. Still, he does have the twenty-five feet of space required for just about any vehicular shots. To further accommodate his automotive clients, Stewart had a heavy bar inserted into the concrete floor of the shooting stage. It reinforces this section of the studio and allows the floor to support a subject of any weight. A 14-foot-high door situated to the left of the cyclorama can be opened to admit any vehicular traffic.

The studio's kitchen (right) is fully functional. The client area (far right) is directly off the shooting stage and is separated by color and light rather than by counters or walls.

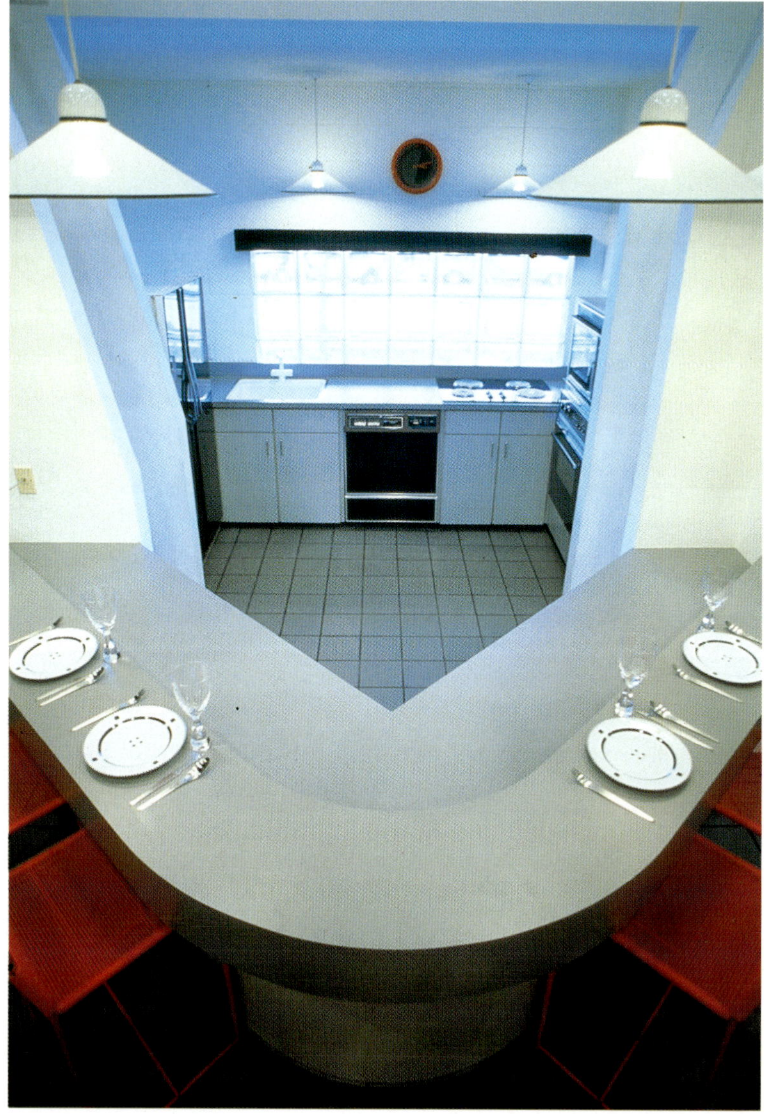

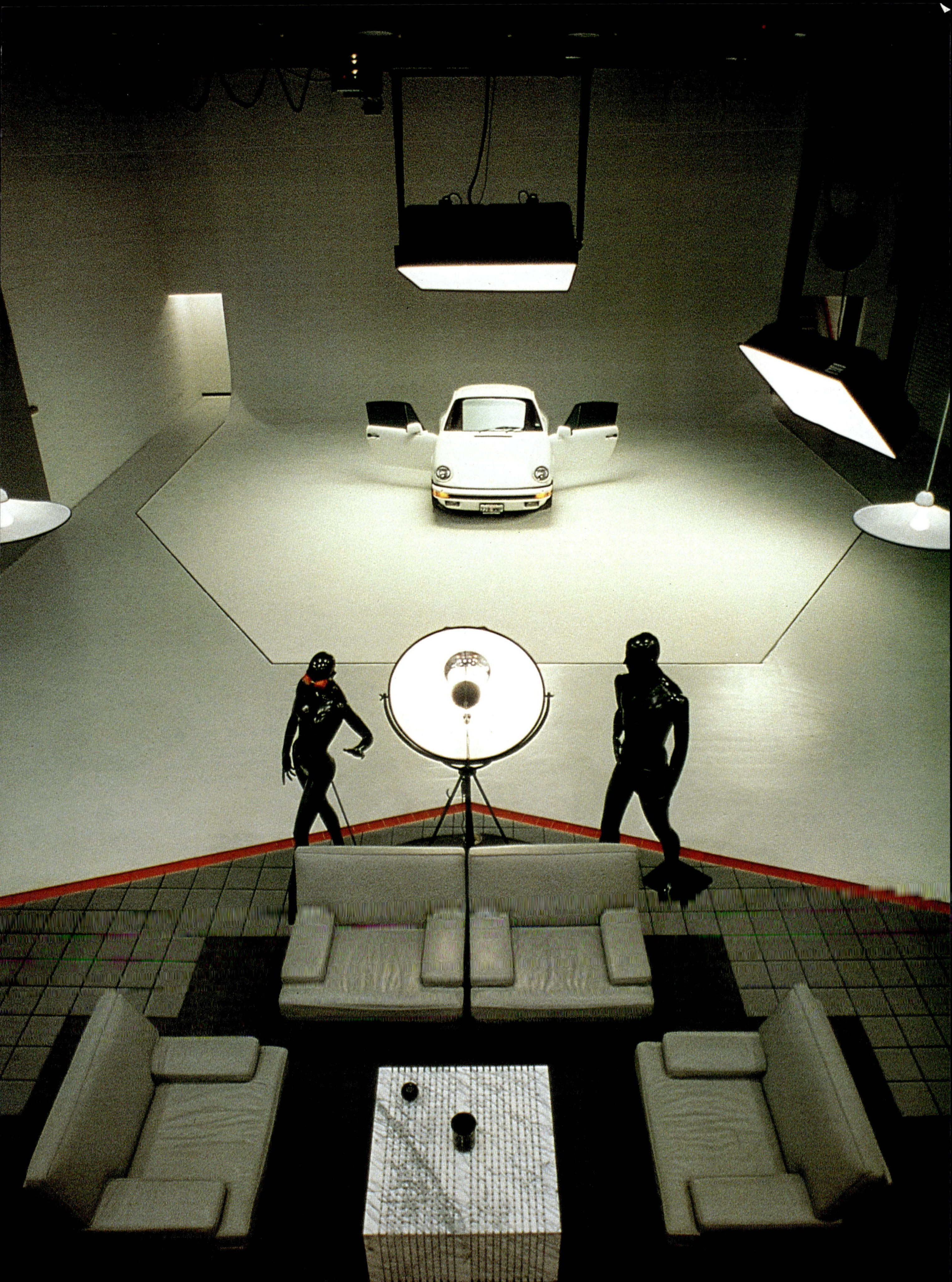

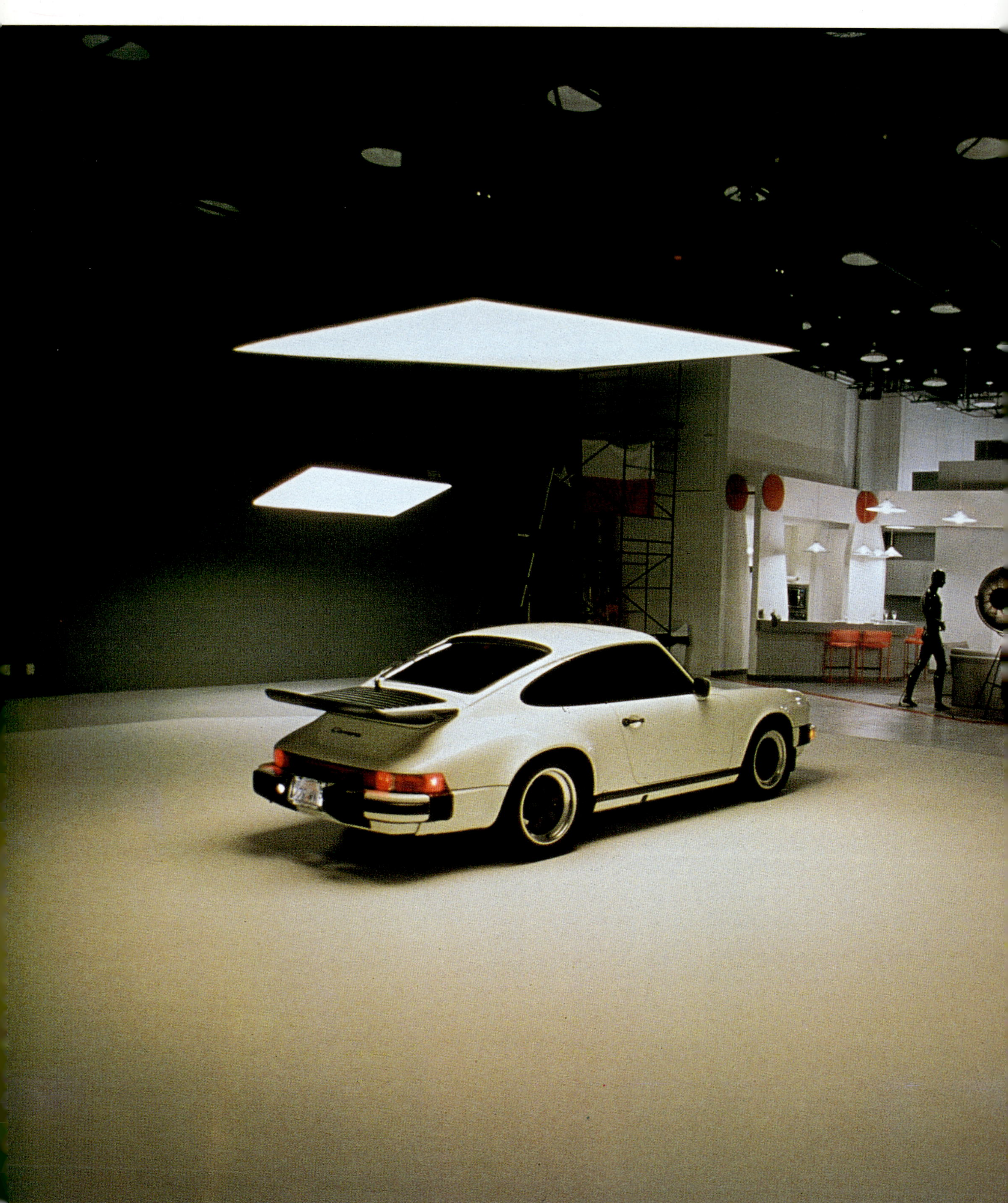

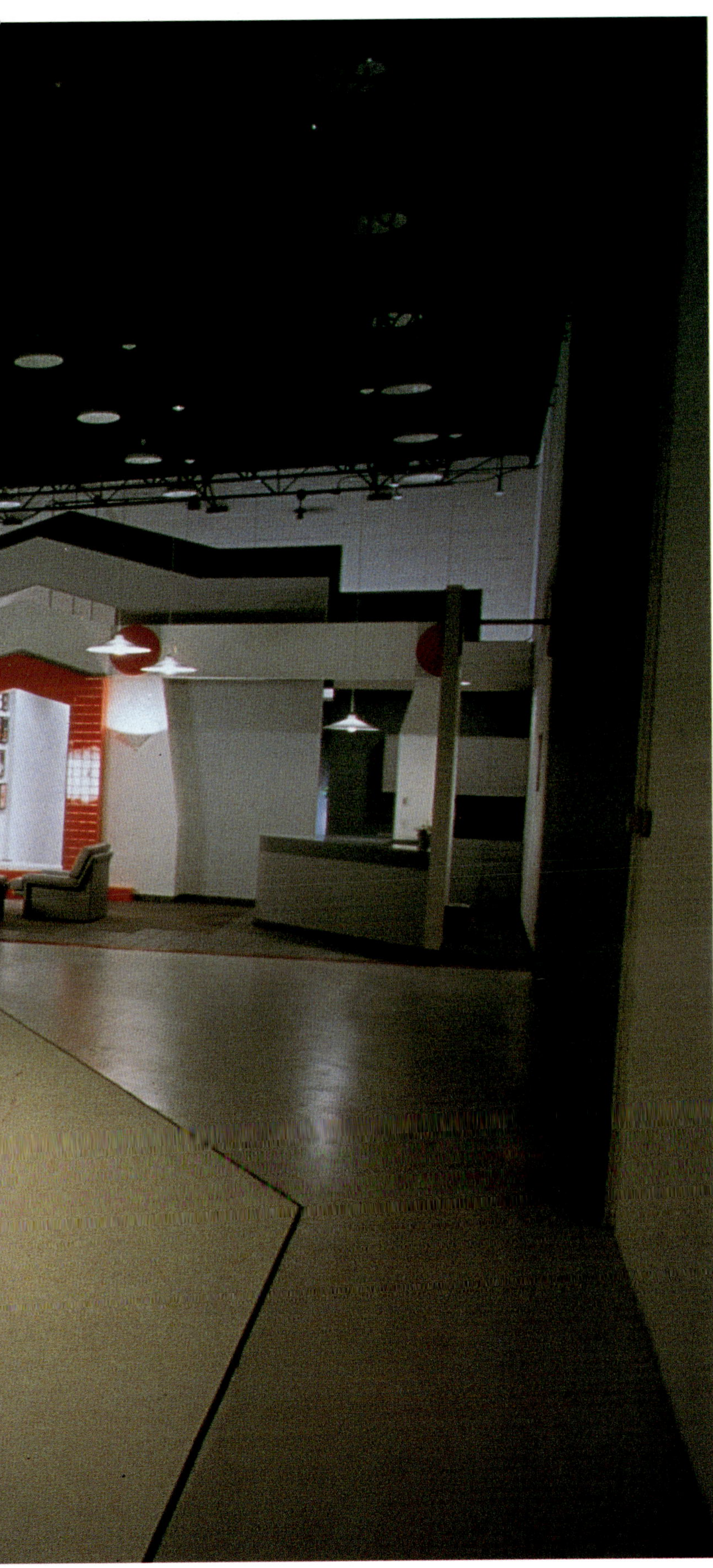

To gain access to the shooting stage, the visitor must walk through three increasingly larger arches. It is a dramatic effect that George Tracy says represents the bellows of a camera. The photographer was impressed. As Stewart explains, "It forces the visitor directly into what I'm selling: the studio. I find that it works wonderfully well."

Without doubt, the most striking feature of the shooting cove is the state-of-the-art Broncolor lighting system that dominates the ceiling. The system is composed of a 3 × 7-foot softbox and a 7 × 8-foot box, both of which are completely motorized. The two units are situated on separate bars that ride on a large grid that covers the entire shooting area. The 12,000 watt/second strobe system and its modeling lights are controlled by a single infrared remote control unit that fits into the photographer's hand. The six strobe heads that make up the unit can be raised or lowered and turned on and off with one motion from anywhere in the studio. In addition, the light ratio generated by the two boxes can be reprogrammed through the same unit. Stewart also has a series of smaller light boxes that stand on the floor and are used for supplemental fill. The photographer has no problem justifying the $100,000 price tag on his Broncolor unit. "The efficiency in speed and time makes it all worth it," he says.

A major point of the Tracys' design was its clean aesthetic: all studio clutter is hidden behind the shooting cove's rear wall. It is here that Stewart keeps flats, rolls of seamless, sawhorses, equipment, clamps, and assorted studio supplies. The pristine white of the shooting stage floor is painstakingly maintained by Stewart, who paints it, he says, almost monthly. Because he is averse to seamless paper (although he stocks rolls in order to fill client demands), the photographer will paint the cyclorama to match any PMS colors a client may request. The two small walls that encircle the cove are painted 18 percent gray both for the visually calming effect the color brings to the studio, and so that they can act as unobtrusive backdrops in [illegible]

A reverse view of the studio shows the entryway through the bright red arch.

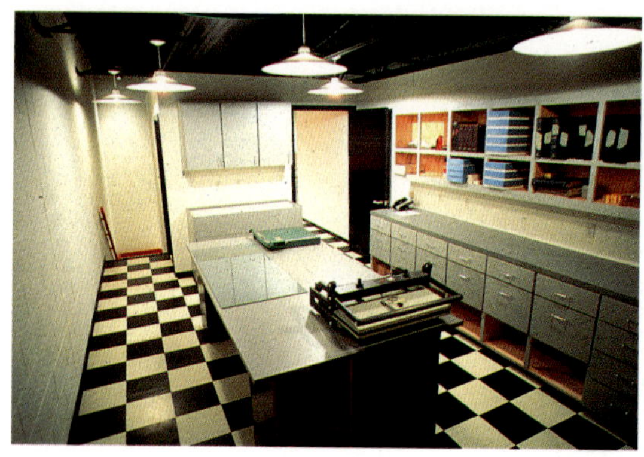

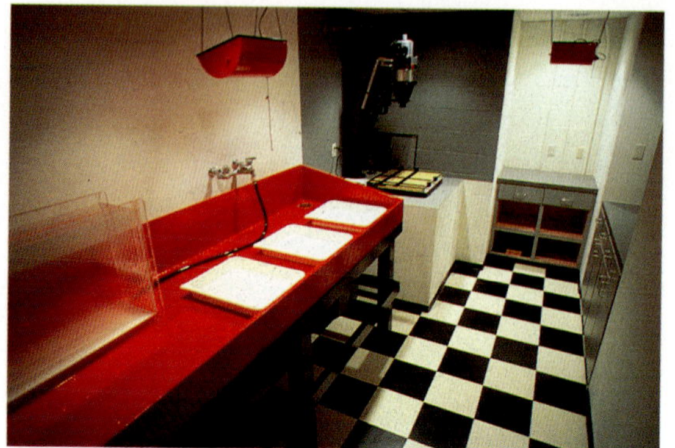

Alongside the prop storage room and behind the stage wall is a studio workroom that contains a large light table, a dry mounting press, file cabinets, a paper cutter, and an assortment of office supplies. Next door is the studio darkroom. All color work is sent out for processing, but Stewart and a crew of freelance assistants develop and print all black-and-white work in house. "I like to have full control," explains the photographer.

The studio's basement houses a well-stocked carpentry shop. "This is where we keep all our paint and wood supplies," says Stewart. An equipment locker and film storage room complete the ground floor. All power packs, heads, cameras, lights, and motor drives are organized on the room's shelves, and a separate security system with motion detection—which is always locked at night—safeguards these essentials.

Stewart is not one to scrimp on either necessities or luxuries. Other studio niceties include 525-amp heavy-duty wiring, three 5-ton air conditioners and four ceiling fans that distribute the air the trio generates, and a private conference room. The studio's exterior, which resembles nothing so much as a fortress, is as striking as its interior.

The project cost Stewart $262,000 for the building and $80,000 for the lot. Although work from many of his oil accounts has lessened, he keeps his business going with annual reports, brochures, and industrial ads. He has recently diversified by going after banking and financial accounts and local retail assignments.

Conventional wisdom maintains that the economy is cyclical and, therefore, what goes around must come back around. When that happens in Houston, Craig Stewart will certainly be ready.

Of all the design plans, "the most original idea, that which was most different from the normal, was what I went with."

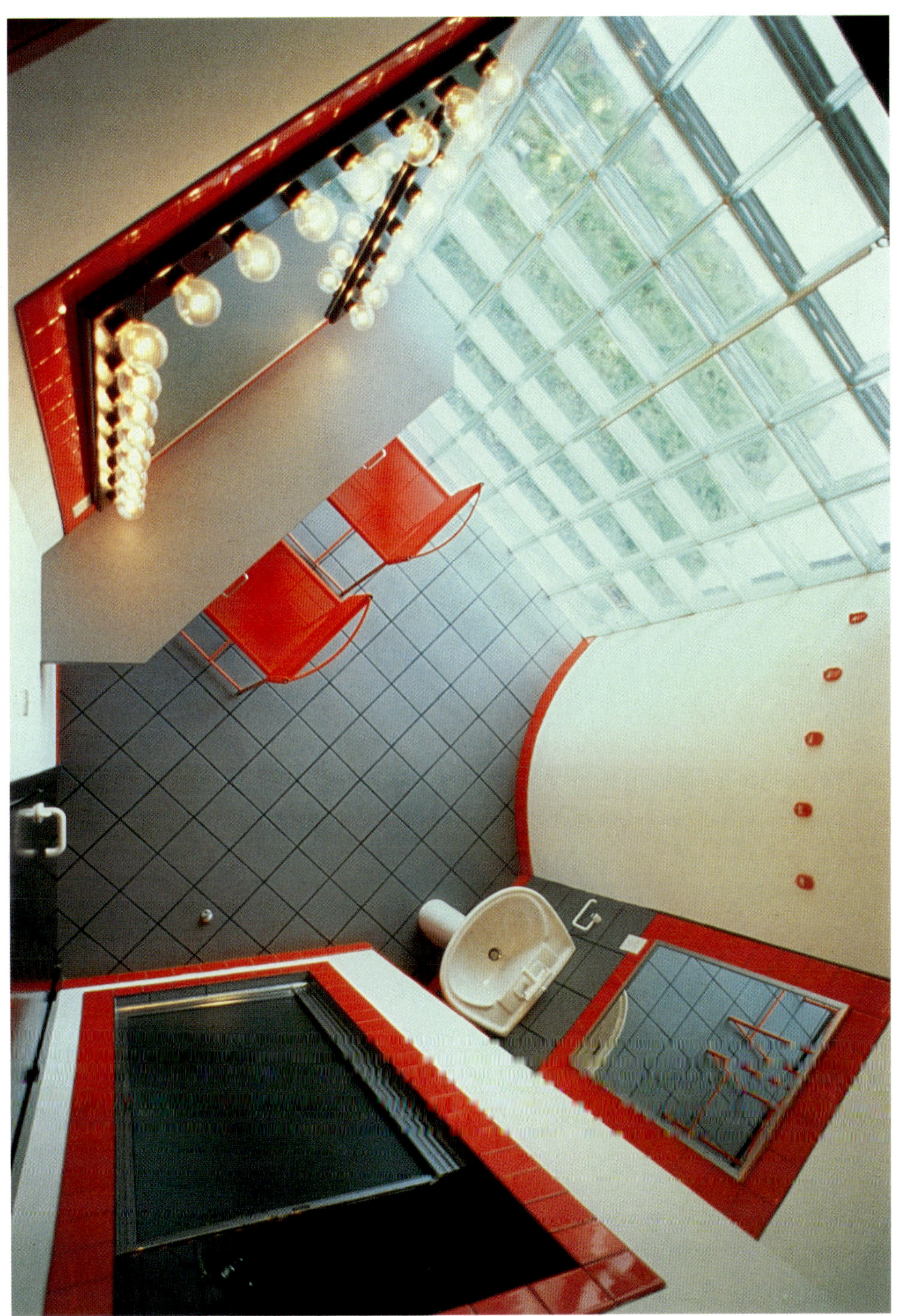

The changing room, used by models and stylists, is small but contains everything necessary for a successful fashion shoot.

MAKING A STUDIO A MODEL OF EFFICIENCY

"I don't come from a photographic background," says Michel Tcherevkoff, "so I had no preconceived ideas about what a studio should look like." Indeed, the New York City-based photographer had originally studied law in his native France. But one summer he accompanied his sister, a model, to the United States. During that trip, he decided that photography could offer him a "more glamorous lifestyle." He switched careers and never looked back.

Rather than learning his new trade by attending school, Tcherevkoff "acquired" his craft by assisting Pete Turner, a noted New York photographer who specializes in photographic effects. After a year and a half, the young Frenchman went on to a number of other jobs. "Many of them taught me what *not* to do," he recalls. Finally, Tcherevkoff decided it was time to open his own studio.

A southern exposure, which means sunlight all day, is but one of the reasons that Michel Tcherevkoff's small but efficient studio works so well.

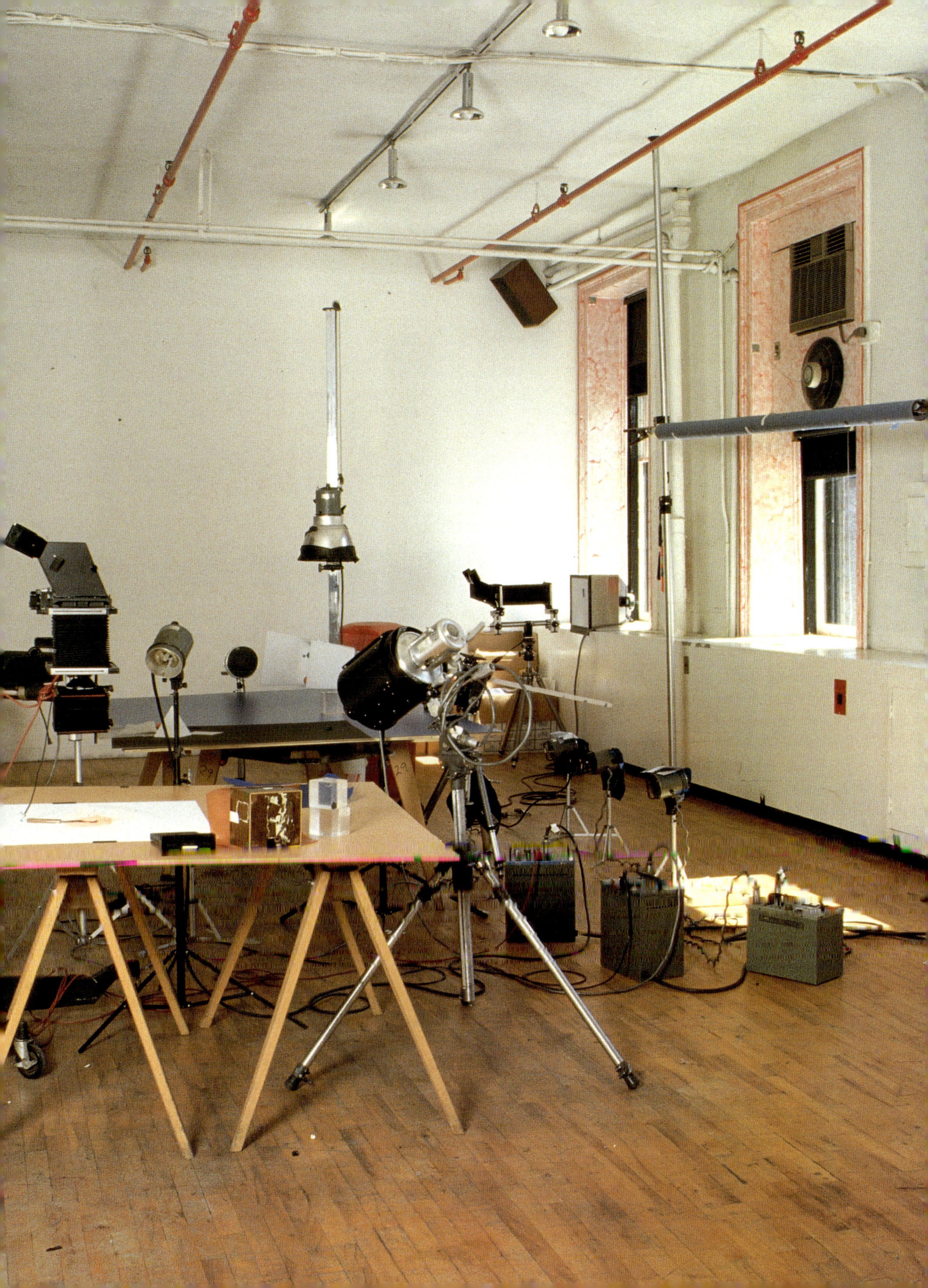

Tcherevkoff's first space, "which I always knew was temporary," was located in downtown Manhattan. Though serviceable, it was small. Because he had been exposed to a number of different studio setups while learning his craft as an assistant, Tcherevkoff now had a clear notion of what he expected from his own space. "Since I was spending so much time in the studio, I wanted something physically and mentally comfortable," he says. "I knew that had to include lots of light, preferably from a southern exposure so sunlight was available all day long. I'd worked in studios that were dark and cave-like, and I found the experience depressing and difficult."

After a brief search, Tcherevkoff discovered an 8,000-square-foot loft space on the seventh floor of a building on lower Broadway. The structure had once housed an upscale department store called Arnold Constable, which had closed in the late 1960s. The facility contains large, unbroken areas of floor space, seven elevator shafts, and 14-foot ceilings. In an effort to make his property more rentable, the building's owner was willing to break up the cavernous space into smaller offices. The location of the building at the edges of New York City's burgeoning photo district, as well as the various amenities it offered, suited the photographer's needs. But 8,000 square feet was far too generous an amount of space for Tcherevkoff. Since his work tends to be tabletop setups, the photographer estimated his needs at roughly 3,000 square feet. The landlord soon agreed to break up the loft and rented the southern portion of the area to Tcherevkoff. "I didn't want a larger space," says Tcherevkoff. "The more space you have, the more expensive your overhead. I didn't want to become a slave to my work in order to finance my studio."

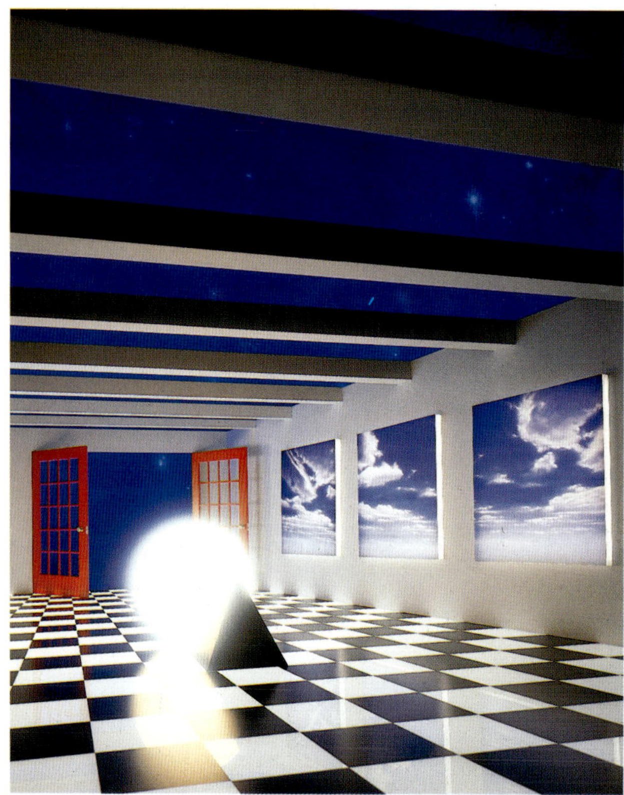

Most of Tcherevkoff's special-effect photographs are done on tabletop sets inside his Manhattan studio.

Cleverly disguised storage areas keep Tcherevkoff's studio well stocked and running smoothly.

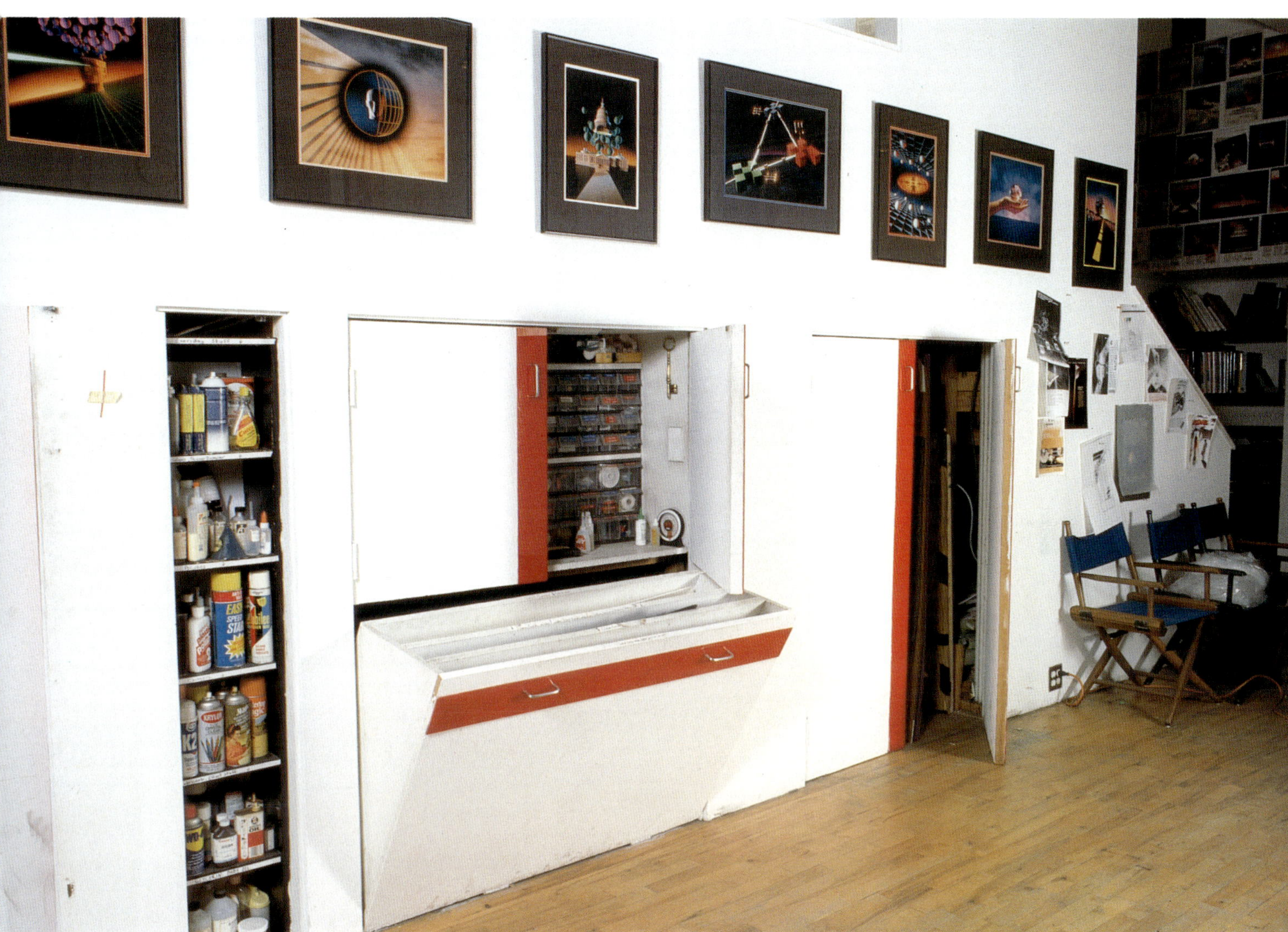

PLANNING FOR EFFECT

Although expenditures might be lower, a small space has very immediate limitations. "I knew that I had to utilize this area to its optimum," notes Tcherevkoff. To do this, he called on a friend, Michael Wolfe, an architect by trade. The two came up with a design that took advantage of just about every available corner of the studio. In terms of both design and comfort, Tcherevkoff's studio is a model of efficiency.

The visitor arrives at a small reception area that, at first glance, seems to be stark white. Opposite the entryway, on top of the small couch, a compact neon sculpture appears to be the only piece of decoration alleviating the room's sterility. This, according to Tcherevkoff, is part of a deliberate effect he has created. "I let my visitors simmer here for about forty-five seconds after they are announced," he says. "That's just enough time for them to sit down and—bang—glance at the left side wall." The wall is covered from floor to ceiling with award and citation certificates Tcherevkoff has received during the past eighteen years. Once visitors have the photographer's professional credentials firmly in mind, they are ready to enter the work area through a steel door that, for security reasons, has no doorknob on the outside.

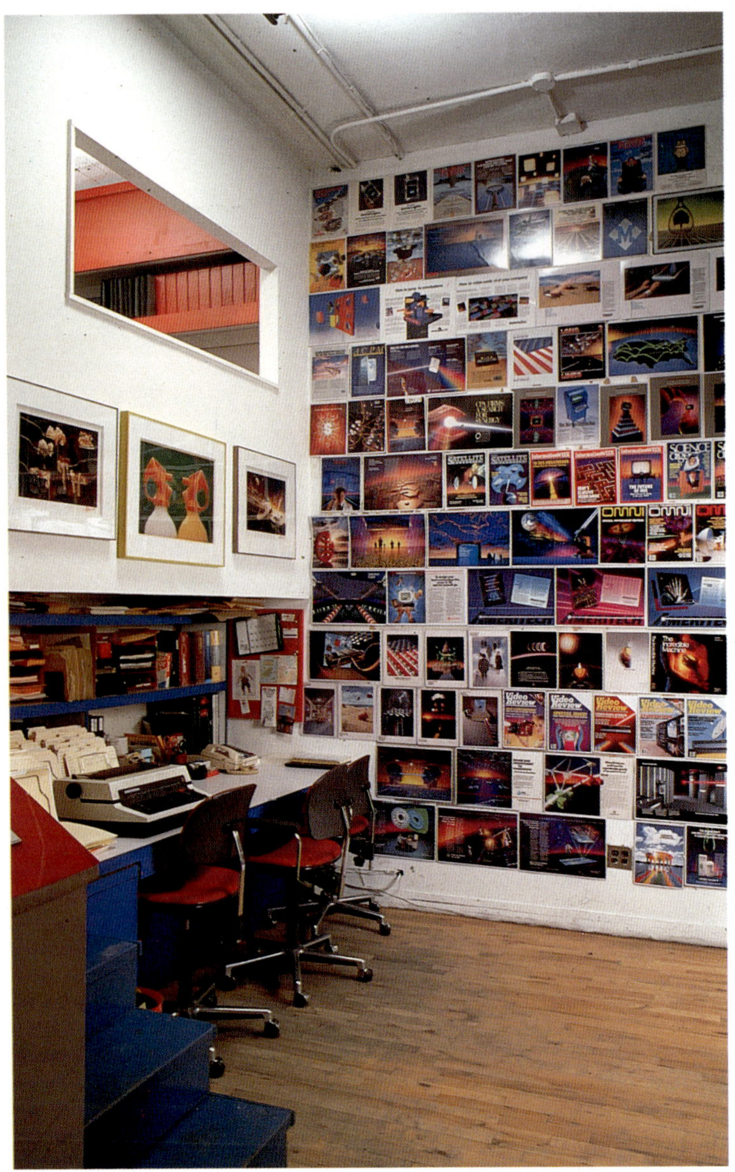

The entryway accommodates a secretary's office, and above that, Tcherevkoff's own loft-based office. The wall on the right features an ongoing, everchanging display of the photographer's latest work.

Upon crossing into the studio, visitors are confronted by a long desk immediately opposite the door. It is here that all office work is done by one of Tcherevkoff's three assistants. A curtain underneath the desk, stretching its length, hides the first of many storage areas visitors will see. The desk is built into a larger wall that extends up toward the ceiling and forms part of a 16 × 13-foot alcove overlooking the entire studio. Wolfe's design has effectively broken up half the studio by incorporating an alcove at the front right of the space, and a darkroom/workroom at the left rear. Yet, because the rest of the studio remains totally open and seven windows run along one entire wall of the space, visitors never feel cramped here.

Originally, Tcherevkoff did a fair amount of food photography and had a kitchen designed to accommodate this specialty. A sink, stove, and refrigerator are part of the overall design. An 8 × 8-foot work island sits in the middle of the kitchen area. Because he "stopped enjoying that sort of work," Tcherevkoff no longer shoots food. Currently, the kitchen is used to heat catered meals, and on busy days the work island often becomes another shooting stage.

The second of the studio's two "rooms" faces the kitchen area. It is divided in two and contains a small darkroom where both black-and-white and color film can be processed. Two enlargers and a dryer occupy this area, as does a large cabinet containing photo paper. Other drawers contain small surfaces, gels, and marbleized backgrounds. Next to the darkroom in the same enclave are prop storage and a work area where small construction is done. Carpentry tools are stored here, as are sawhorses, very large glass surfaces, and a clothes rack. The top portion of this "room" is used for more storage.

The remaining studio space, measuring 21 × 42 feet, is given over entirely to shoots. Polecats hung with backdrops act as dividers. Tcherevkoff points out that up to five small shooting stages can be set up here. The main focus of the shooting area is, of course, the seven windows that admit an immense amount of light. In keeping with his theme of optimum utilization, the photographer had a series of enclosed shelves built underneath the window area. As a result, the studio remains clean and uncluttered at all times.

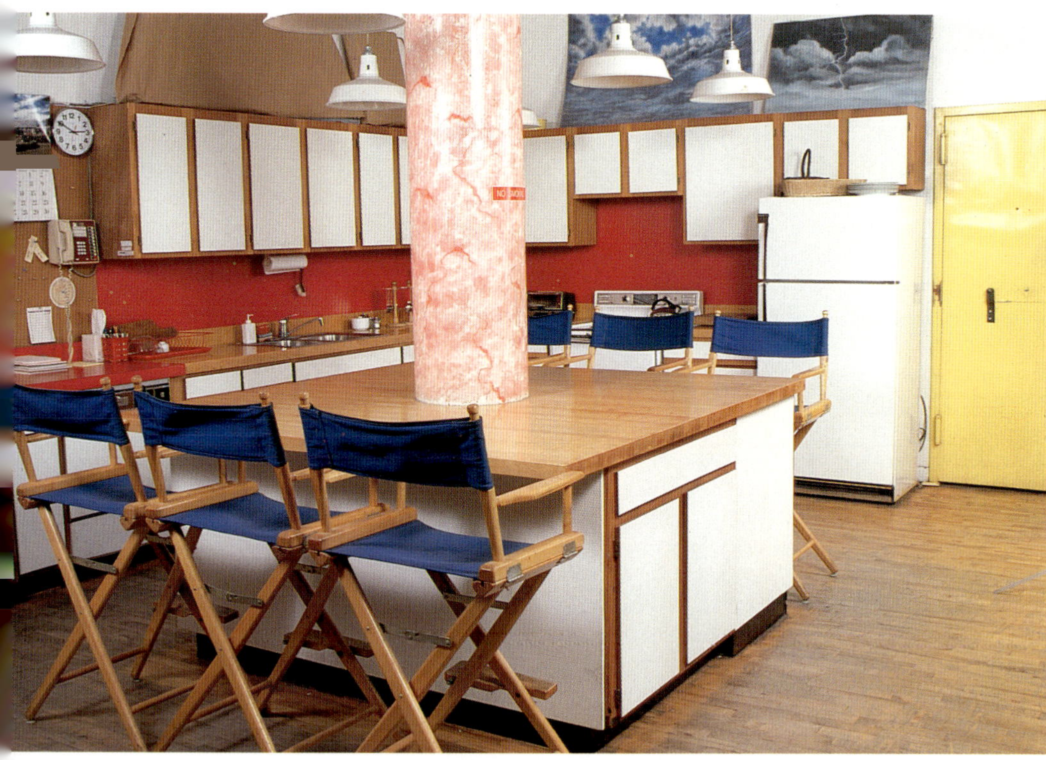

The kitchen area with its work island contains more storage space.

Tcherevkoff's darkroom is also contained within his 3,000-square-foot space.

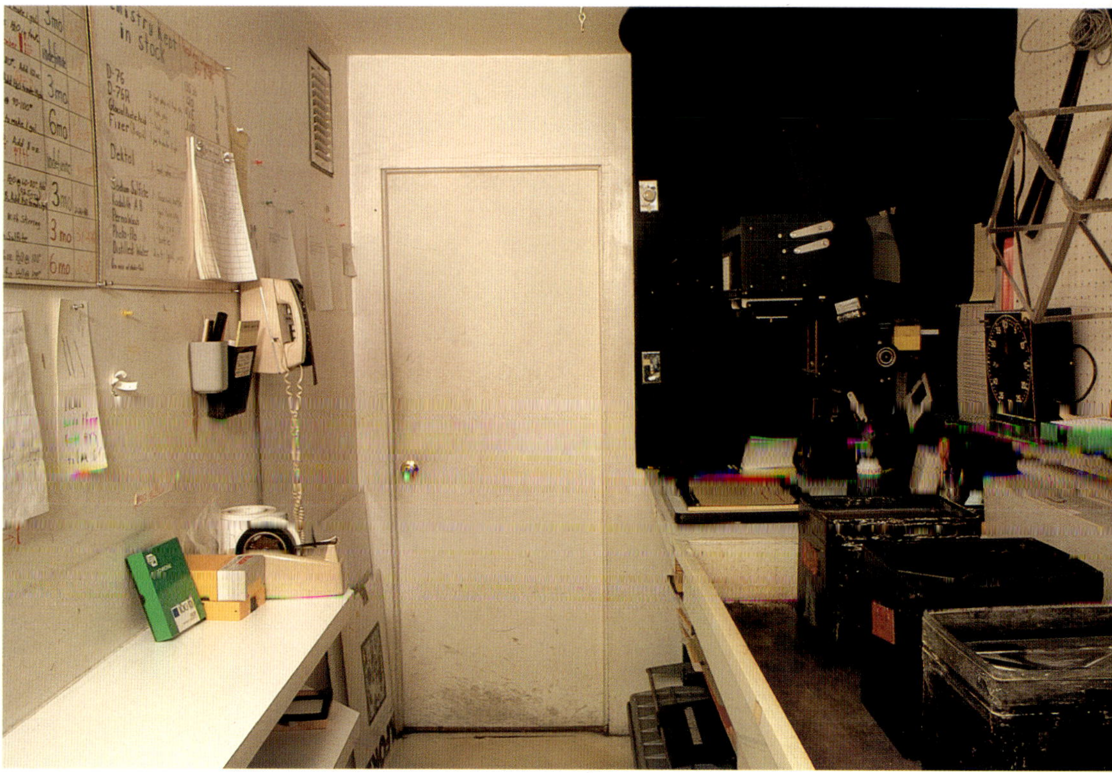

A staircase to the left of an assistant's desk provides access to the alcove, which is also Tcherevkoff's office. Glassless "windows" on three sides allow the photographer to see and hear everything that takes place underneath the alcove. A desk extends against the 16-foot alcove wall; all the studio paperwork is kept here until it is outdated, when it is stored at another location. The desk overlooks the studio's shooting area, allowing the photographer to direct assistants even as he takes care of other matters. A series of flat files face the desk. It is here that Tcherevkoff keeps all his images, both 35mm and 4 × 5 transparencies. One drawer of files contains a lightbox, which can be pulled out to supplement the lightbox that sits on top of the cabinets. A banquette occupies the entire length of the alcove and is situated directly opposite the studio entryway. Tcherevkoff points out that the bench is hollow, and the cushions hide more storage space for records, paperwork, and files. In fact, the alcove sits above a group of closets specifically designed by the photographer and the architect to suit Tcherevkoff's individual needs.

The largest of these closets faces the shooting stage and has a series of vertical dividers and a few horizontal shelves. Tcherevkoff keeps all his background surfaces—plastic, Formica, glass, rolls of diffusing material, and flocking paper—and tripods here. Next to this walk-in space are smaller cabinets and shelves. Photographic supplies, such as clamps, wires, tape, and miscellaneous studio needs, are neatly stored here, as are cleaning and household supplies (in other, smaller cabinets). The back of the alcove faces the studio's kitchen. Another series of closets is built into this area. This is where Tcherevkoff keeps all his "hardware," such as cameras, lenses, and flash packs. The photographer estimates that one-third of these closets is reserved for his equipment, which includes five large-format 4 × 5 cameras, collapsible bank lights, and a series of reflectors.

To visitors, it appears as though Tcherevkoff has solved all of his space-related problems. When questioned, the photographer thinks for a moment, then laughs and says, "Maybe so, but the abundant light has caused a problem I'd never thought of. The studio is always hot." Then Tcherevkoff pauses, glances around his model space, and concludes, "I don't spend any money heating my studio, just cooling it."

"I didn't want a larger space. I didn't want to become a slave to my work in order to finance my studio."

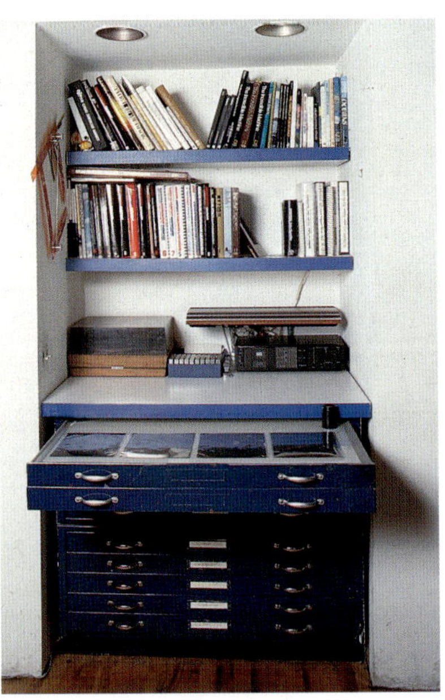

A recessed nook is used to hide slide and volume storage (above). The complete shooting stage (right) accommodates three different jobs simultaneously.

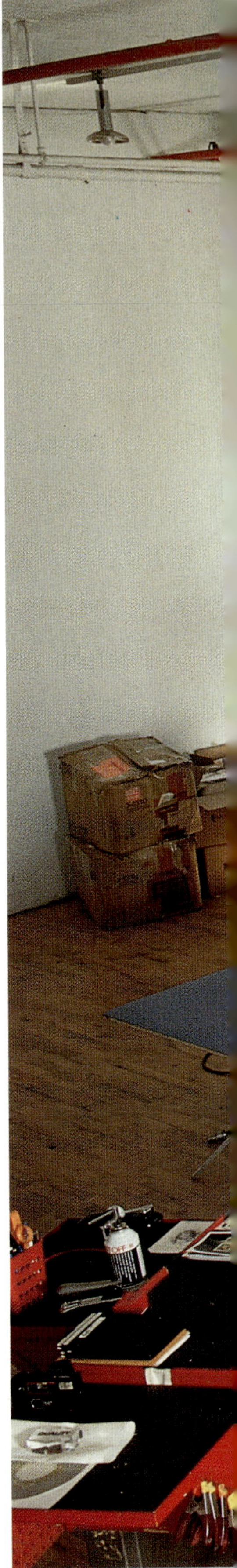

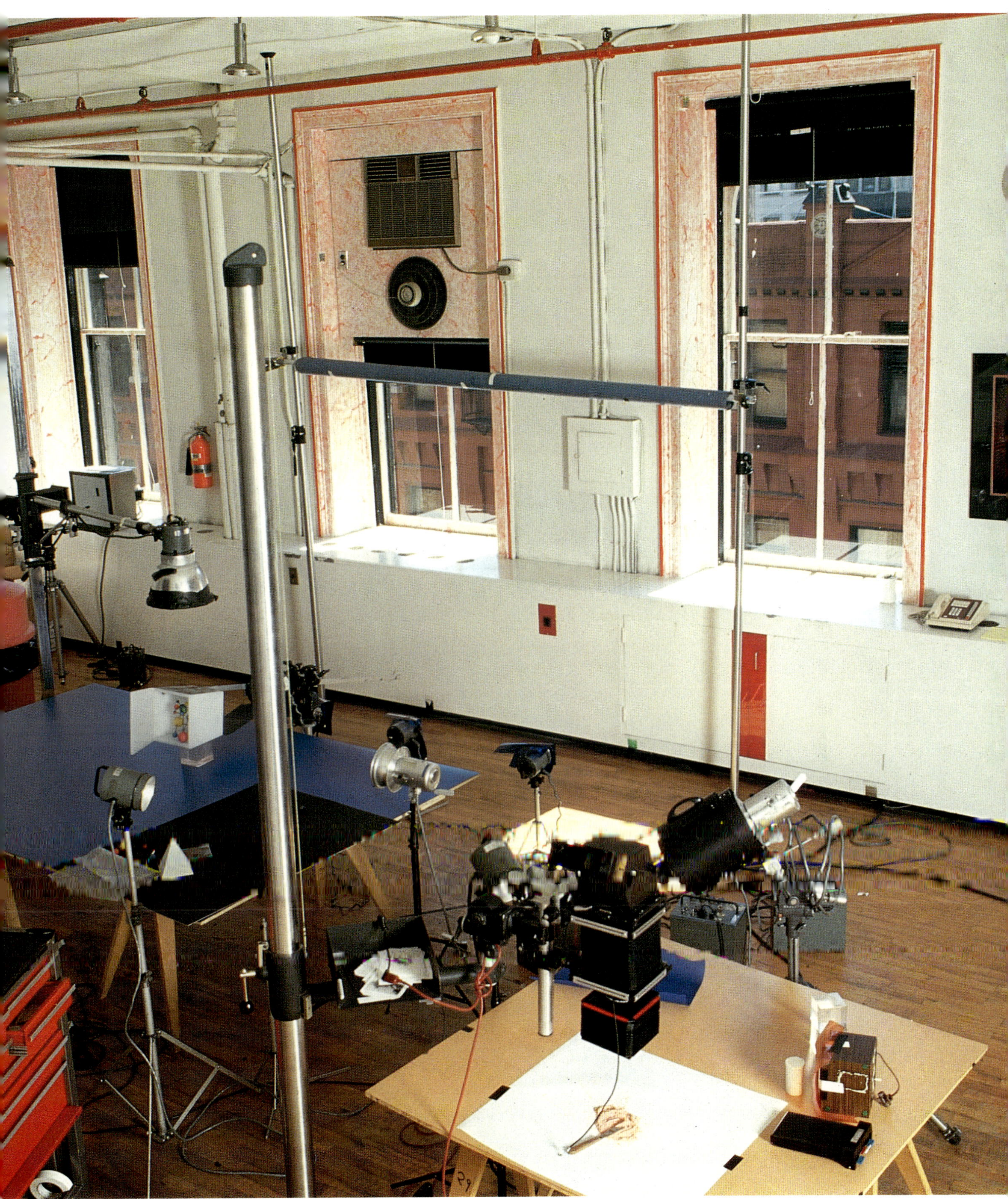

SHARING A STUDIO

The standard success formula for commercial photographers includes a long list of creative assignments, well-known and highly regarded clients, and perhaps most conspicuous of all, a busy studio designed to satisfy the photographer's every need. But in New York City, economic realities often dictate a different scenario. Rather than consider their setup—shared studio space plus two photographic tenants—to be a problem, J. Barry O'Rourke, who specializes in beauty, travel, and celebrity photography, and his partner, Robert Kligge, whose specialty is still-life photography, have made the arrangement work to everyone's benefit. **O**'Rourke, the seasoned shooter of the team, began his photographic career during the Korean War taking pictures of high-speed guided missiles for the navy. After his discharge, he went to the Art Center in Los Angeles, graduating four years later with a major in photojournalism. While struggling to get editorial assignments from magazines, O'Rourke shot photo essays for a syndication service and did architectural assignments as well. One of these features was picked up by *Playboy* magazine for its "Bachelor Pad" column and generated additional work from the publication. This eventually led to a staff position as a general shooter. After four years at Playboy's Chicago offices, the photographer decided it was time to try his luck in New York City.

The open design of J. Barry O'Rourke and Robert Kligge's studio makes it easier for the photographers to share the space.

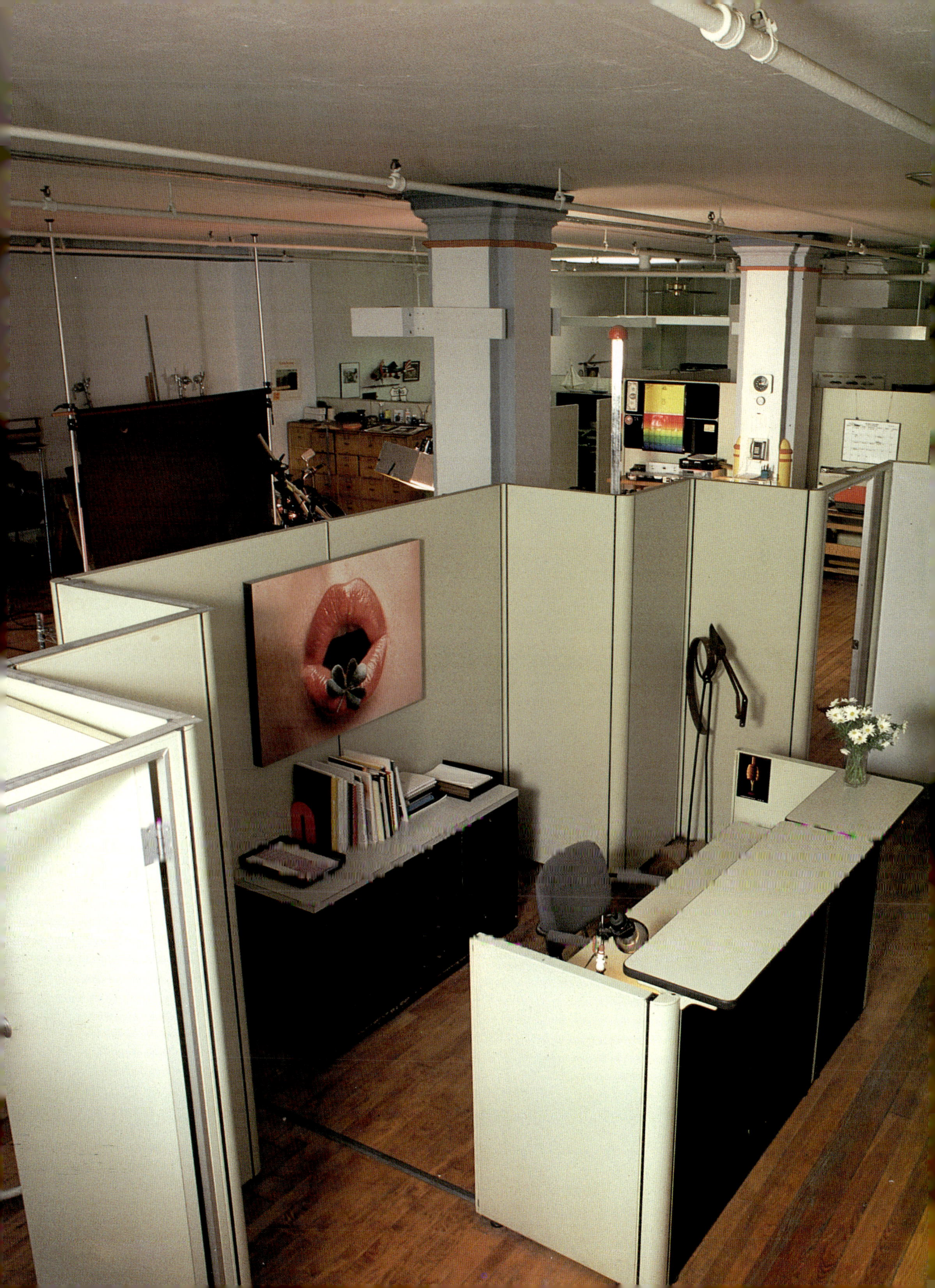

JOINING FORCES

Shortly after arriving in New York, O'Rourke rented a small studio (1,200 square feet) near midtown Manhattan and began getting beauty assignments. But the neighborhood was changing, and, as a result, his rent continued to escalate. "I decided that I wanted to change my whole approach to the business," he recalls. "I wanted a big space in which to work, and it occurred to me that several shooters could pool their resources toward this goal." He decided to explore this option. He continues, "I knew that years ago it was a stigma if you shared a studio; it meant that you couldn't afford your own space. I decided to challenge that notion."

O'Rourke teamed up with one of his former assistants, Robert Kligge. Kligge had studied at New York City's School of Visual Arts and had been introduced to the already established O'Rourke through a friend. A few freelance jobs assisting O'Rourke eventually led to a permanent position for Kligge, who learned a great deal about the business from O'Rourke. "But after 3½ years of working together," says Kligge, "I felt that the time had come for me to leave." In 1979, he set up his own studio in New York and began doing a lot of catalog and still-life work. "After a bit of hustling, the work started rolling in," says the photographer. Yet, although the bills were getting paid, the overhead that Kligge's rent alone represented was staggering. "In 1983, Barry and I discussed sharing studio space," says Kligge. "But because of the terms of each of our leases, we were locked into our separate arrangements."

The photographers kept their idea alive for two years while O'Rourke quietly went about looking for the ideal space where they could realize their joint goals. "I wanted a decent neighborhood where celebrities and models would feel safe," says O'Rourke. And, he says, both men wanted "a big freight elevator, a twenty-four-hour building with heat, hot and cold running water that came directly into the building at all times, ceilings that were at least 12 feet high, and lots of electrical power—about 200 amps."

Though O'Rourke and Kligge share one studio, their work is dissimilar. O'Rourke specializes in beauty, travel, and celebrity photography, whereas Kligge produces mostly still-life images.

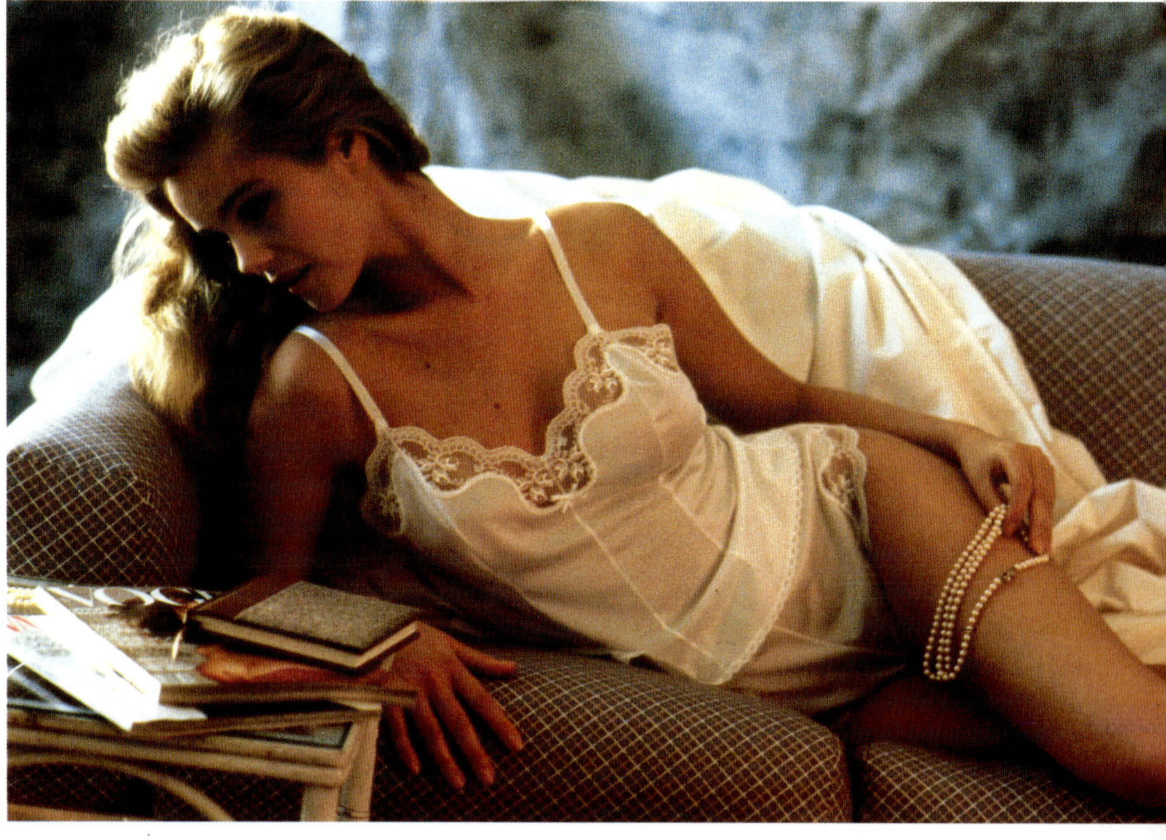

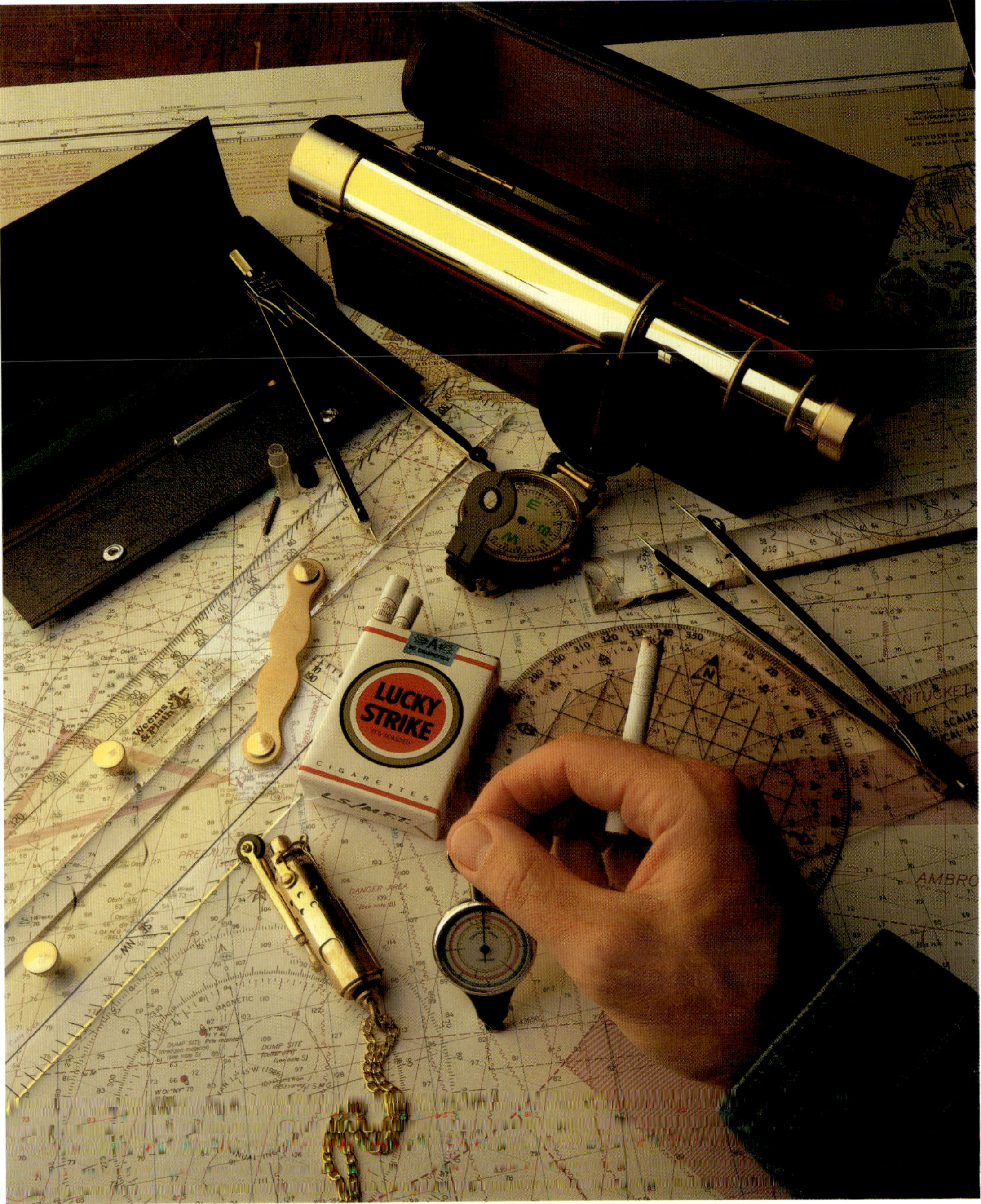

At the start of 1985, O'Rourke found a large loft in a soon to be renovated building on the fringes of Manhattan's SoHo district. "When I first saw this place, it was very dark," explains O'Rourke. "It had been a sweatshop, but the quality of light from the front windows was absolutely beautiful." This alone, however, was not quite enough to sway the photographer. "I also noticed that the building was being redone by Zuberri Associates, the people who had renovated another building I'd once worked in," he says. "They do beautiful work, and once I knew they were responsible, I was convinced it was the right place."

O'Rourke called Kligge, whose own lease was about to come up for renewal, and asked him to see the loft. At first, Kligge wasn't impressed "since hardly any work had been done." But he soon noticed that the large windows in the front of the building admitted a dazzling amount of light. "I could see that with all this light there was a lot of potential here," notes Kligge. The two photographers agreed to rent the loft and signed a ten-year lease. They also agreed to take on two subtenants: Caroline Greyschock, a fashion and portrait shooter, and Randy O'Rourke, who does travel and editorial work. "It would have been nice to buy space," says O'Rourke, "but this arrangement was more feasible for all parties concerned."

RETAINING AN "OPEN" FEELING

The photographers hired the design firm of Scruggs and Meyers, which, although it had no experience with photographic studios, had created interiors that both shooters were impressed with. "We had a loose discussion with them," explains Kligge, "in which we detailed our basic requirements. We told them we needed a large kitchen, plus we wanted a separate processing room and printing room." And, he continues, "The loading room had to be up front and not on the shooting floor so that four people could work comfortably here." Other than those few specifics, the designers had free reign.

The result: the studio layout retains the open feeling of the original loft. No floor-to-ceiling walls break up the space. Through careful placement of equipment and partitions—Herman Miller modular walls are used throughout the space—the various photographers have been assured of individual work areas that offer a large measure of privacy.

Visitors enter the fifth-floor studio directly from the elevator and are greeted by a medium-sized reception area in which an assortment of work by the four photographers is displayed. To the left and right of the receptionist's desk are identical doors. The entryway on the left leads onto the shooting stage, while the opening on the right provides access to the kitchen and studio offices, circumventing the work area. For the convenience of the four photographers, each has an office. And, for the comfort of the clients, there is a meeting room.

Directly off the shooting floor is a dressing room used by models and makeup and hair stylists. Along one wall of the room there is a mirror with makeup lights, but they are rarely turned on. "The windows admit so much light that it makes life easier on the hair and makeup stylists," O'Rourke explains. Next to this area is a small loading room used for processing black-and-white film and changing 4 × 5- and 8 × 10-sheet film.

Another convenient feature is a large storage room in which all flats and various props are kept. This room has a separate entrance that can be reached via a freight elevator. In this way the studio can be kept clear of any cumbersome object needed for a shoot. Next to the storage room, running along the studio's outer wall, are a fully equipped darkroom used primarily by O'Rourke and Kligge and a loading room used by Greyschock and Randy O'Rourke, Barry's son.

A second storage room overlooks the shooting stage. The usual jumble of photographic accessories—for example, clamps, wire, and gaffer tape—is stored here. "We didn't want pegboards around the studio," notes O'Rourke. "It would have made the space look too cluttered." This idea is reflected throughout the studio. There is nothing hanging from the ceiling to obstruct the continuous line of the loft, and none of the cubicle walls reaches the ceiling.

One consequence of the desire to keep the studio spare, says O'Rourke, "is the lack of closet space. There isn't one in the entire place. We keep a rack in the changing room in order to hang coats."

The lack of closet space is, in fact, a minor complaint. According to Kligge, the cost of renovating the studio was approximately $150,000. He and O'Rourke had some trouble with their contractors. "Because of the amount of money involved, I insisted that everything get done as we wanted," Kligge explains. The project, which took close to one year to complete, was finished by the photographers themselves. They say that they would do very little differently, and the few changes they would like—a gas stove instead of an electric range, 6,000 square feet instead of 5,000, and taller ceilings—are nonessential.

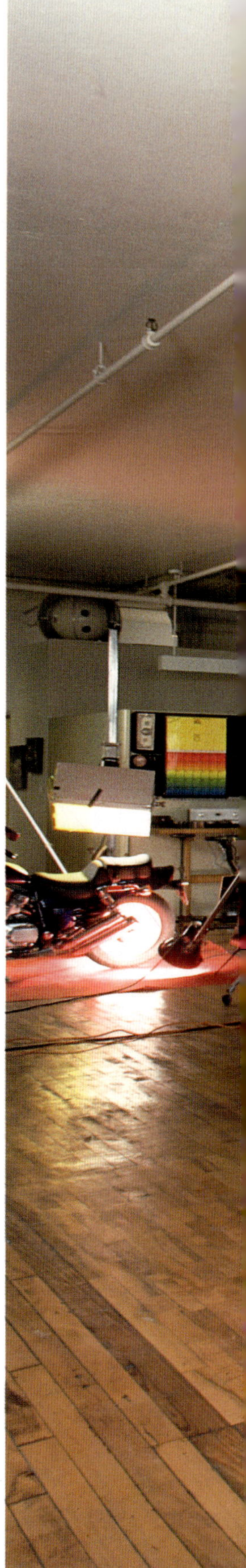

The shooting stage of the joint studio is kept clear unless a job is in process. Lightstands and polecats are then used to differentiate the work areas.

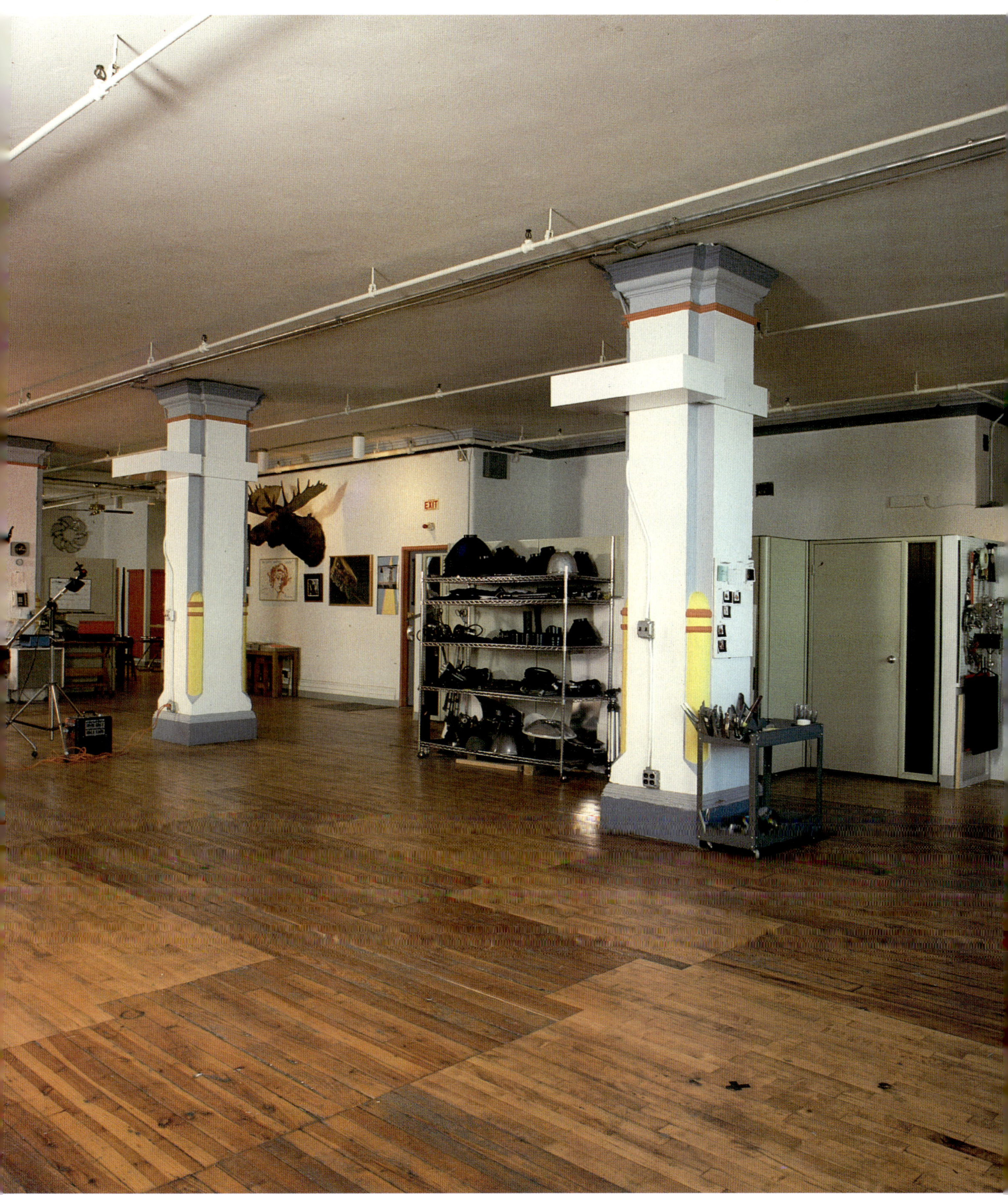
EXIT

The kitchen is, arguably, the heart of this studio. Its white formica countertops, cabinets, and bar make it a natural gathering place for visitors and staff members alike. Stools running along one side of the bar offer comfortable seating, as do the chairs that match the large table. But the kitchen serves a multitude of purposes. In addition to the beverages and snacks, fully catered lunches and sometimes dinners are often prepared here. All the cooking and styling for O'Rourke's food photography is done in the kitchen. And, on occasion, the room becomes the set where the prepared food is shot.

Beyond the kitchen is a fully appointed bathroom. Besides the usual assortment of fixtures, O'Rourke had one unique modification put in: a shower stall with a glass wall that faces out into the larger studio. The shower is shielded by a waterproof set of blinds for regular use; however, when O'Rourke is doing a beauty or advertising shot, he can set up his camera outside the shower, away from the moisture and steam, and get a sharp yet accurate image.

Another special feature is an equipment closet. Because of its small cubicles that face each other, the closet area is a direct contrast to the other half of the loft space, which is completely open, spacious and airy. One entire wall of this section is taken over by windows. They "provide a western exposure," O'Rourke says. "The best light is available during April/May and September/October. I use it *all* the time."

In deference to the available light, this portion of the studio was designated the shooting stage, even though no design elements—colored walls or tiled floors—physically separate this space. Instead, light banks of assorted sizes, poles holding backdrops and seamless, and tables with still-life setups are pushed around the shooting floor in order to form impromptu "work cubicles." Up to four shoots can be set up here, and with care, all four can take place at the same time. Much thought was also given to the choice of artificial lighting. "We wanted nice light in the kitchen, dressing room, and offices," says Kligge. "I didn't want fluorescents." The studio is illuminated by a specially designed configuration of sources (a mixture of metal halide and sodium tubes) that projects a soft blue and pink glow.

One aspect of their business life works extraordinarily well for all involved. "When you share a space with other photographers, no one is allowed to get a big head. Nothing and no one is taken too seriously," O'Rourke explains. "And it's beneficial to all because if someone is too busy, we can pass the work around."

The glass-walled shower (right) is kept open only during beauty shoots. Otherwise, a venetian blind obscures the bathroom. The kitchen (far right) is also used as a client meeting room.

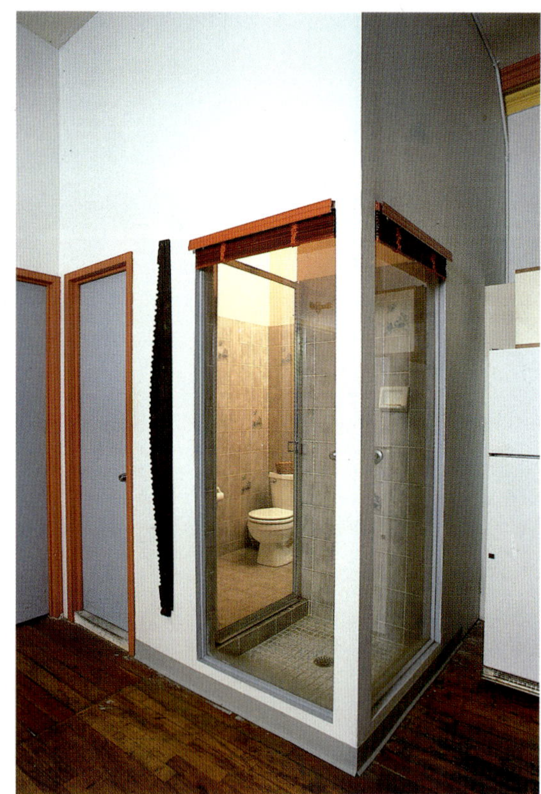

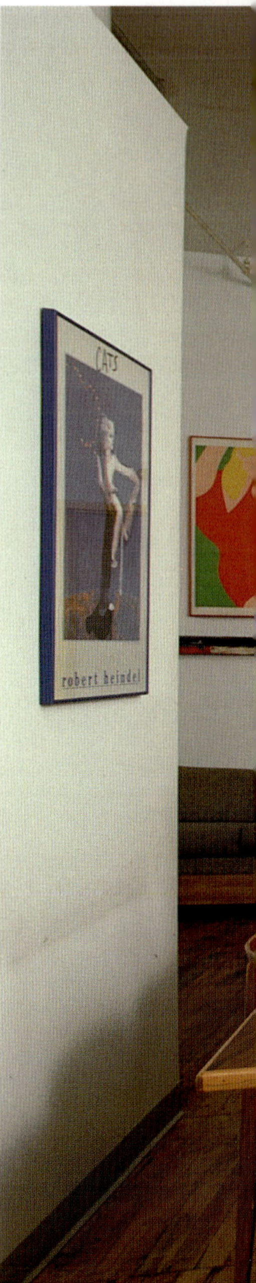

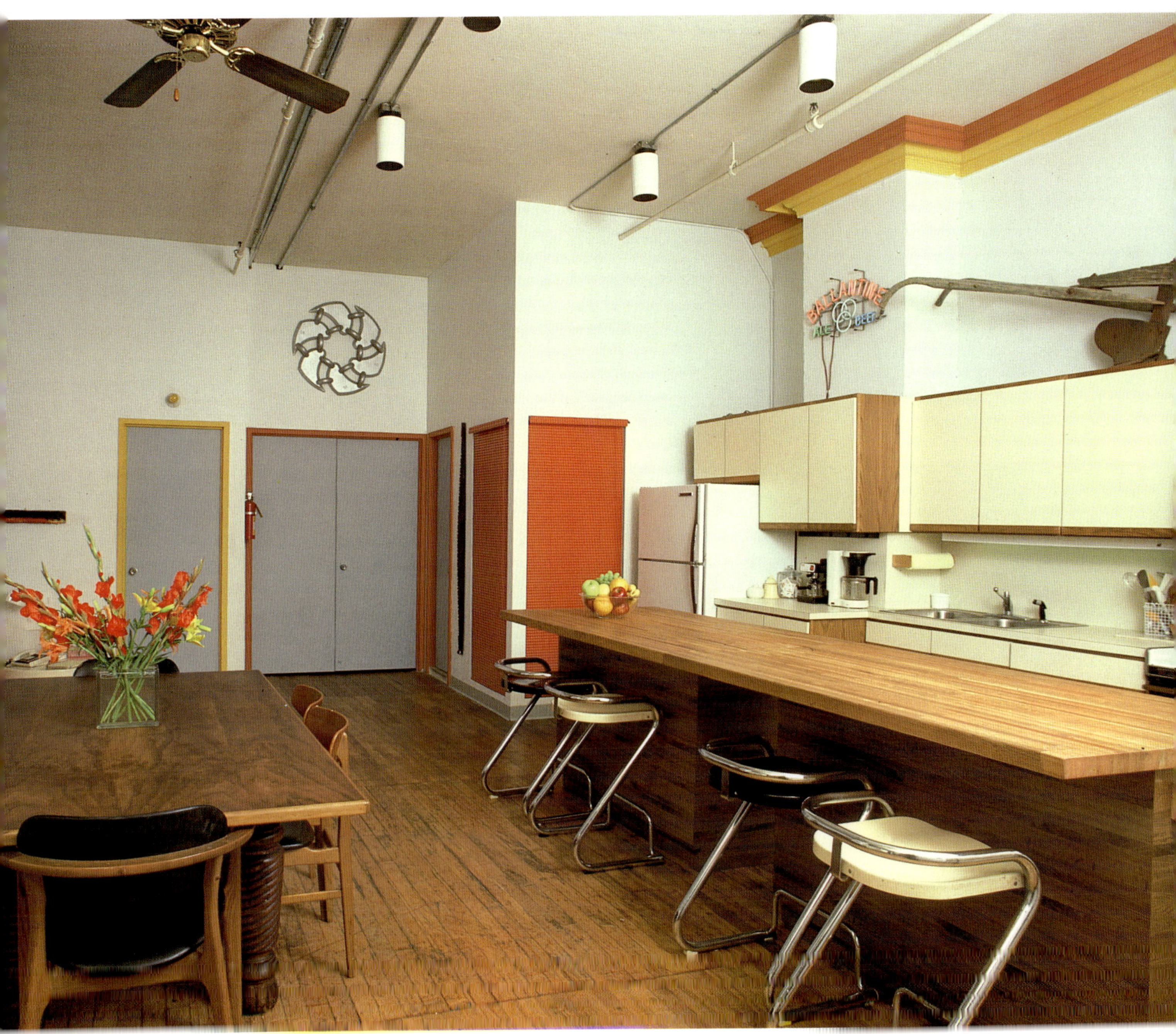

"Years ago it was a stigma if you shared a studio; it meant you couldn't afford your own space. I decided to challenge that notion."

CONSIDERING CLIENT NEEDS

As in so many other areas, Canadian photographers have, to some extent, been eclipsed by their more well-known American peers. However, although fame might be impressive, it does not necessarily indicate quality, as the industry knows. The Canadian photo industry, located primarily in Toronto, might not be as well known as its New York City counterpart, but it is certainly as effective—and as diverse. Currently, Toronto boasts the cultural and business supports that keep the art and business of photography thriving. This is one reason why Robert Wigington, a Toronto native, has successfully parlayed an interest in the medium into a lucrative career. **W**igington attended Queen's University in Kingston, Ontario, and majored in geology. But upon completing his freshman year in 1961, he "grew sick of school," he says, and "decided to do something more artistic." After a bit of thought, he set his sights on photography.

Robert Wigington's Toronto studio is located on a residential block in that city's South Annex.

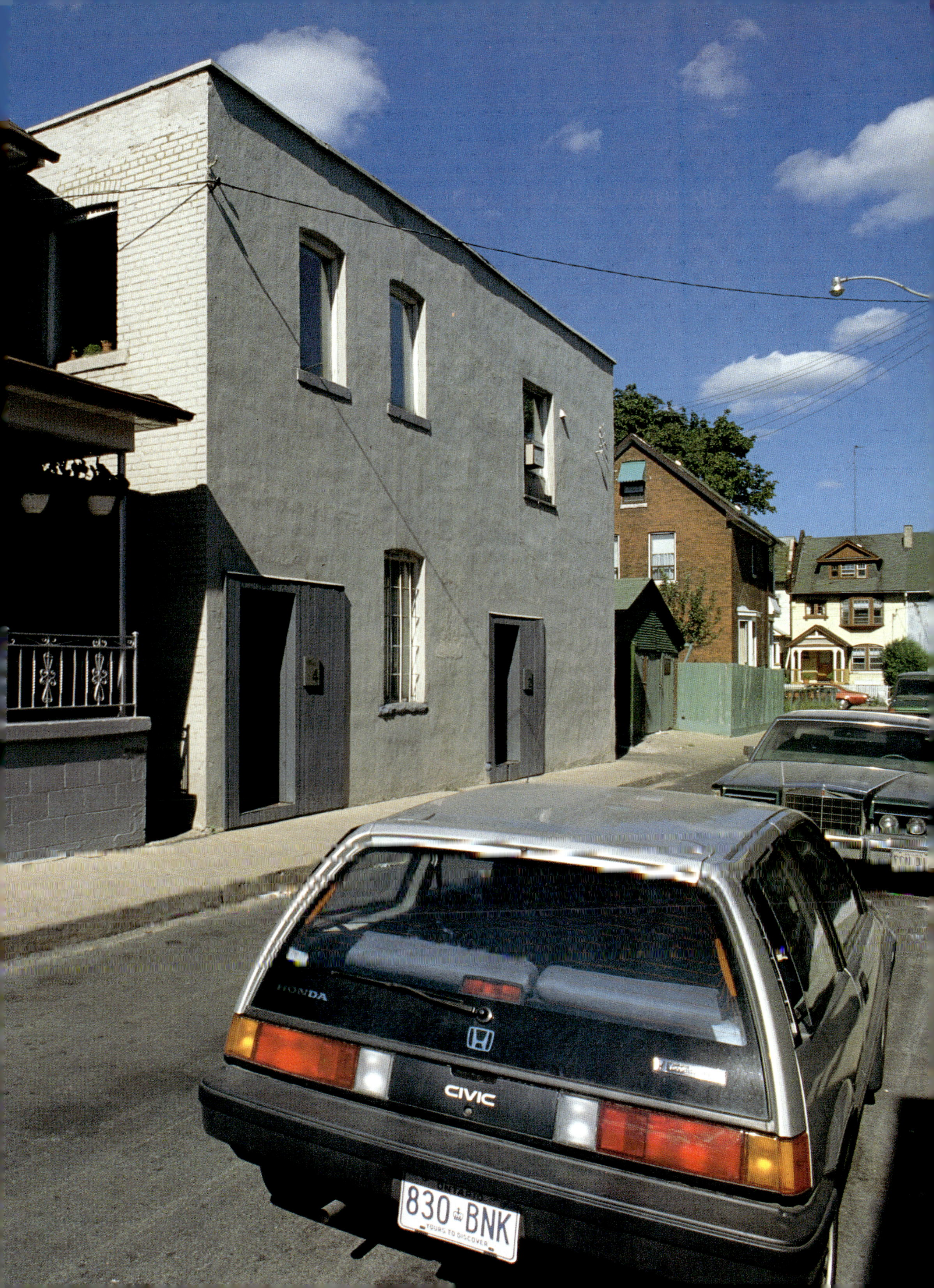
HONDA
CIVIC
830 BNK

ACCOMMODATING AN EXPANDING BUSINESS

In the early 1960s, there were few independent freelancers in Toronto; most photographers banded together and formed small companies to handle general work. So Wigington found a job in a catalog house. It was the perfect starting point for a beginner. From the outset, the fledgling photographer shot many different subjects in a vast range of sizes. "I photographed everything from large cars to tiny pieces of jewelry," he recalls. But catalog work, though it pays well, rarely leaves room for much creativity, and Wigington's experience confirmed that. "It was excellent training, but dull work," he says. So, after eleven years, he ventured out on his own, opting to become a freelancer, which remained a relative rarity in Toronto even in the early 1970s.

Wigington began working as a stills shooter for a television production company. An assortment of jobs followed, during the course of which the photographer developed a specific interest in food photography. Wigington worked—and continues to work—on both editorial and packaging assignments. "My temperament seems to suit the patient, careful pace of tabletop work," he notes. "In addition, food is a lucrative business, plus it's not affected by recession as other businesses are."

As his client roster grew, Wigington found that he needed more space. He rented a small studio in a warehouse section of downtown Toronto. Although his setup was adequate, the photographer wanted to own his space rather than rent it. Unfortunately, the area he was then located in was rapidly being occupied by artists looking for the large spaces found in old warehouses, and real estate costs, already hefty, were quickly rising. "Luckily, my real estate agent was interested in funky old buildings," recalls Wigington. The agent showed the photographer a two-story building in an emerging residential neighborhood known as Toronto's South Annex. Located on an alley-like street right near the subway, the spacious turn-of-the-century building suited the photographer's needs, and, says Wigington, "It was going for a song."

Graceful propping and sensuous lighting are only part of the way in which Wigington makes food look mouthwatering.

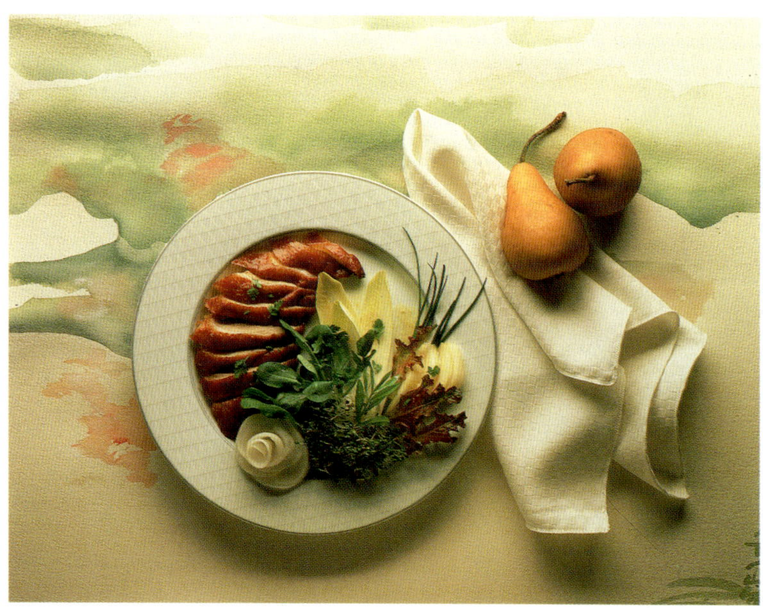

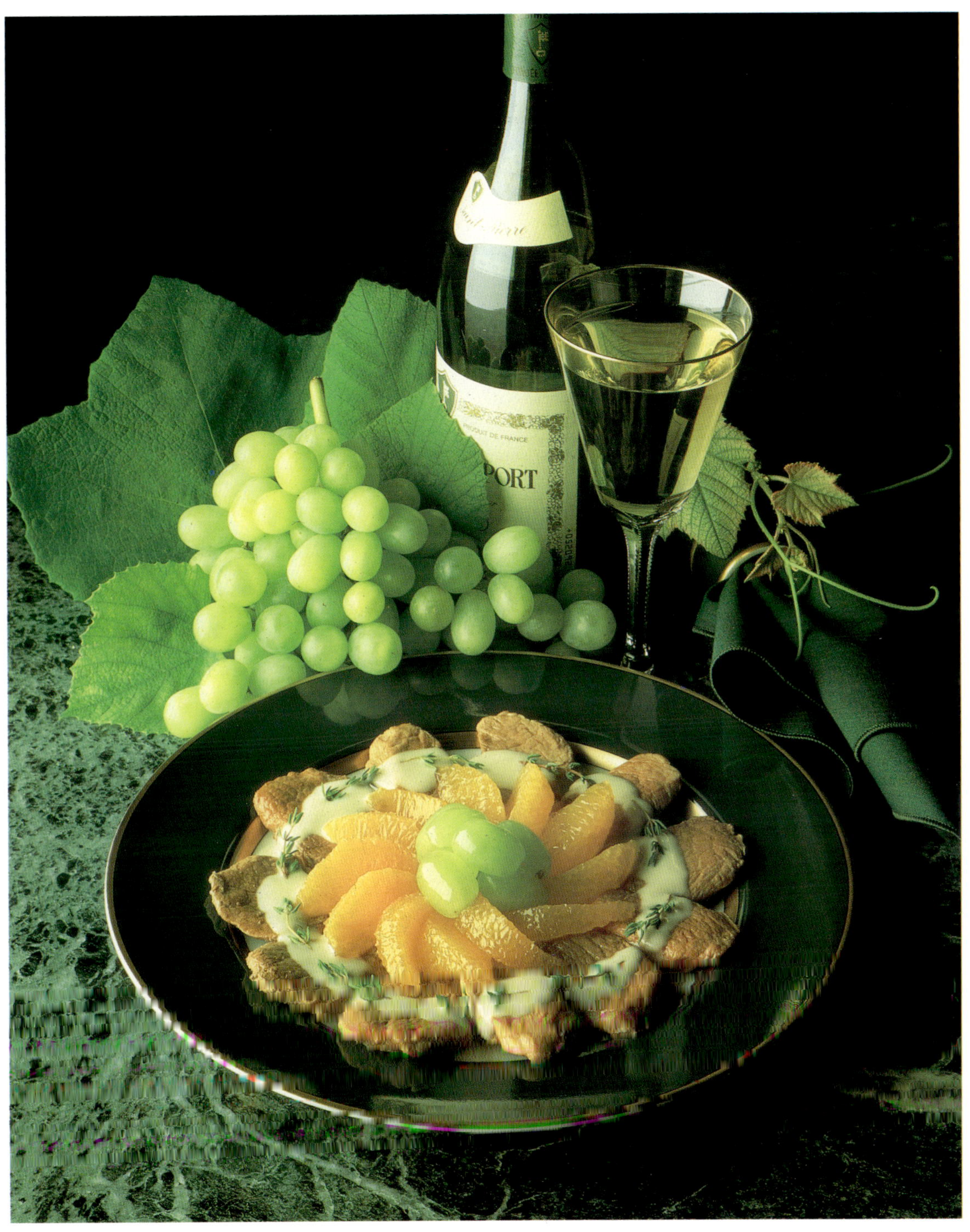

SIMPLE BUT EFFECTIVE IMPROVEMENTS

The photographer decided to keep the top floor for himself and recoup a part of his investment by renting out the ground floor. (It is currently occupied by two graphic designers.) He renovated only his studio, leaving the choice of the ground floor's renovation to his tenants.

Wigington had the studio's brick walls sandblasted in order to reveal the original textures, which had been obscured by years of clumsy paint jobs. Aside from the installation of a comfortable kitchen, the 2,400-square-foot space needed very little work. "All I did was knock down one pillar, which stood right in the middle of the shooting area," says the photographer. He later had that section of the floor reinforced. "I kept it all fairly simple," Wigington explains.

The studio, though hardly glamorous, is warm and airy. The visitor enters through an unpretentious doorway at the street level, walks up a flight of stairs that leads to the reception area. This is a stylishly decorated, somewhat spartan room. Directly off the reception area is the 40 × 22-foot shooting area. Two large windows and a pair of 3-foot lightboxes dominate the space. Ladders, clamps, tripods, and other, smaller light sources are carefully stored around the room. The back wall of the studio has a light table, slide projector, and drawing table for visiting art directors.

Since Wigington sends all his film out for processing, he doesn't need a darkroom. Therefore, he has only a small loading room, doubling as a storage room for rolls of seamless paper.

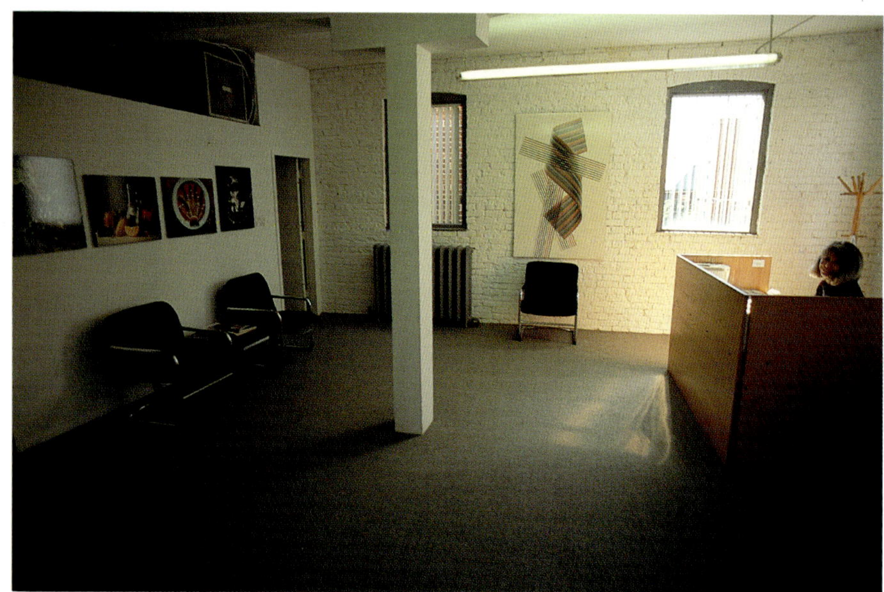

Wigington's reception area (above) is stylish but unpretentious. The shooting stage (right) is where most of the tabletop work is done. The ceiling is painted black so the photographer can control any reflected light.

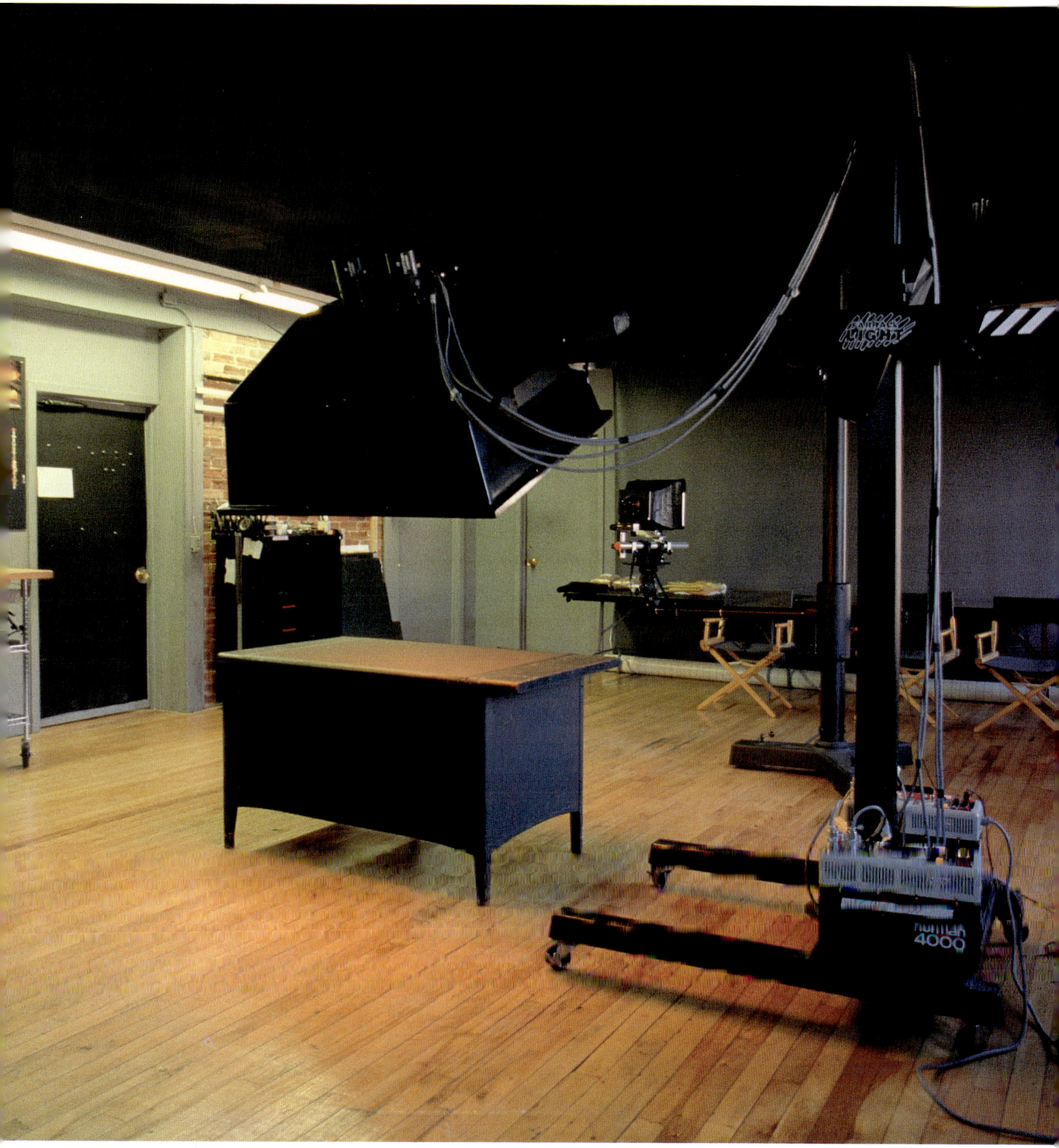
4000

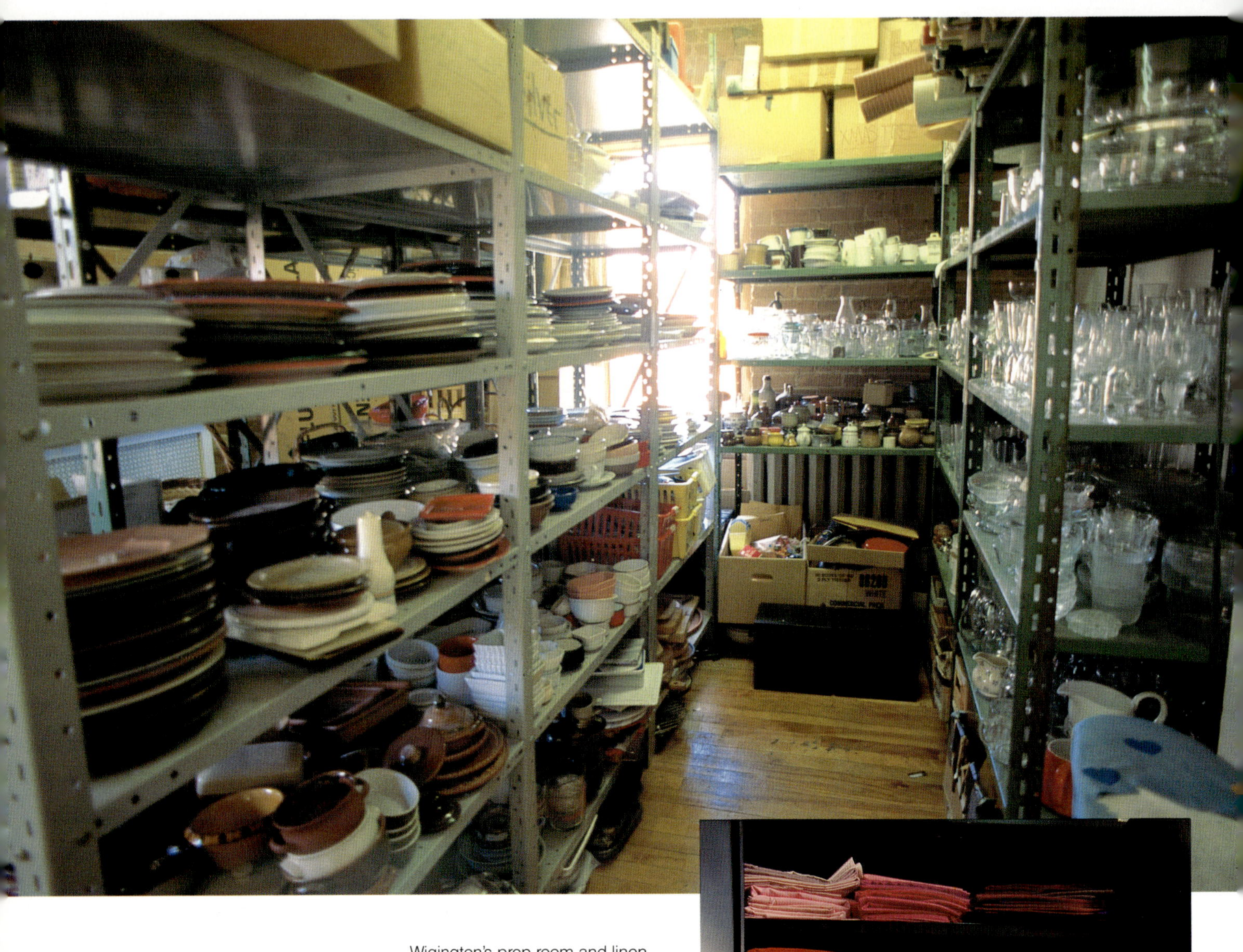

Wigington's prop room and linen closet are where most of the utensils, table settings, and backdrops are stored. The kitchen (opposite page) is shown during a rare calm, uncluttered moment. Aside from the shooting stage, this is the most important room in a food photographer's studio.

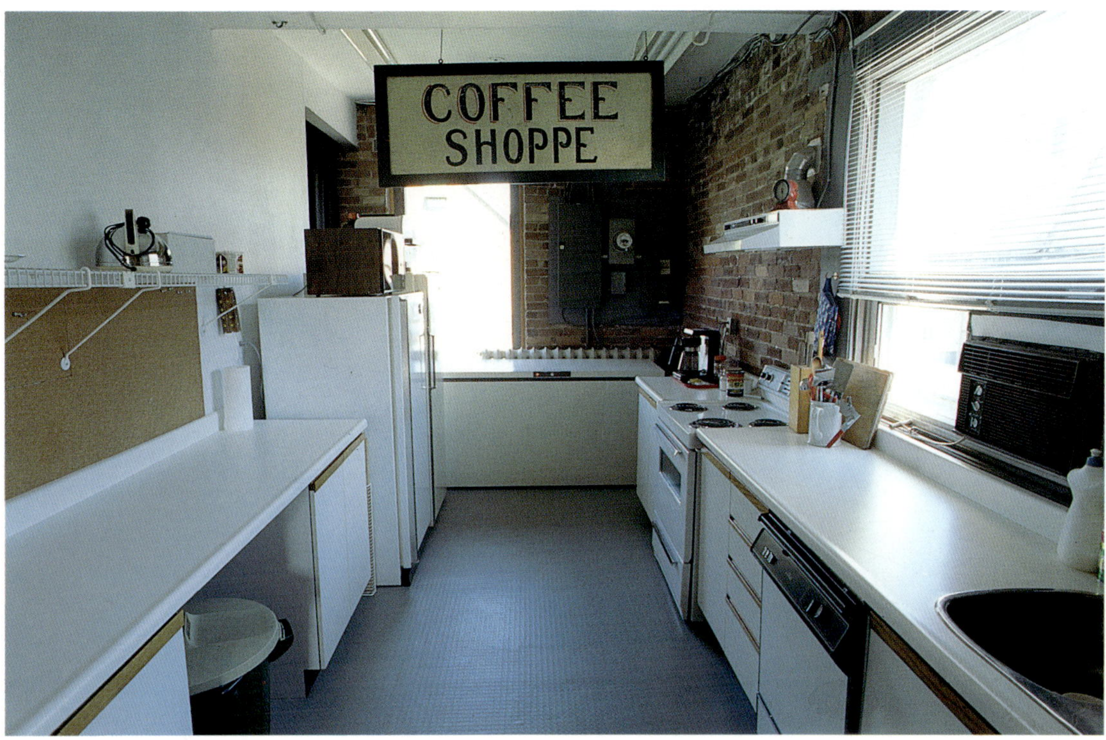

Tucked behind the shooting area is another storage room. It contains neatly stocked shelves filled with a mind-boggling array of utensils: dishes, platters, soup bowls, glasses, flatware, pitchers, creamers, sugar bowls, and even pots and pans neatly arranged by category. "I keep everything," explains Wigington, "because tableware, like everything else, goes in and out of style. One year, brown plates may be the rage, and the following year they are impossible to find." The photographer also maintains a closetful of material in a spectrum of colors, textures, and designs. These double as backdrops and table linens. Wigington also collects surfaces, such as wood, marble, and plastic, that can easily be used to add further interest to his compositions.

Alongside the studio, but separated from it by a thin wall, is the kitchen. In a space he owned earlier, Wigington discovered that when the kitchen is tucked away, food stylists don't get in his way when they set up for a shoot. This allows the photographer to prepare his own sets more effectively. "I wanted them to be within speaking distance," he says. "But the smells, smoke, and noise of the kitchen should not directly affect the shooting area, nor should their light interfere with the light being used to illuminate the subject." Wigington continues, "I could have put a lot more money into it, but I knew that food stylists can be very hard on kitchens. In the course of working, they can burn and scar countertops, and that's just the beginning." Yet the photographer also knew that the results of the preparations done in this environment were his primary resource, and he wanted those who worked there to feel comfortable. He interviewed a number of food stylists and discovered that they preferred to work in a location with abundant shelf and counter space, so he incorporated their advice into his final design for the kitchen.

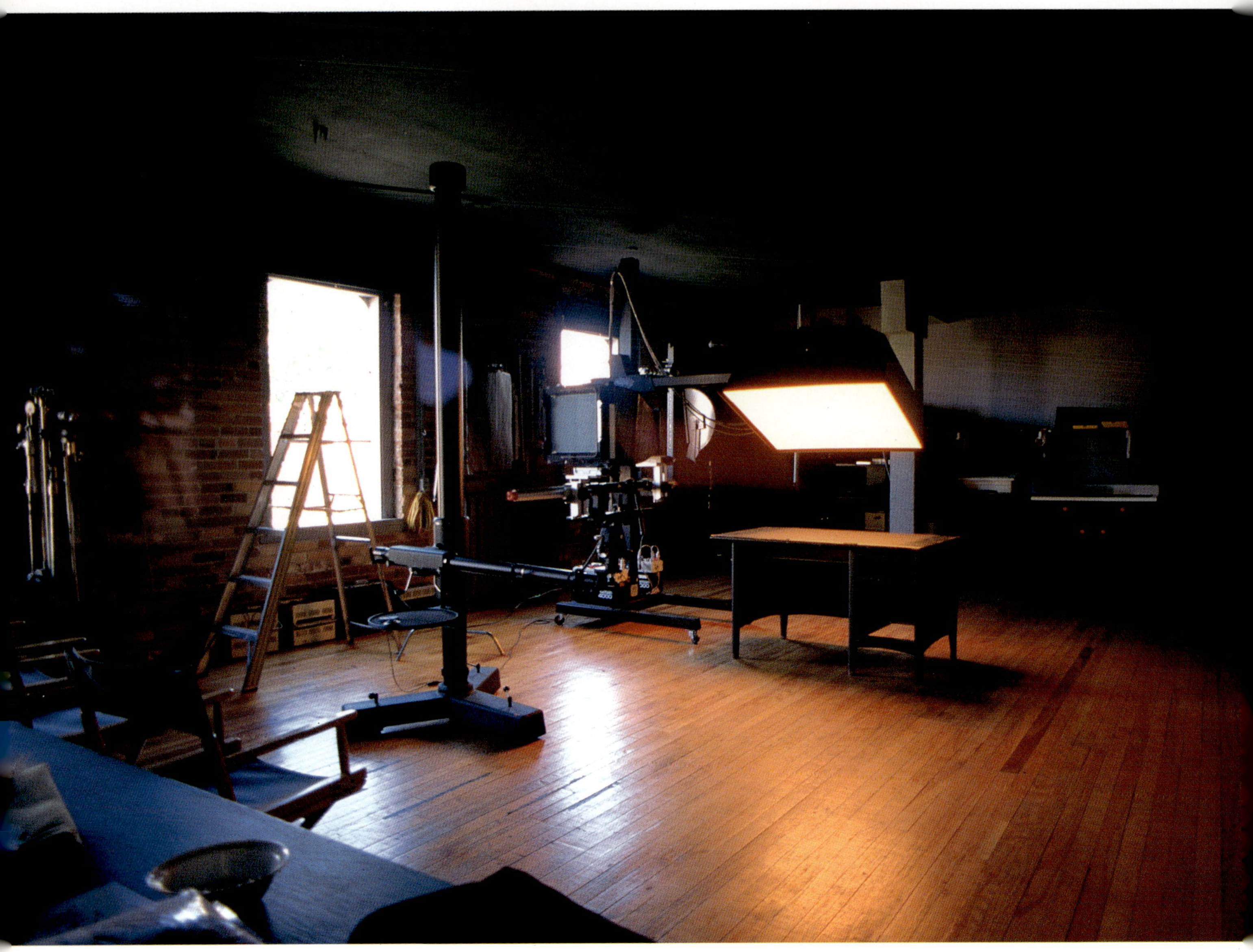

This reverse view of the shooting stage (above) clearly shows the ambient light that can be highly reflective and problematic. The client meeting area (right) is also bright and sunny. The studio's roof terrace (opposite page) is used during the warmer months for meals and lounging.

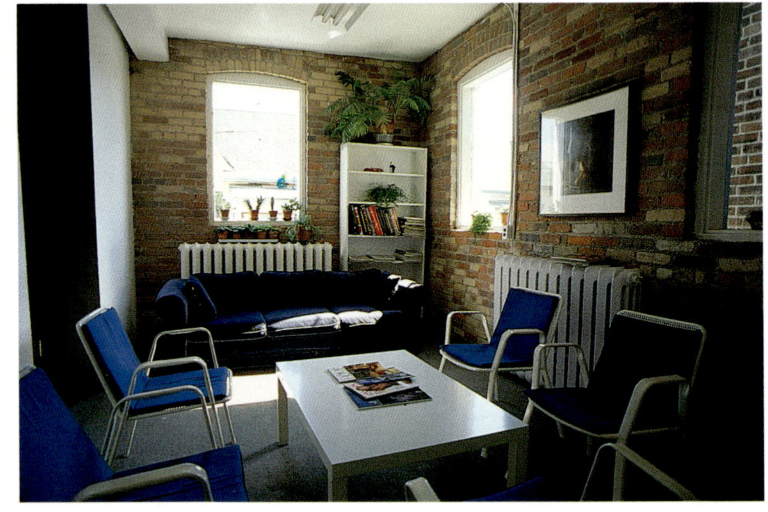

SPECIAL FEATURES

The most striking aspect of Wigington's studio is the ceiling: it's painted a deep, rich black. This prevents any reflected light from bouncing around the studio, explains the photographer, and in a specialty where the sets are generally small and the lighting formula crucial, it's another element that the photographer prefers to control. The windows also sport black shades to avoid further light discrepancies.

Beyond the kitchen is the client/conference room. Unlike many photographers whose studios feature a formal table-and-chair setup, Wigington furnished the room as if it were a living room. The room has a cozy feeling to it, enhanced by couches, chairs, and a cocktail table backed on two sides by exposed brick walls, well-stocked bookcases, and a number of flourishing plants.

A door behind the couch opens to a staircase leading to the roof, where Wigington has built a deck up, used as a dining area during the spring and summer months. "I'll bring in ethnic foods and have the caterer cook the meal in the studio's kitchen. In this way, the food is fresh, the view is spectacular, and the client is always impressed."

To visitors, Wigington's entire operation is impressive. "Eight years ago, I put in between $40,000 and $50,000 Canadian to get my business going," he says. Though not a particularly large enterprise, it is run in an organized manner. Wigington has one full-time assistant who can also do propping. On the occasions when he needs extra help, he hires freelance talent. The photographer is pleased. "Right now, my overhead is very low. I have income coming in from the work I do, as well as from the downstairs rental, plus the building has been completely paid off." Still, you would think that successful photographers are no different than any other human beings. When a visitor asks Wigington if he has any requests about his studio's design, the photographer thinks for a minute, then smiles, and says, "Well, one day, I'll probably upgrade the kitchen." Like the studio he inhabits, Wigington's needs are simple but very efficient.

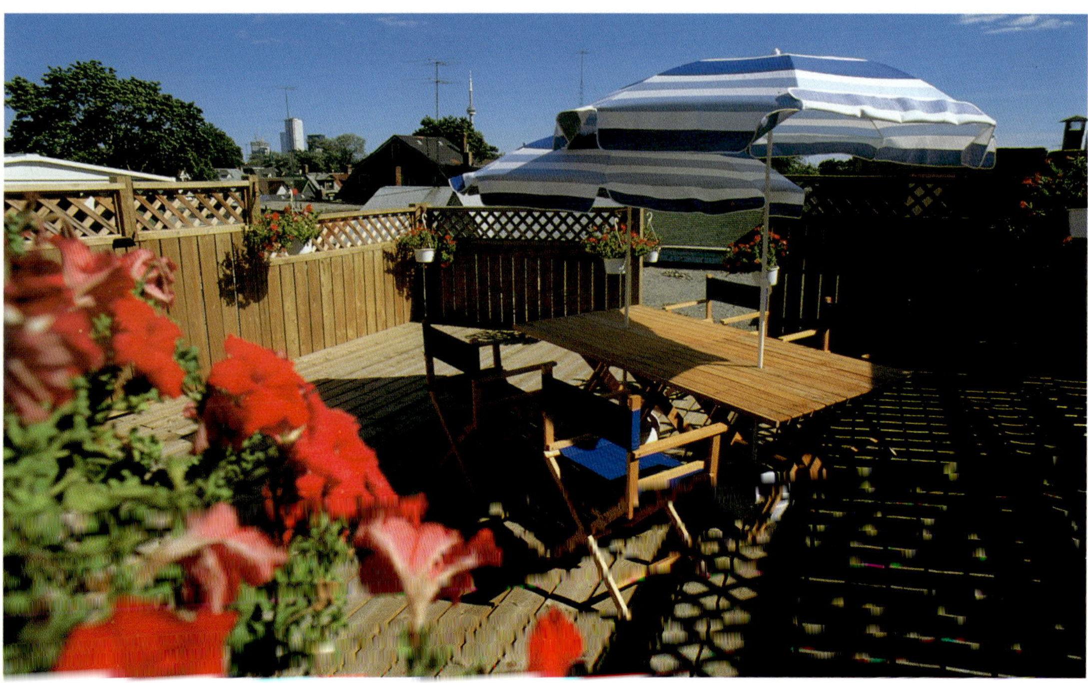

Wigington's entire operation is impressive and is run in an organized manner.

CREATING A STUDIO TO ATTRACT CLIENTS

In Los Angeles, the movie industry dominates almost all aspects of the city's economy. Los Angeles is a difficult place in which to build a name for yourself as a still photographer, particularly in advertising photography, because stills are so clearly overshadowed by film. But Jay Silverman hasn't let that stop him. **A** native Angelino, Silverman attended California's Brooks Institute of Photography, where he majored in commercial photography. After graduating in 1975, he moved to New York City and, taking the traditional route, found a job as a studio assistant. Neither the city nor his status as an employee made the photographer comfortable. Six months after Silverman's move, he returned to Los Angeles, determined to make it as an independent shooter. He rented a small studio space and began to compete within that city's limited market.

The stark exterior of Jay Silverman's Los Angeles studio belies a client-pleasing interior.

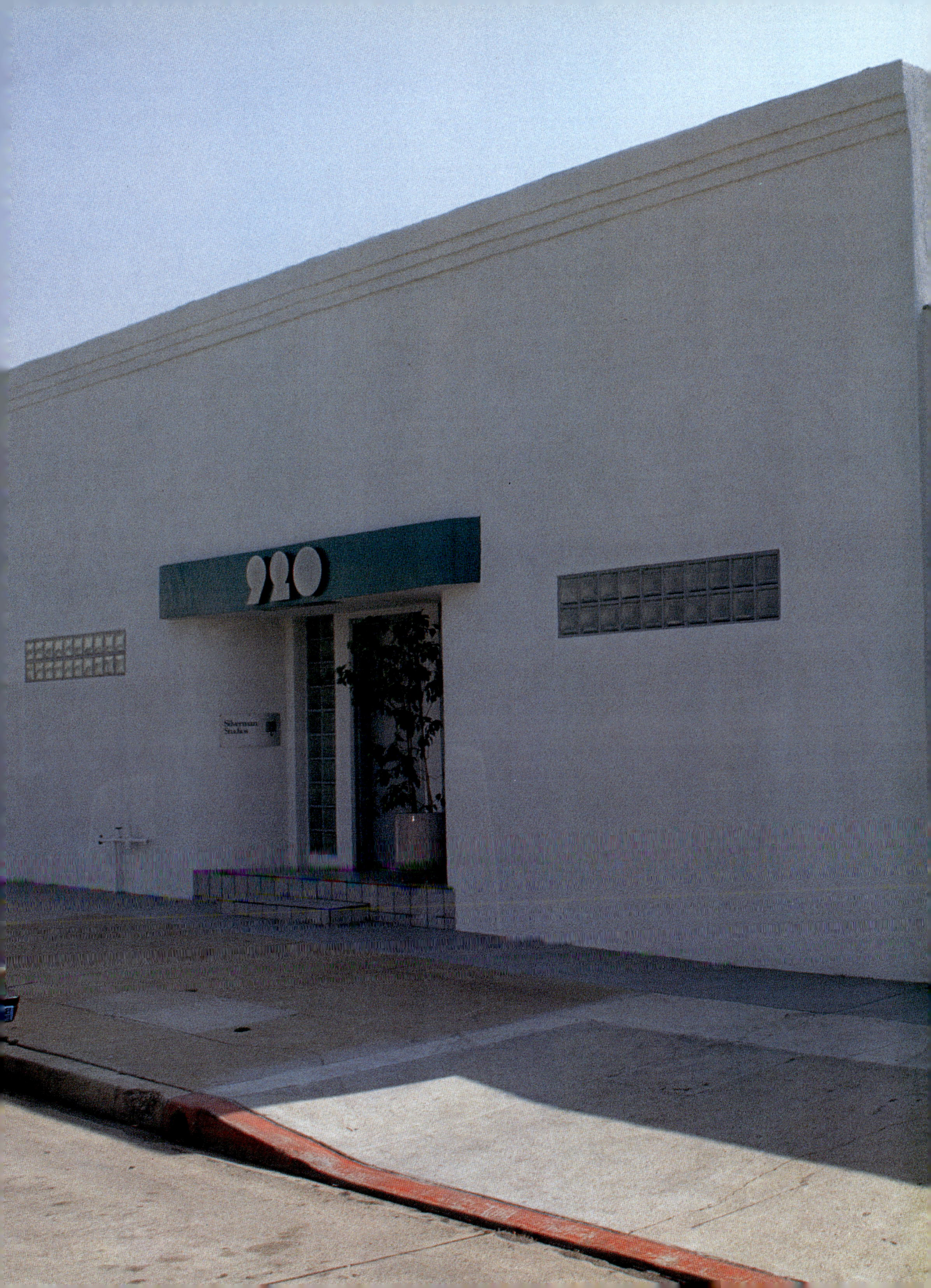
920
Silverman
Studios

THE IMPACT OF ASPIRATIONS

Silverman had set his sights on having a world-class clientele, knowing that most of those accounts, as well as the agencies representing them, were located outside Los Angeles. To win their business, Silverman had to convince them that he could offer all the amenities of the best studios in the country—and then some. Silverman never doubted his photographic abilities, but he had to be able to offer a space in which to impress potential clients. Naturally, that meant a bigger, glitzier, state-of-the-art studio in which to work.

In 1983, Silverman decided to purchase a work space, and he spent a full year searching for the right property. While driving through an industrial section of Hollywood, the photographer happened upon an art deco die-cutting factory that had gone out of business. Its high ceilings and open interior were exactly what he had been looking for; he acted immediately, and the financial and legal transactions began the following day.

It was more than the building that convinced Silverman that his new location was ideal. The block onto which he was about to relocate featured one of the best print labs in Los Angeles, as well as the most prestigious prop house in the city. In addition, E-6 and Kodachrome processing were available within easy walking distance of the studio.

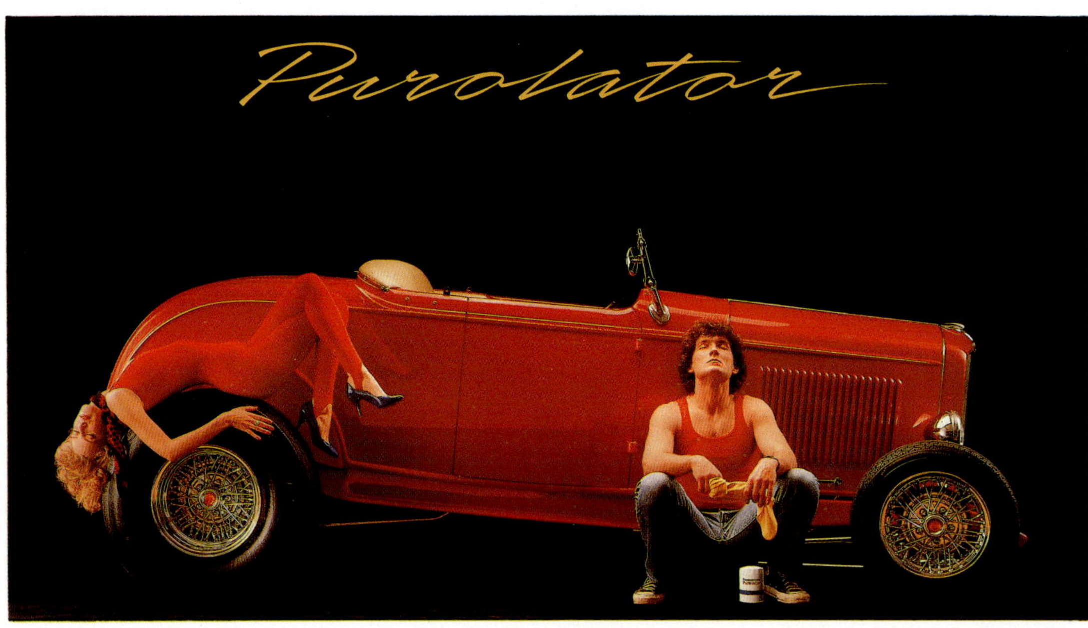

Silverman's cinematic style has brought him attention from art directors outside the Los Angeles area.

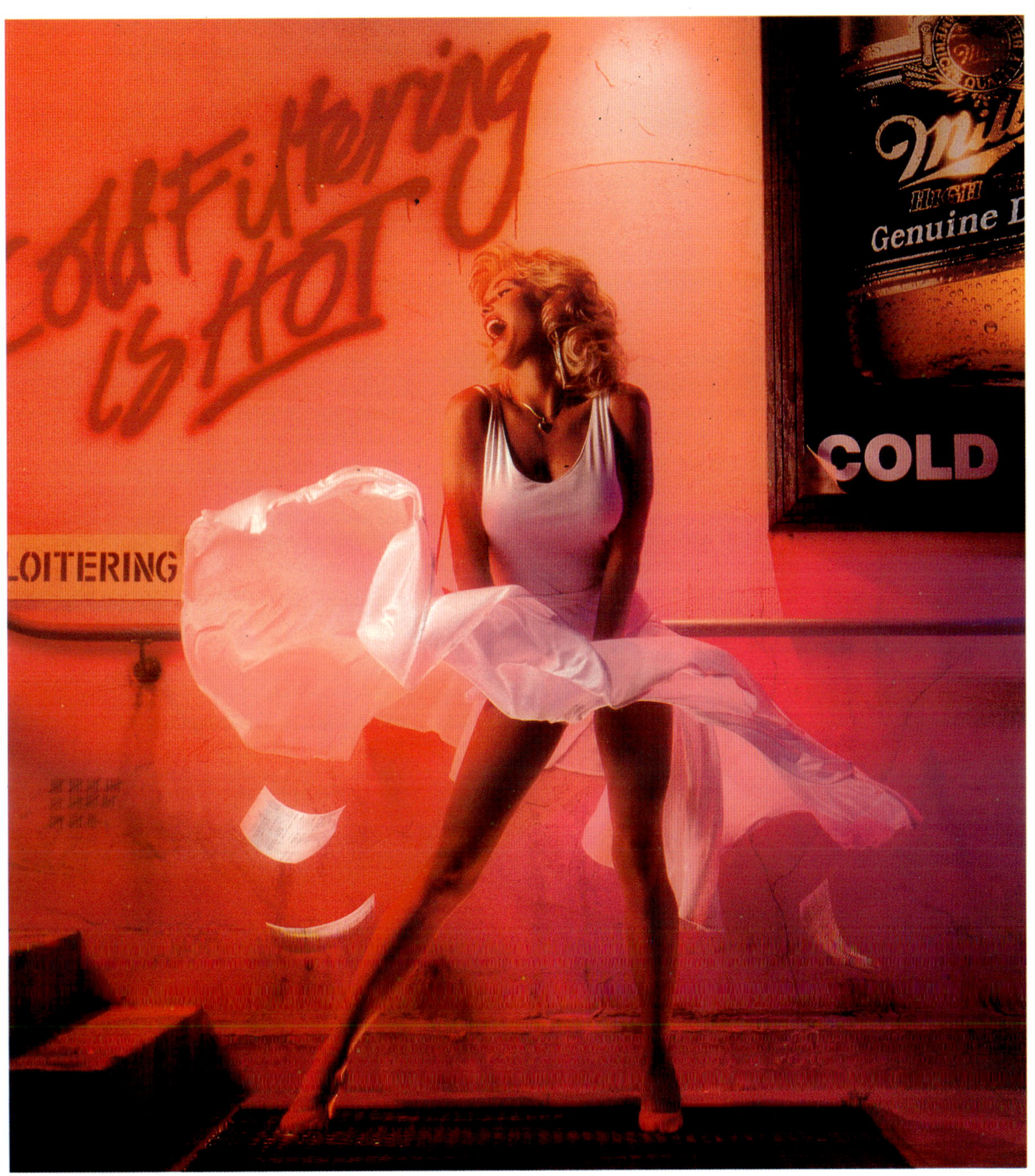
Cold Filtering is HOT
LOITERING
Genuine D
COLD

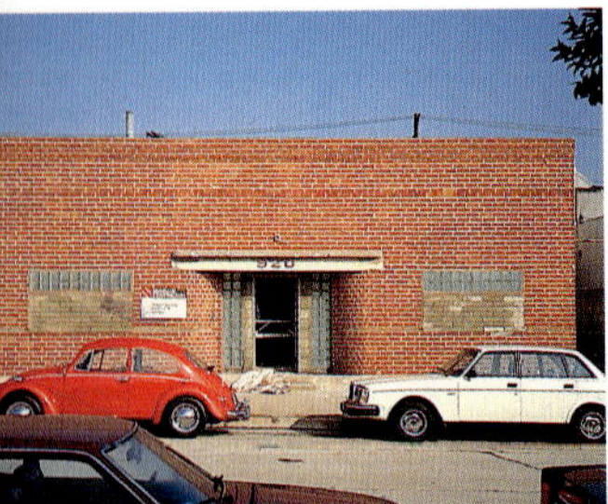

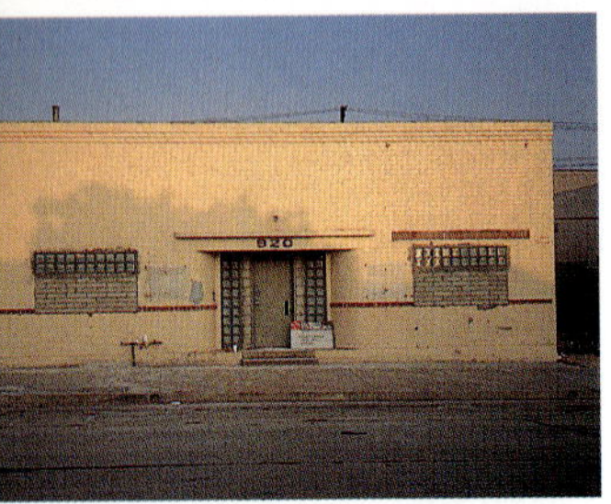

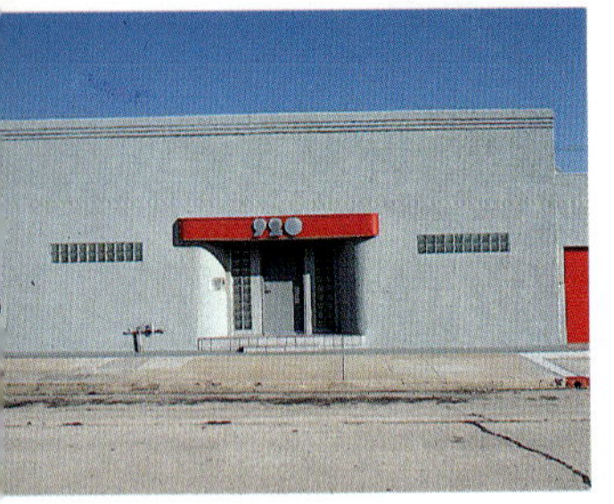

The evolution of the studio façade maintained the art deco character of the architecture.

Most of the work done on the interior of the studio, as well as the restoration of its façade, was carried out by the firm owned by the photographer's brother, Lynn Silverman Construction. The interior design was handled by Silverman's former client and close friend, Brad Donenfeld.

The exterior was cleaned and painted, and "the art deco character of the architecture was played up," says Silverman. Because the structure had been completed in 1942, the pipes were not in good condition. Silverman, anticipating a potential problem, arranged for entirely new plumbing to be put in before any other work began. Then he had the electrical system rewired. "The building already had a 400-amp capacity," he explains. "But we had to get the plugs and light sockets in the right place." The new design has 30-amp sockets positioned every ten feet throughout the shooting stage, plus four 30-amp plugs in key spots within the studio. In addition, Silverman installed a central vacuum system with outlets in every room of the studio, run by a compressor situated behind the building. "This was a major smart move," says the photographer proudly. "The system is so quiet that my crew can clean up while I'm working, and they won't disturb me at all." And with a vacuum outlet in every room, the photographer and his staff need never worry about heavy canisters and wires damaging furniture and tripping up visitors.

Once all the interior wiring was completed, Silverman had a 4-inch concrete slab inserted beneath the floor to steady it. This would ensure a workable area where vehicles and other oversized subjects could be securely photographed.

In the conference room, the attention paid to detail is evident. A glass-topped table seats twelve people comfortably, and a large leather couch can accommodate six more. "We've had production meetings in here with up to twenty-five people," notes Silverman. The room also doubles as a screening room and is furnished with video equipment suitable for projecting 24-inch, ¾-inch, and ½-inch footage.

Behind the conference room is the studio's kitchen. It is situated in the right-hand corner of the largest "room" in the studio, the shooting area, and offers a good view of the shooting stage. All the cabinets are custom-built Formica and have European closings. In addition to the standard appliances, Silverman had a dishwasher and microwave oven installed. As in most studios, this small section is often the area where staff and clients tend to congregate between shots. But if a particular production requires a bit more space, the counter, which is fitted with wheels, can quickly and easily be rolled out of the room. The kitchen has also been used as a preparation area for the occasional food shot that Silverman may be called on to do, and once, in the case of celebrity Vanna White, it was used as a set.

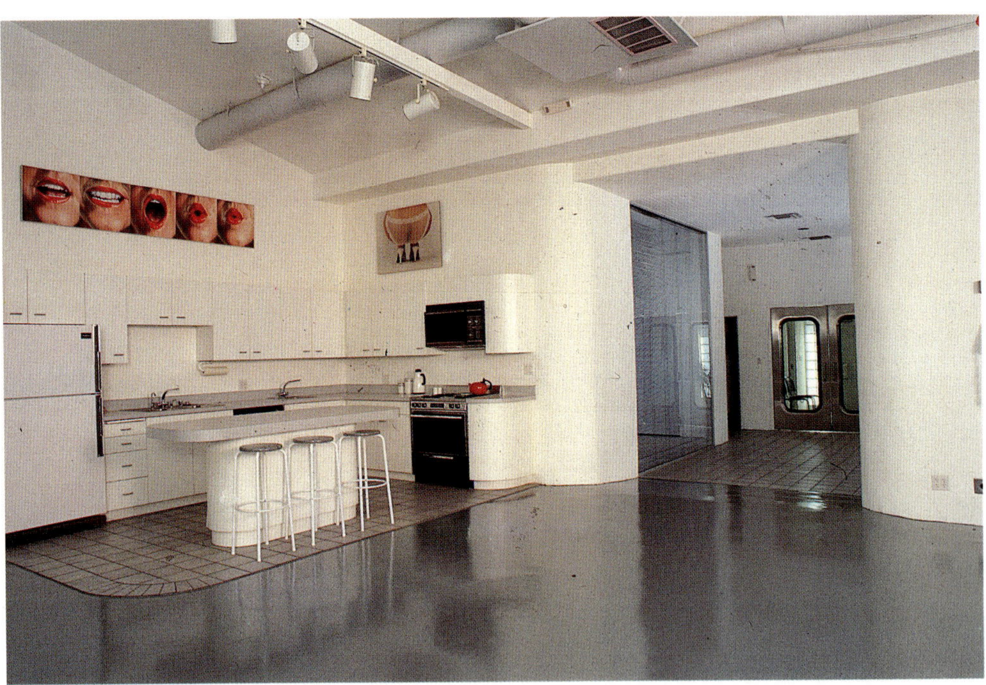

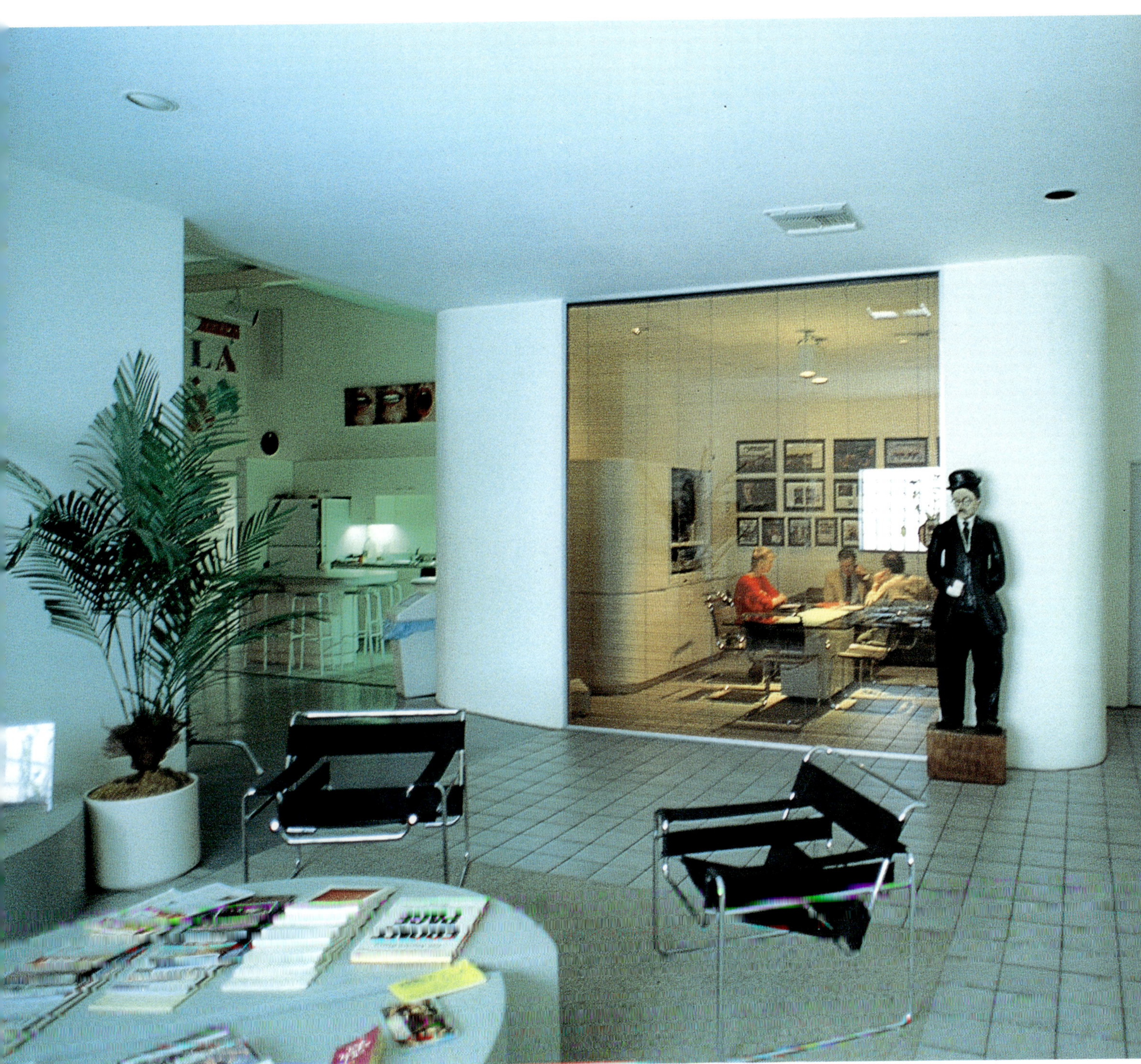

The waiting area (above) is done in muted, yet modern tones. The kitchen (left) can be found directly off the shooting stage.

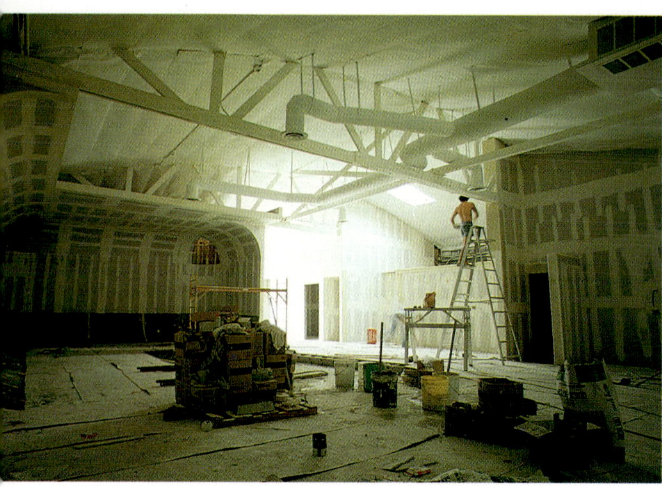

The stage is virtually free of clutter. There is no equipment hanging from the walls, and, aside from the cyclorama, which is in fact the back wall of the stage, there are no obstructions that might ruin crucial camera angles. Furthermore, no light banks hang from the 16-foot-high ceiling. "We build all our bank lights as we need them," notes Silverman. When asked why he insists on a workplace this pristine, the photographer says, "I see this space as a slate waiting to be used according to my immediate needs." The gray floors and white walls are painted frequently, so that the studio appears to be as spotless as possible. To ensure an immaculate appearance, all necessary equipment is kept in rolling supply chests that can be moved from set to set as needed, and wheeled into a storage area behind the cyclorama when not in use. This same storage area also holds flats and props.

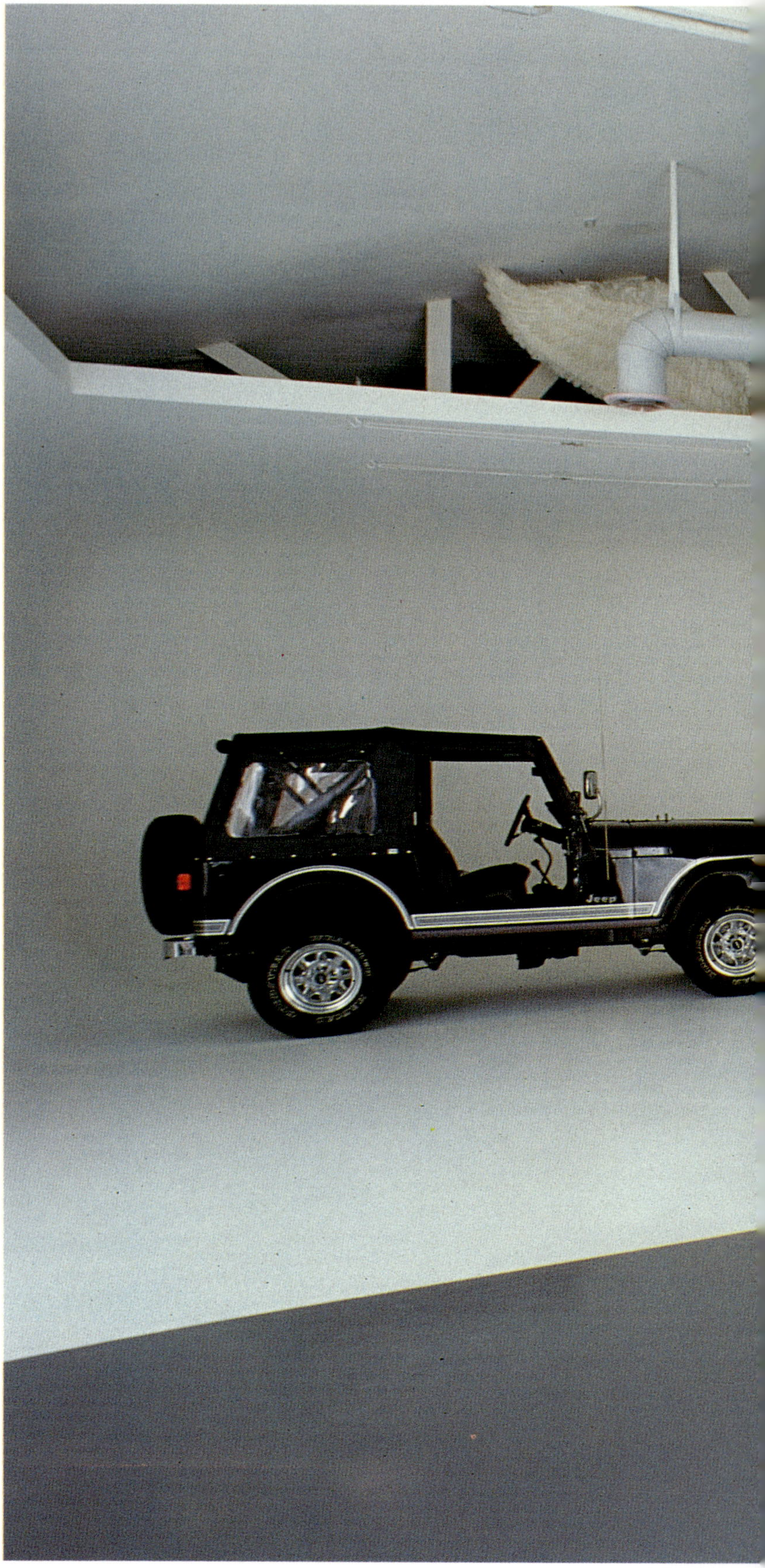

The shooting stage was constructed to be as versatile as possible.

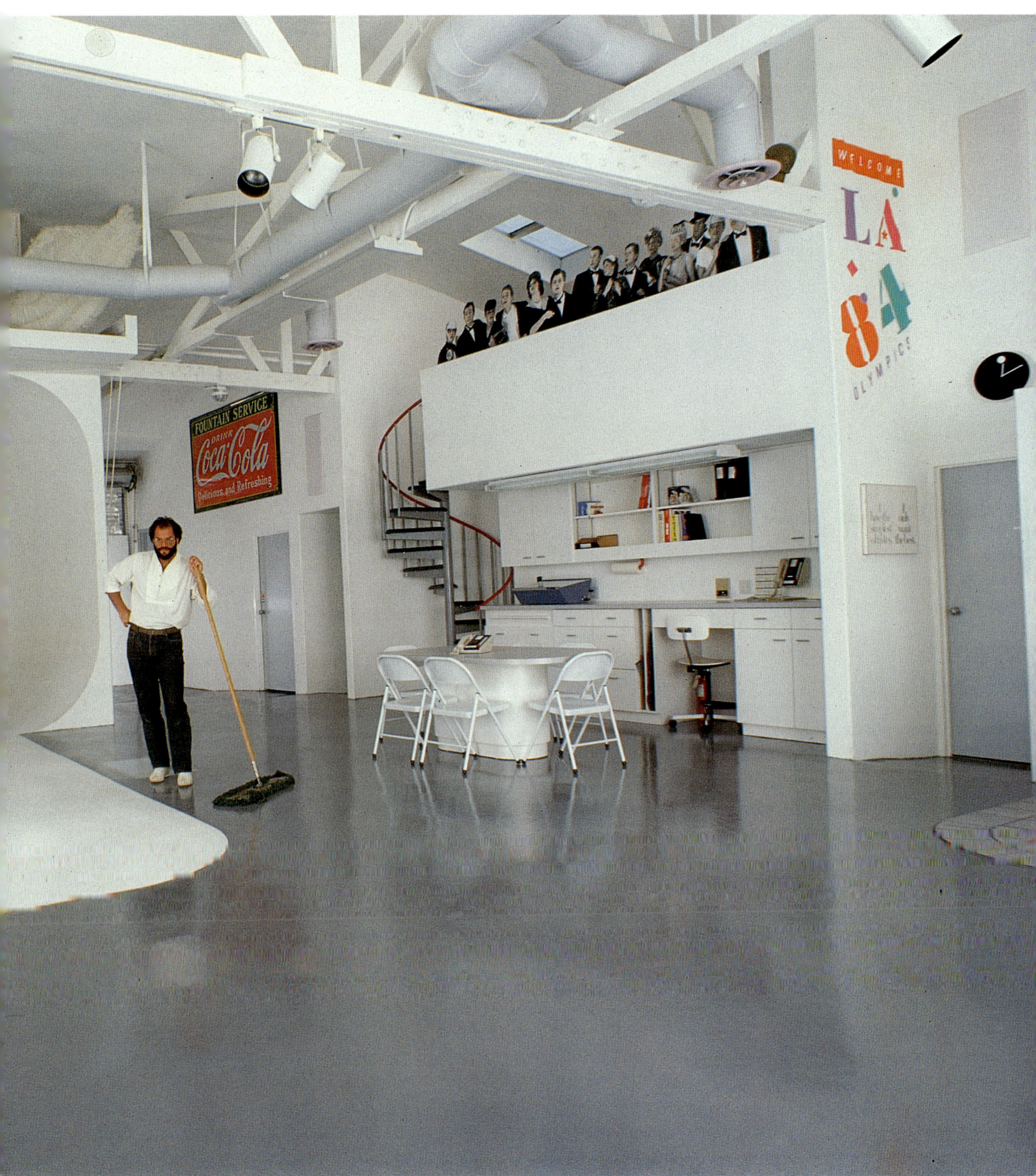
FOUNTAIN SERVICE
DRINK
Coca-Cola
Delicious and Refreshing
WELCOME
LA
84
OLYMPICS

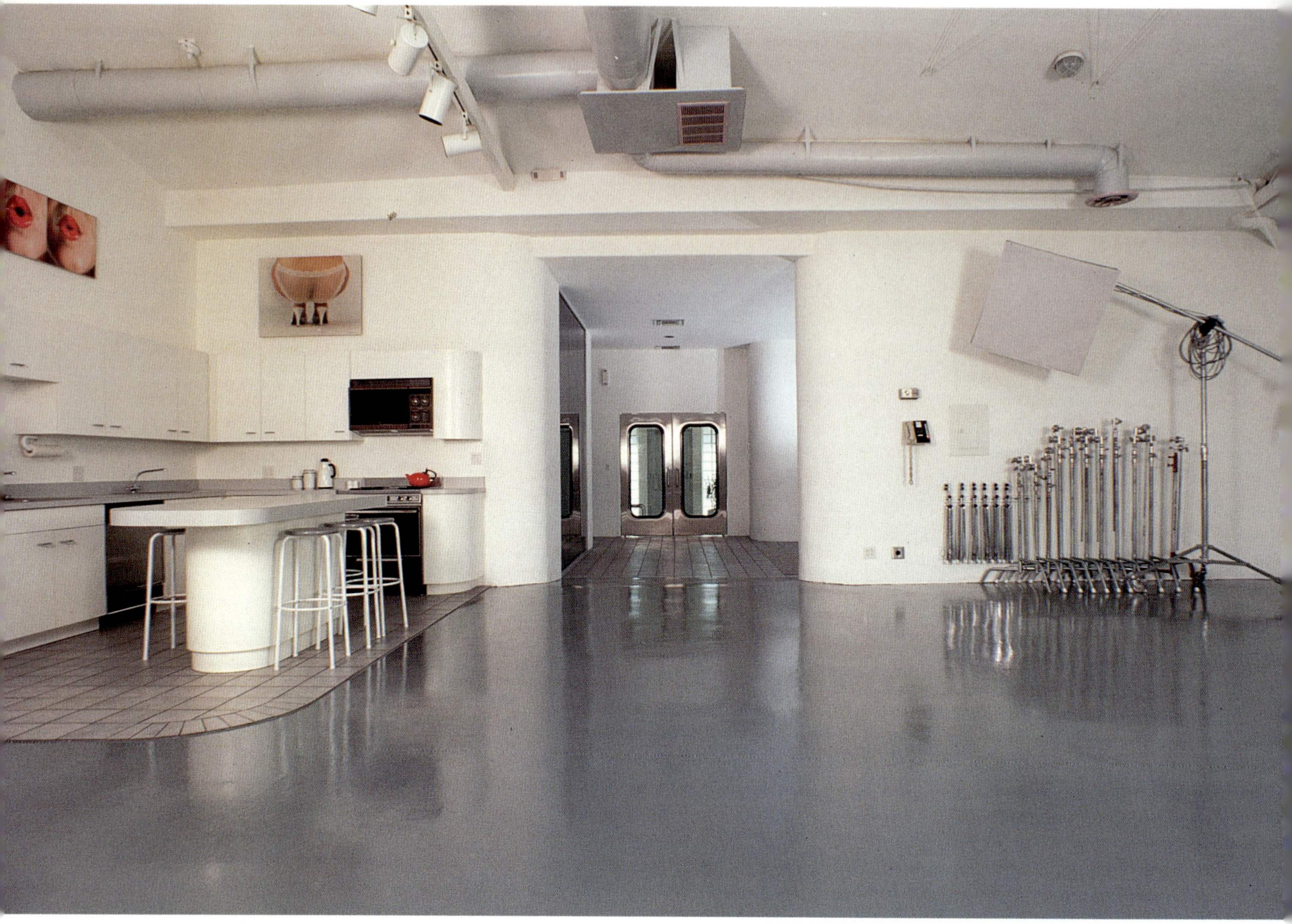

This view of the shooting stage (top) shows just how spacious it is. The parking area (right) is located behind the studio building.

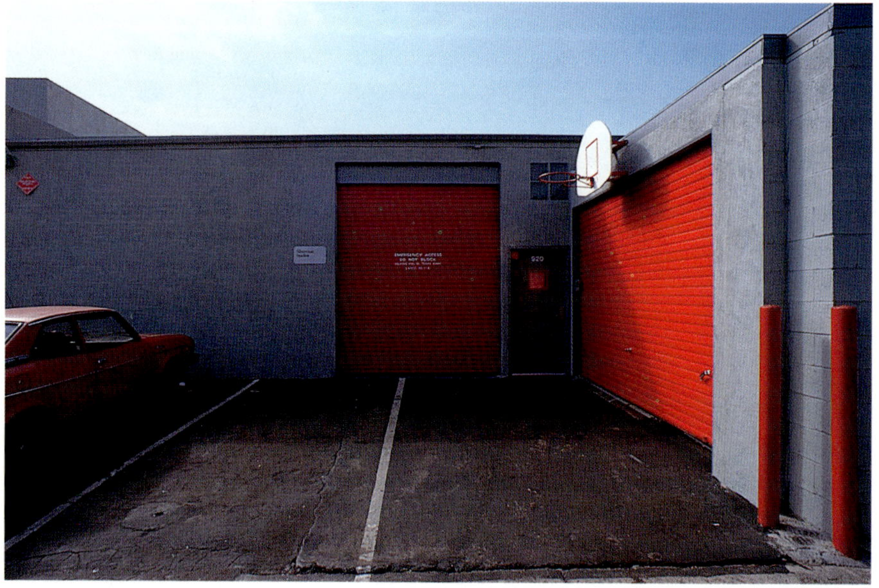

Discreetly hidden between the kitchen and the art director's work area is a door that leads to a honeycomb of smaller rooms, each serving a specific purpose. Directly behind the kitchen is another studio rarity: a mailroom in which just about every postage need can be expedited. Silverman keeps his seven portfolios here, and he can package and send them out within moments of a request. All his stock photographs are stored here, too. The photographer admits that stock images are not his most lucrative enterprise, but his extensive file of celebrity photographs do draw queries. "Once the mailroom was one of two darkrooms," Silverman says, "but I'm constantly evaluating the efficiency of the studio. This facility is more in keeping with my current business needs."

Behind the mailroom is a darkroom, albeit a small one. These days almost everything that Silverman does is sent out for processing. "I do some black-and-white printing, though," says the photographer. "But the option is used mostly by media buyers who can get a bit extra out of black-and-white advertising." A finishing room, with equipment for editing and dry mounting, as well as storage space for transparencies and tearsheets, is situated next to the darkroom and mailroom. This room also serves as a storage room for new jobs before they are sent out to the client and as an office for Silverman's assistant. A tiny film-loading facility is accessible from the finishing room, as is a luxurious bathroom. Every room in which film or equipment may be handled is hooked to a central compressor system, so that compressed air, used for blowing away dust, is always available.

A prop room and additional storage areas are located at the back of the studio, as is a garage door through which cars and trucks can be driven into the studio and onto the shooting stage. (Silverman also has a second storage facility across the street from the studio.) A garage at the side of the building acts as a holding tank for vehicles that will be photographed. This is also where Silverman's assistants do any construction and preparation work for future shoots. At the back of the studio is a small parking area with five spaces. Three more spots belonging to the studio are out front.

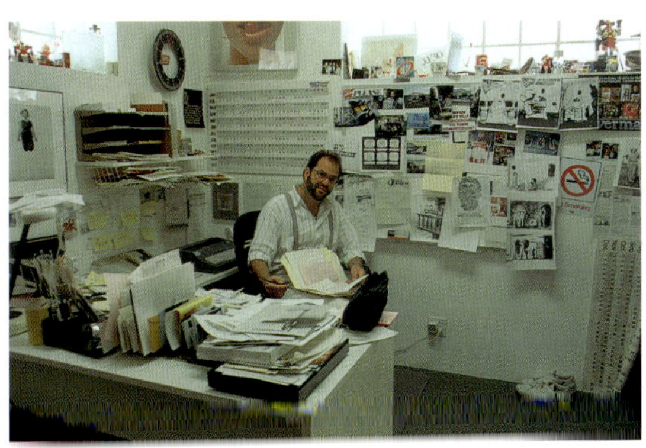

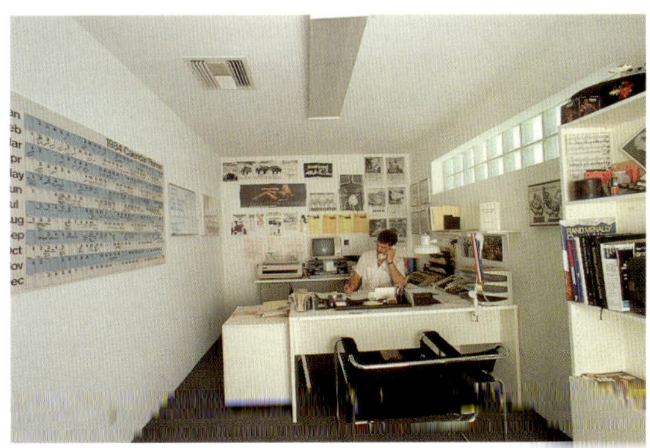

The offices where Silverman and his assistants take care of the business side of running a studio are located behind the kitchen

When the structural corrections were completed, Silverman and Donenfeld were able to turn their attention to the fine points of the studio's design. A small lobby, a glass-enclosed reception desk, and a striking pair of stainless steel doors greet visitors. "This tiny area, with its aura of inaccessibility, was designed with messengers in mind," Silverman notes, "so they could be kept out of the studio completely." The photographer is especially proud of the double doors, which Donenfeld persuaded him to buy. "They've become a trademark," Silverman says. "People *always* remember them." And with good reason: the highly polished doors—which cost $3,500 apiece—dominate their surroundings. Because they are solid rather than hollow, the doors are too heavy to be opened with only a push. Instead, they are controlled by a special mechanism that extends a foot deep into the ground and eases their opening.

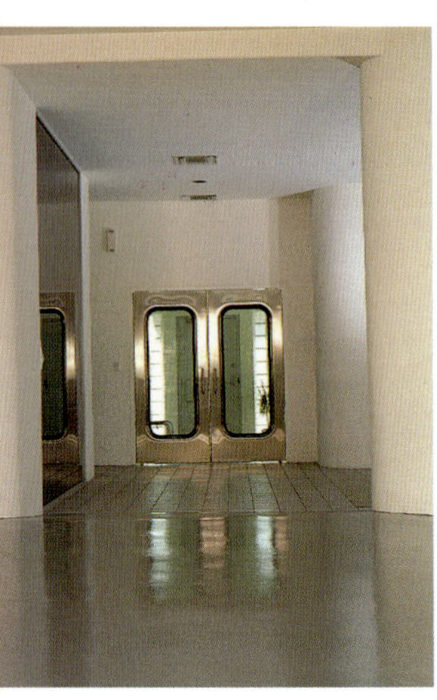

Silverman is particularly proud of his stainless steel doors (above) because, he says, "people always remember them." An assortment of knick-knacks and curved walls (opposite page) give the studio a distinctive look.

Beyond the doors, a square vestibule "carpeted" with custom-glazed ceramic floor tile separates the waiting room and the studio's conference room. "The waiting room is generally not for client leisure," Silverman explains. "It's mostly used to seat models while we're casting for a shoot." On occasion, it also holds spillover equipment when the studio gets too crowded. The curved couches and circular table that furnish this room were designed by Donenfeld to echo the art deco theme that is prevalent throughout the space. The rounded furniture mirrors the curved walls that are a prominent feature of the studio. "I wanted the walls to curve, so that the eye was never stopped by any corners," says the photographer. "This device makes the space look bigger and gives the impression that I have 10,000 square feet instead of seven."

Along the same wall as the kitchen, but recessed more deeply, is an art director's work area. Besides the light table and drawing board, the desk is stocked with everything an art director might need, including razor blades, tracing paper, colored pencils, and reference books. It's an amenity seldom found in photography studios. "That's because most photographers forget about who their clients are," says Silverman. "I view it as an absolute necessity." More than that, though, the work space is a pragmatic decision by an efficient, foresighted manager who prefers that his employees put in normal working hours. "My time, and that of my staff, is more valuable than anything," he admits. "I can't wait for an art director to return to his office because I don't have what he or she needs."

Directly behind the work area is a spiral staircase that leads to a small balcony overlooking the shooting area. It is shielded by a lifesize mural of celebrity look-alikes. This gallery offers a second feature that few photographers provide for clients: an area reserved for *their* privacy. The mural can be removed, in which case the loft affords a clear view of the entire shooting stage without disturbing the actual photo session. Underneath the balcony are two changing rooms and a makeup room that is also used by stylists and hair specialists.

The studio cost $350,000 to renovate, "and that was at mostly wholesale prices," Silverman cautions, "because my brother did the bulk of the work." Although the sum may seem exorbitant, it has produced the desired result. "I have a really unique position here in Los Angeles," he explains. "There are very few people here that have studios on this scale. Without doubt it has helped to attract many of my clients, 99 percent of whom are from out of town." The studio's accounts include Budweiser, Miller, Yamaha, and Levi-Strauss.

Obviously, Silverman has a lot to be proud of. But he insists on sharing the credit with his staff. "My support staff helps me get repeat business," he says. "The volume and quality of my clients can't be solely due to me." Silverman employs a staff of six: a secretary, two assistants, an office manager, a studio manager, and a rep. "I'd have to employ a seventh person if it weren't for my excellent location," says Silverman. "But because we're within walking distance of both prop and processing houses, my staff can come and go with extraordinary speed."

It would seem to visitors that Silverman has achieved his original dream, but the reality far exceeds even the photographer's initial expectations. Silverman has also ventured into filmmaking. "I've always wanted to be a film director," he says, "but right now my career in stills is peaking. I'm not sure which route to take." At the moment, Silverman's biggest concerns seem to be how best to utilize the space he has and how to ensure some free time for himself. This year alone, he estimates that he has had an average of four days worth of work a week, and that in stills alone. When asked, in retrospect, if he would do anything differently, Silverman ponders the question carefully. "I'd probably get a bigger place," he admits. "Not that bigger is necessarily better, just that it would be easier to work in."

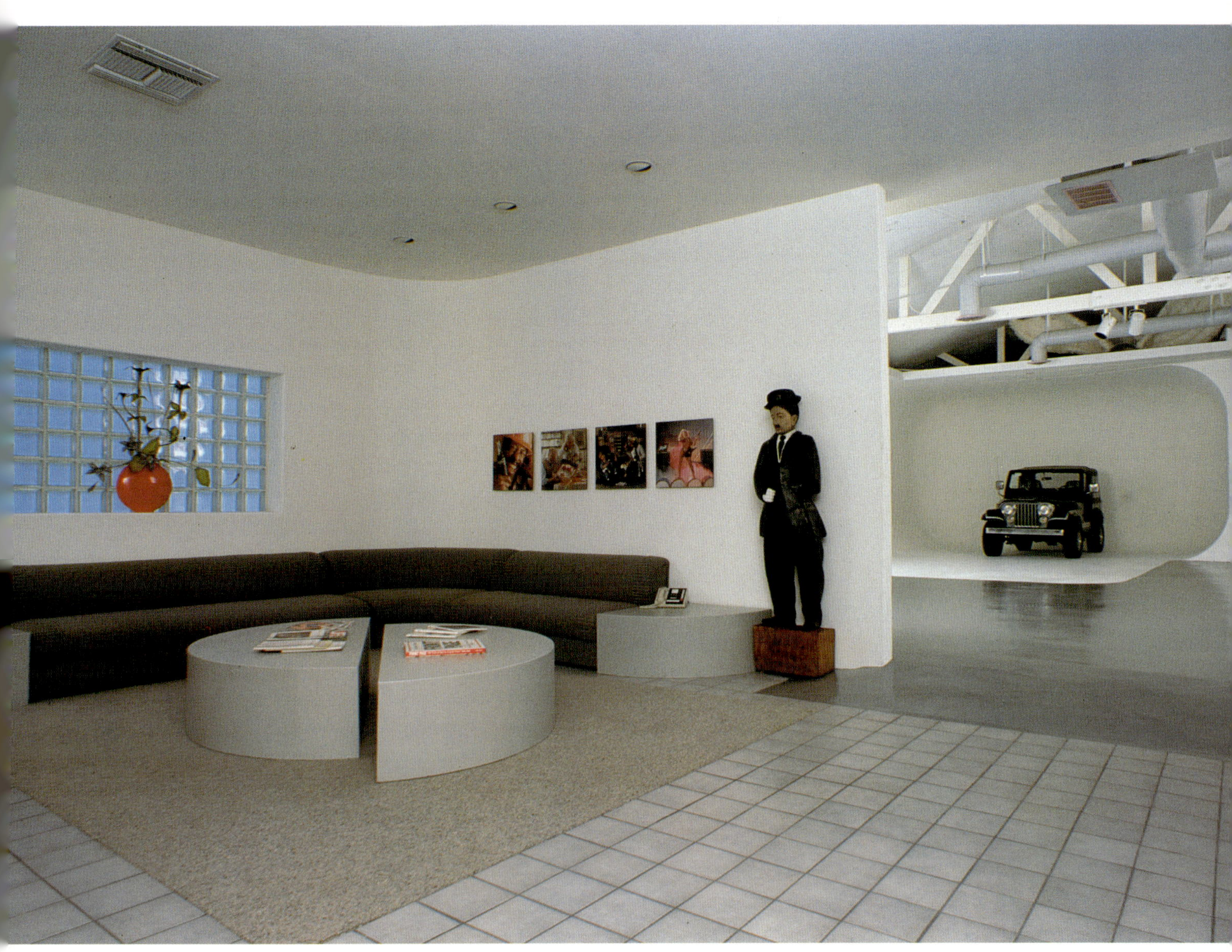

Silverman has achieved his original dream, but the reality exceeds his expectations.

PLANNING AN ORGANIZED STUDIO

The cost and problems of setting up a large, multipurpose studio can be defrayed in many ways. Some photographers establish equal partnerships and share their studio space; others rent out sections of their studios to freelancers and, in that way, offset their own costs. One option, rarely exercised in the United States but fairly common in Canada, is called an associateship. Here, a photographer or a group of photographers, organizes a studio and hires a staff of younger, less-established shooters to work for and with them. The studio owners pay their associates a weekly salary and collect a commission from each job the associate shoots. In Toronto, Westside Studio is a showcase for the success of this method. **L**ocated in what was once a decaying industrial neighborhood, the business is co-owned by photographers George Simhoni and William McLeod. Three other photographers, Silvio Calcagno, Jean Desjardins, and Garth Grosjean, round out the associateship.

The entryway of Westside's Toronto studio is cleanly modern.

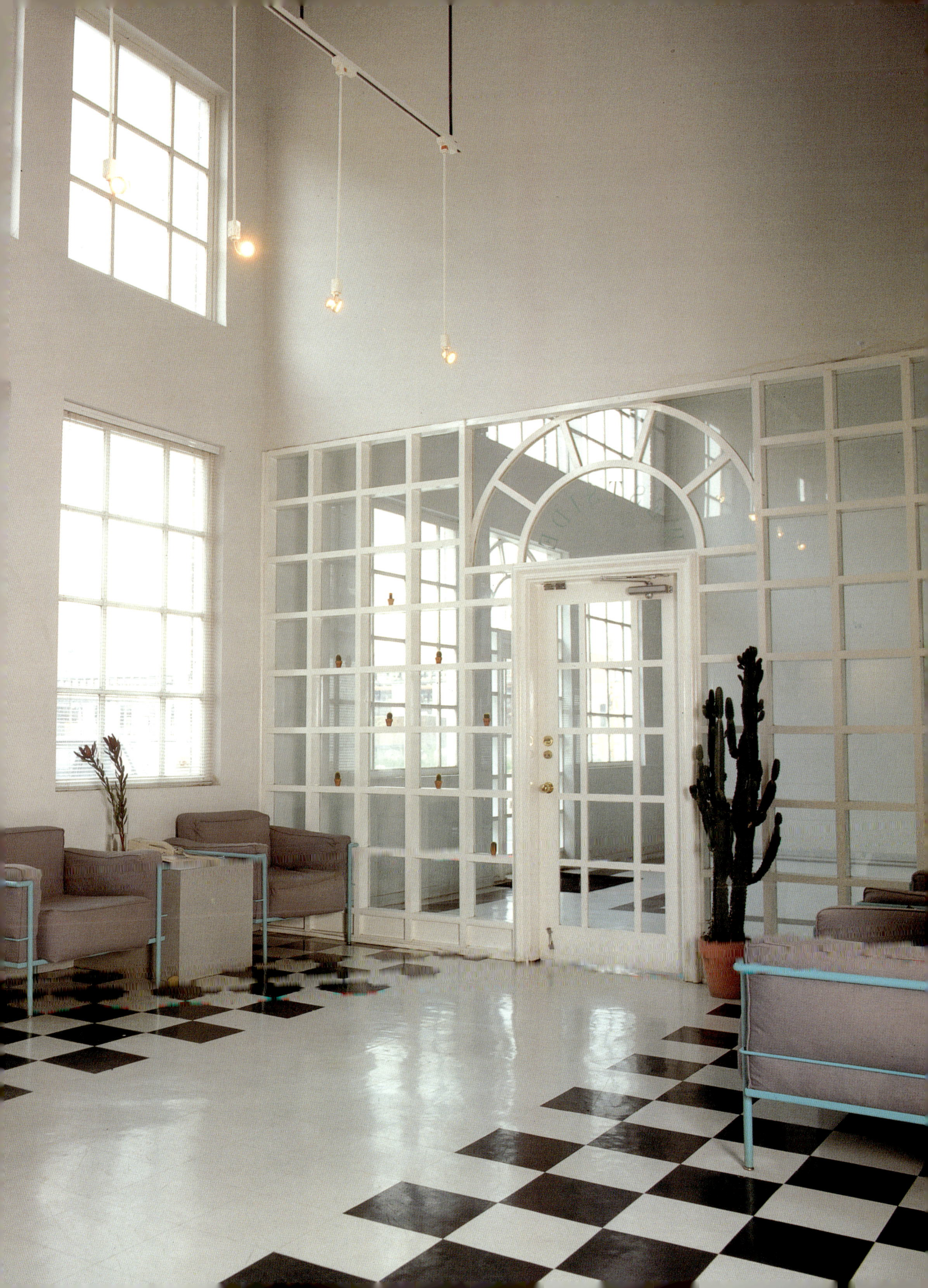

FORMING A PARTNERSHIP . . .

Westside had its beginnings when Sandi Strauss was the manager at a studio where McLeod was an associate. The two were dissatisfied with that setup, mostly because they felt that they had very little input into the business. They approached Simhoni, who was an associate at another studio. In 1984, the three decided to form a business of their own.

It took them almost a year to put the entire project together, including seven months to find the space they currently occupy. The neighborhood was rapidly deteriorating, and the landlord, sensing an opportunity to gentrify not only his property but also its environs, agreed to renovate to the photographers' specifications.

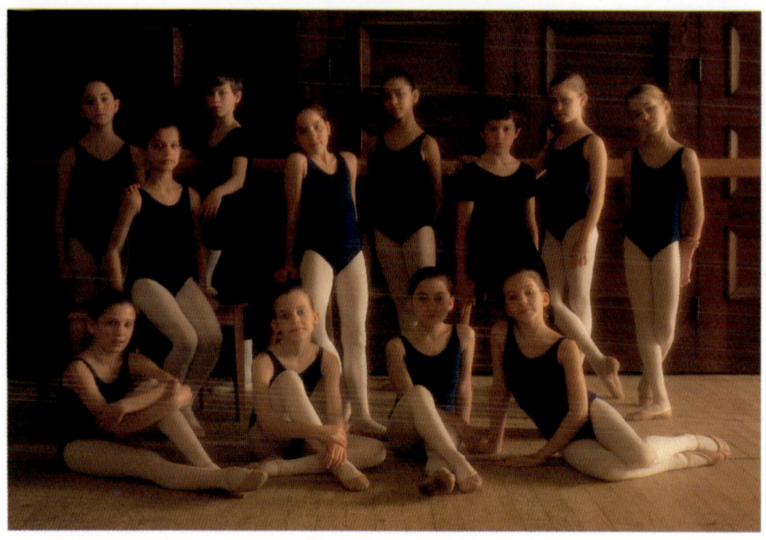

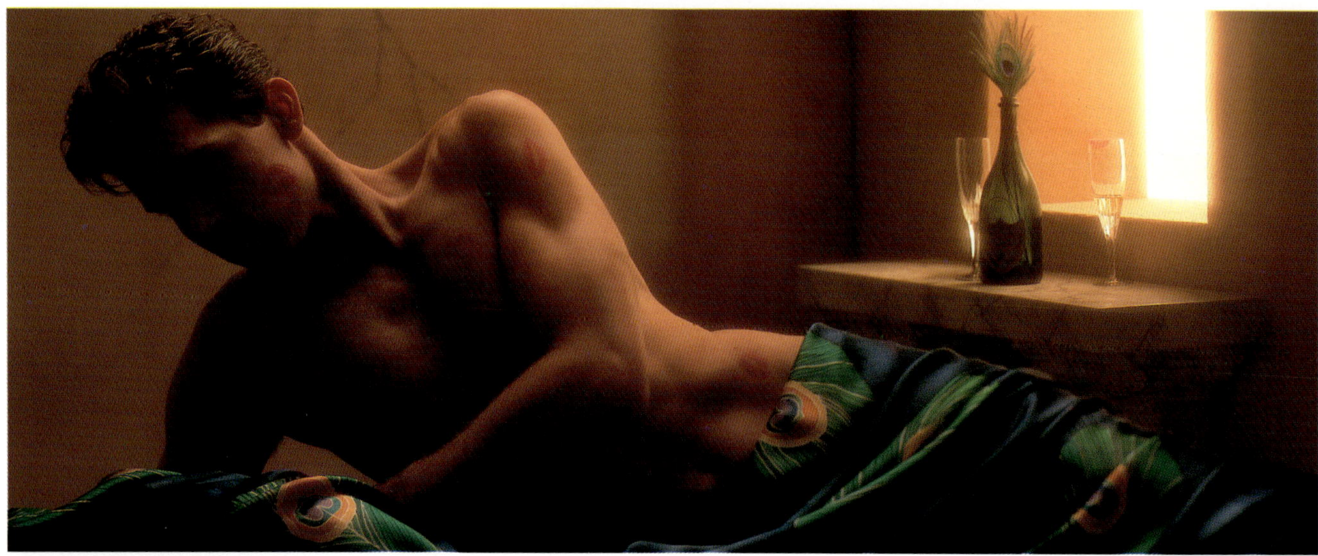

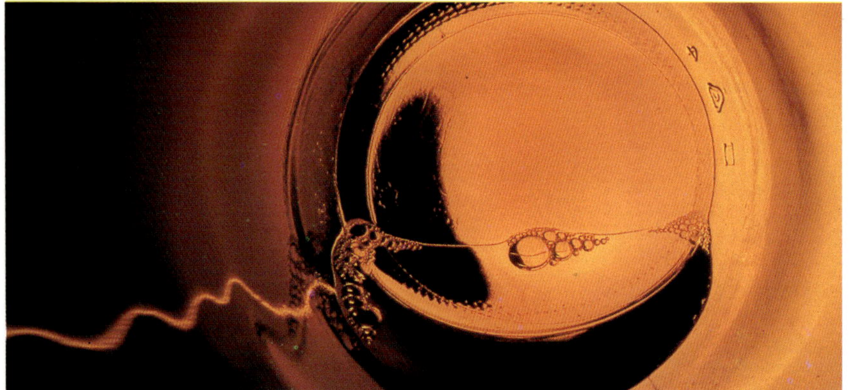

Here is a variety of work by the studio's principals: ballet dancers by William McLeod, a textile ad by George Simhoni, a Taylor Browning ad by Garth Grosjean, an Apple Cider Lite ad by Jean Desjardins, and a fruit still life by Silvio Calcagno.

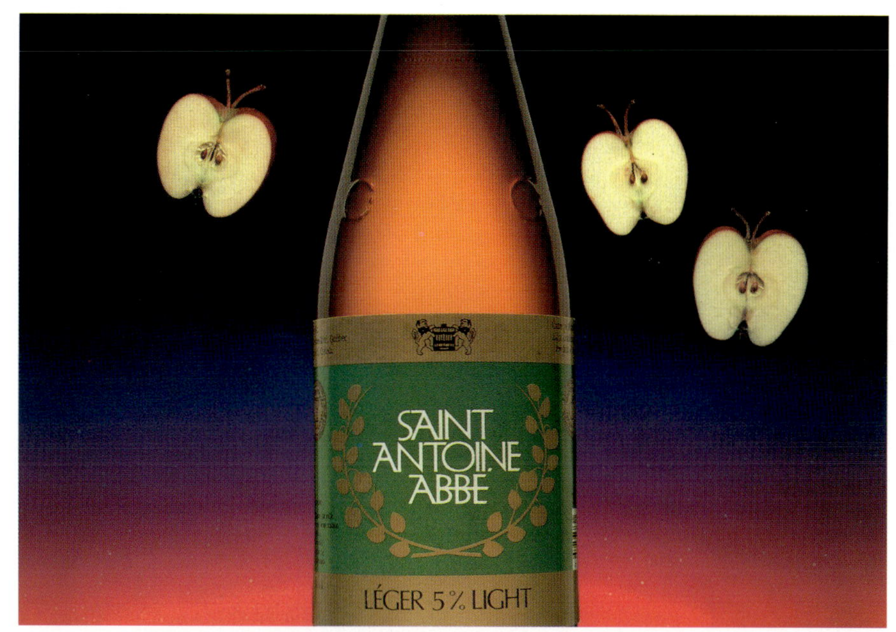
SAINT ANTOINE ABBÉ
LÉGER 5% LIGHT

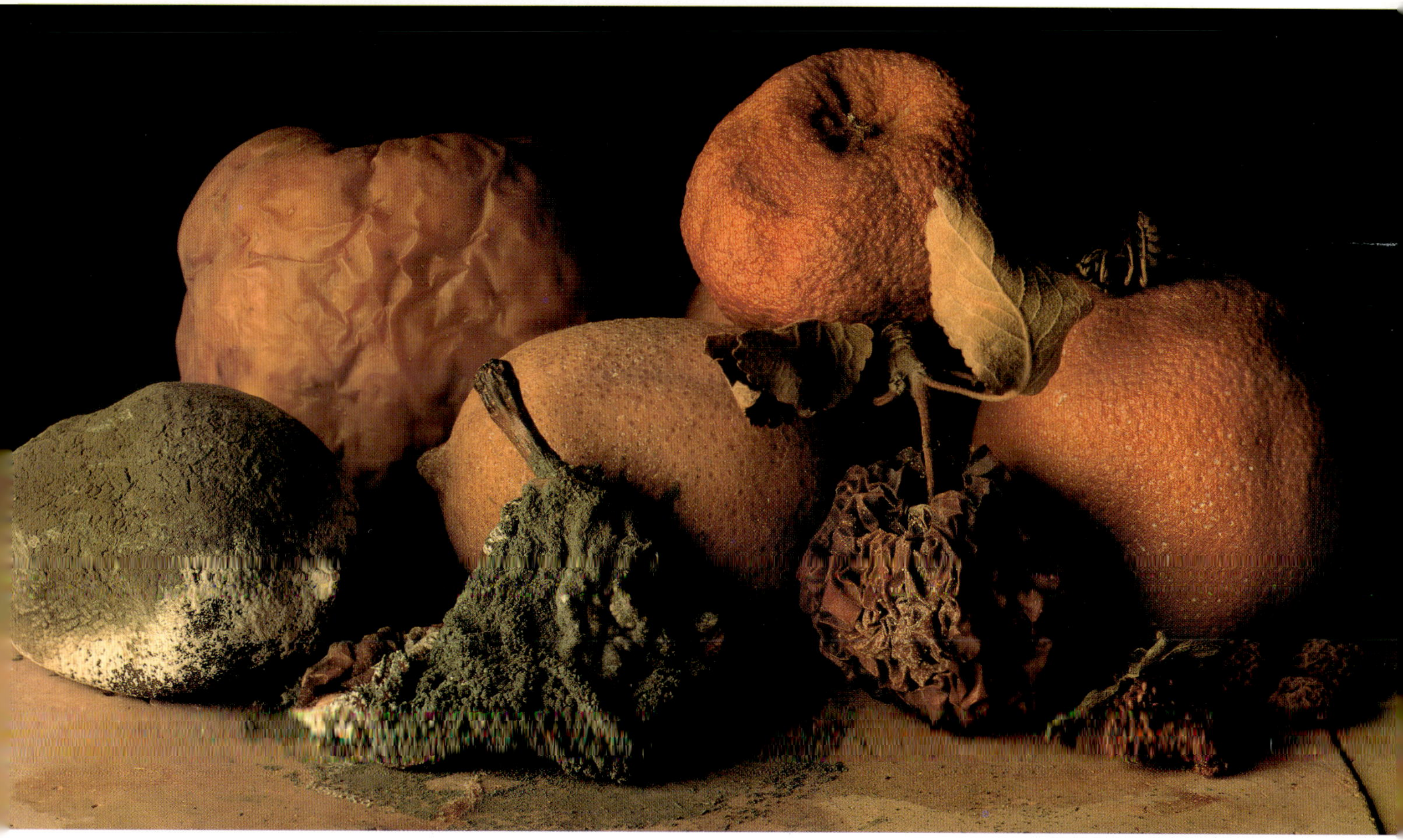

ACHIEVING A MODERN LOOK

The studio itself is part of a former factory complex situated near Toronto's downtown area. The landlord broke up the factory area and leased approximately 10,000 feet of space to Westside's owners. The entire renovation took six months to complete. One of the space's assets was the "I-beam configuration." Rather than columns spread all over, which would have meant a lot of rearranging, the beams were arranged within a row and could be left intact. What the space desperately needed, however, was a level floor. Over 7,000 square feet of concrete was poured to that end.

Though the block that Westside Studio is on still has dark, smoke-stained vestiges of its former life, the studio's interior is bright and inviting. Visitors enter through a doorway composed of small glass panes and are greeted by an airy, high-ceilinged vestibule. Black-and-white floor tile and white cement block walls give the reception area a modern, graphic look. Sea green accents border the chairs and the top of the reception desk, as well as run along the staircases leading to the second-floor mezzanine area, adding a pleasing bit of color.

This view of the reception area is from the mezzanine-level offices.

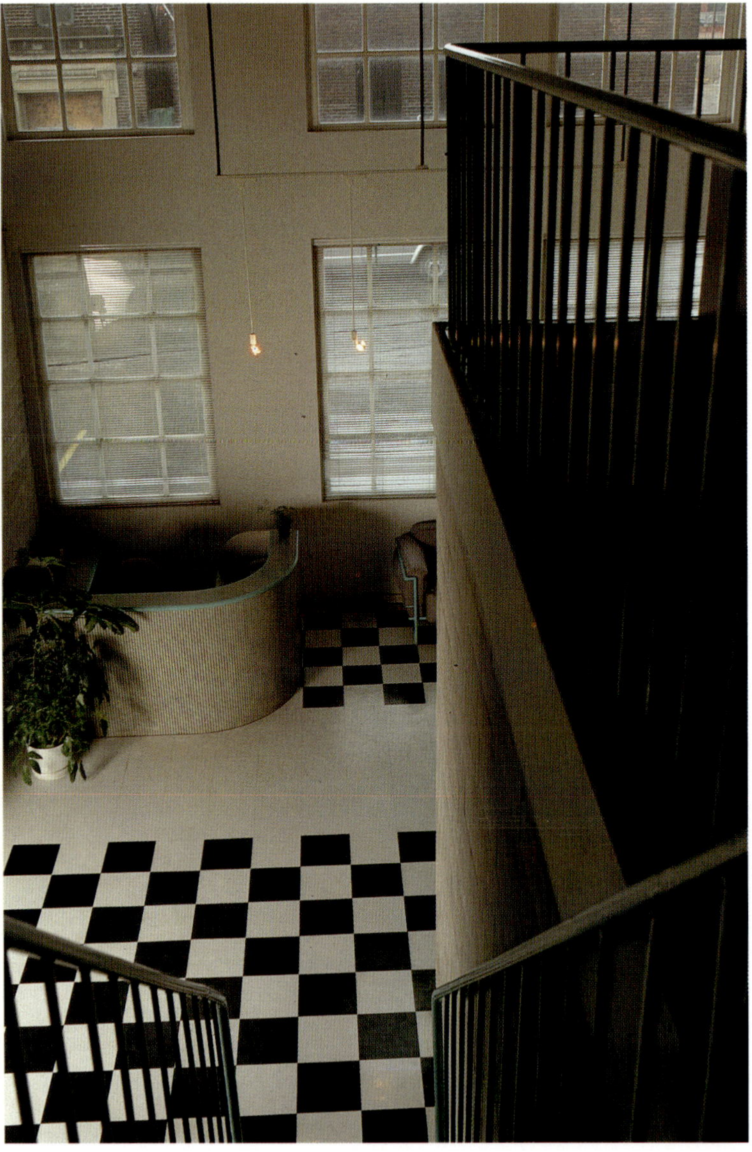

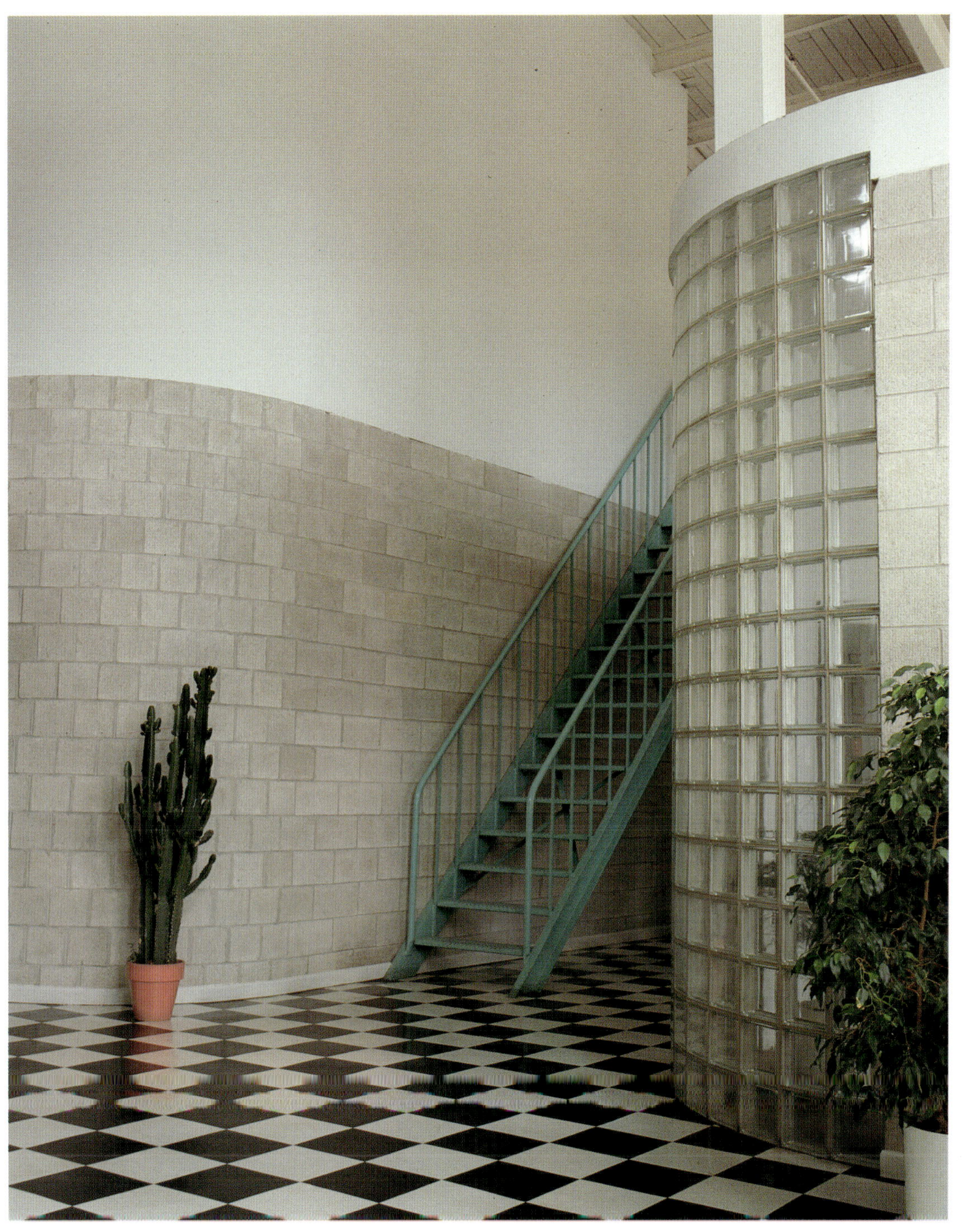

A staircase leads to the offices
of Westside Studio.

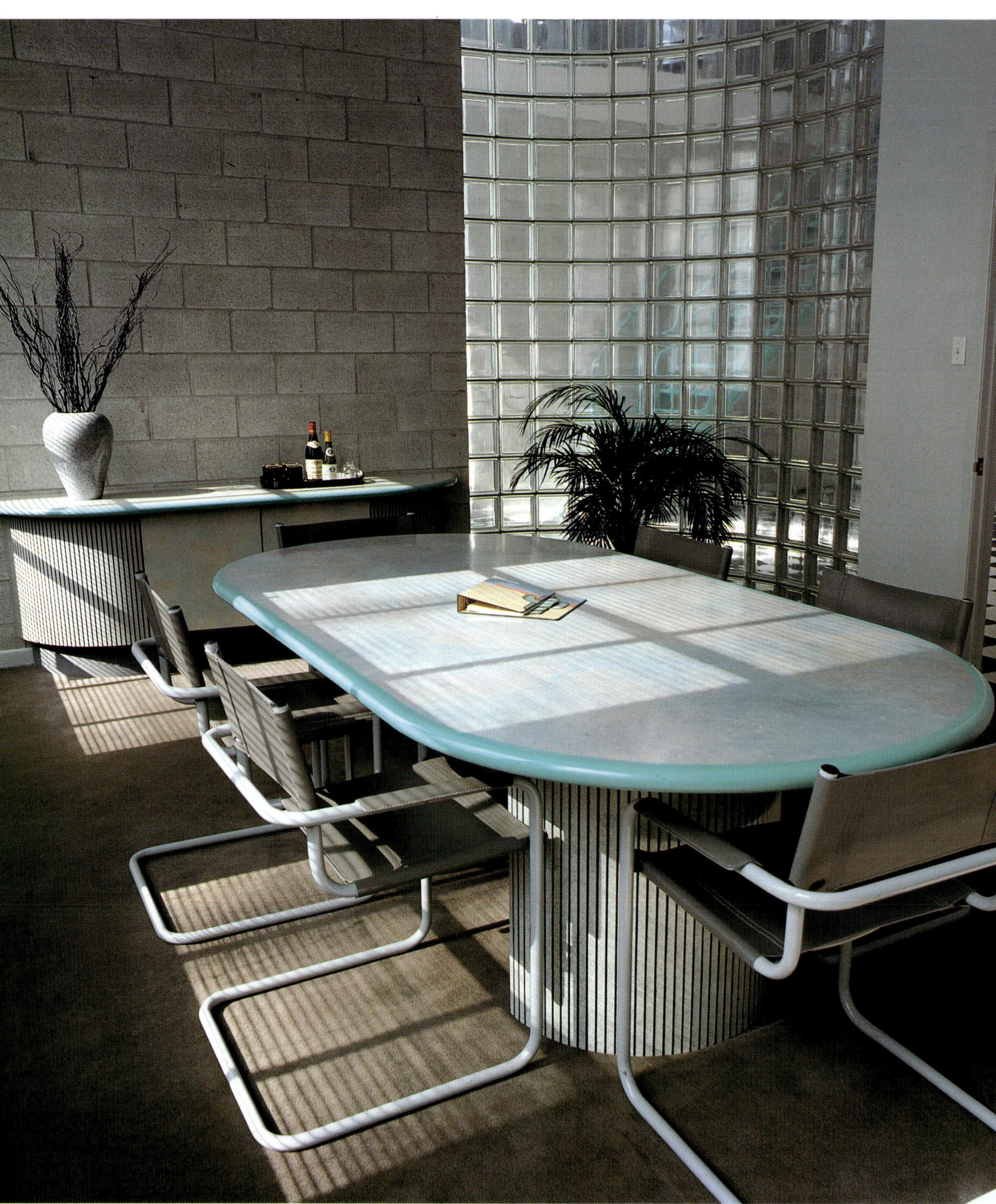

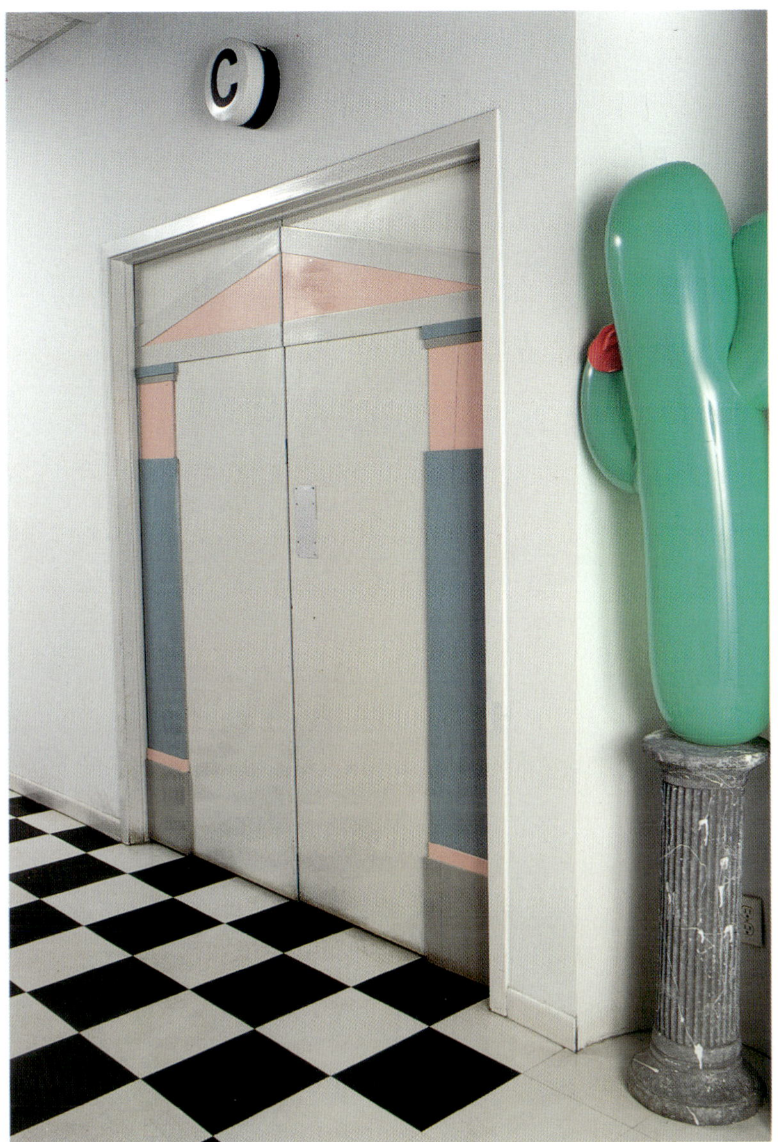

Directly behind the receptionist's desk is a curved wall, made partially of white cement block and partly of glass tiles. Behind this façade is the conference room, where all initial business transactions are handled. Like the reception area, this room teems with the light coming through a series of windows at its front. A conference table, a television set, and video equipment are the only furnishings in this room, giving it a modern yet minimalist feeling.

A long, wide hallway, with a series of doorways on either side, extends from the conference room at the front portion of the studio all the way to the opposite end of the space. The black-and-white tile theme is carried through the hallway, along with touches of the entryway's sea green coloring. A series of pastel accents in the form of geometric columns, both real and painted, along the doors add a sense of whimsy to this area. Also present, but set into a small alcove, is the studio mascot, a large, inflated cactus; it is an echo of the studio's logo.

In one corner of the biggest shooting area, but overlooking the shooting bay, is a kitchen space, which is not fully enclosed. A checkerboard floor differentiates this space from the larger studio surrounding it. The kitchen is functional and modern, but not overly equipped. It has cabinets, a sink, a stove, and a refrigerator. A table-and-chair set provides both extra work space and a lounging area for the staff.

Here are the studio's shooting room (left) and one of the studio's three kitchens (right). The hallway that runs through the space (above) connects the various studios and is decorated in the whimsical manner now identified with Westside's promotional efforts. The light above the studio door is lit when work is going on inside.

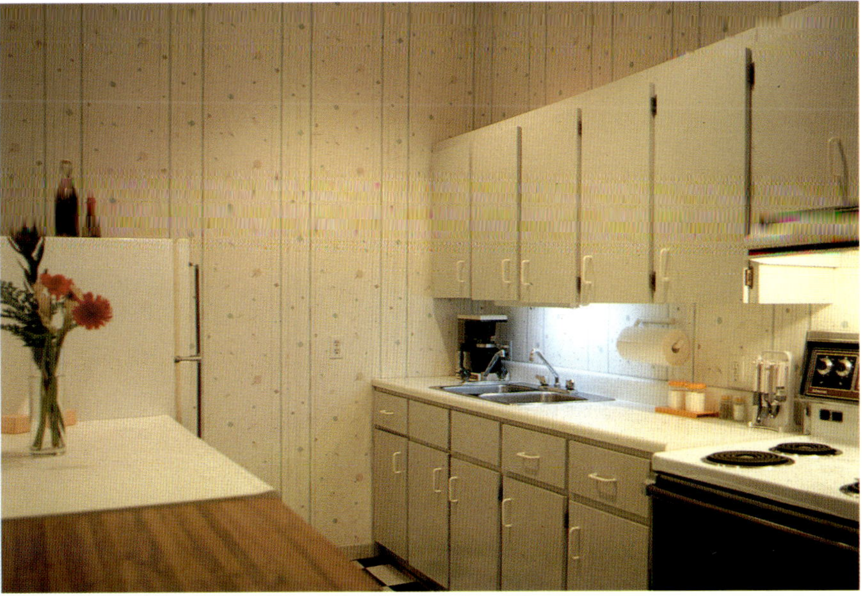

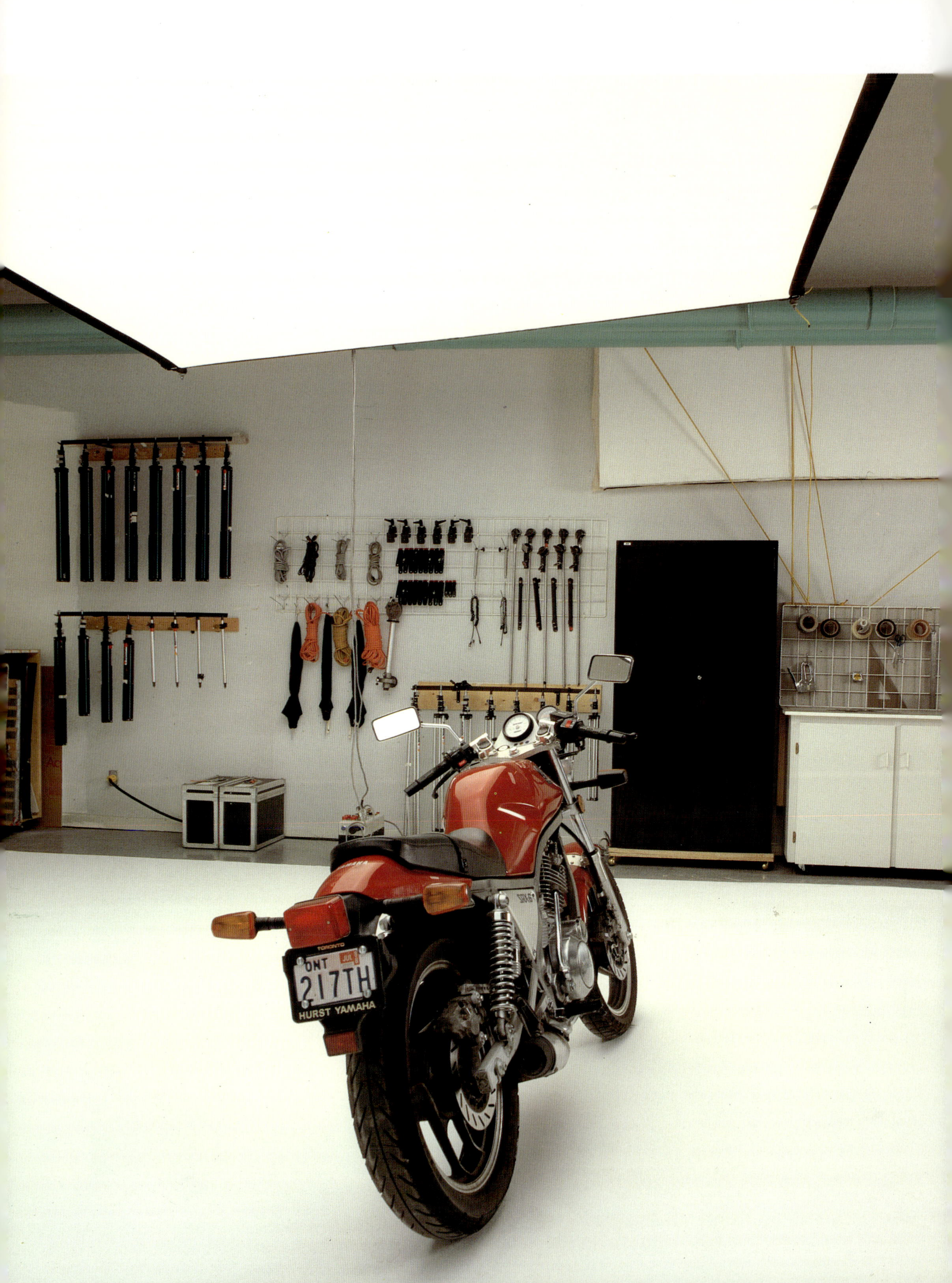
TORONTO
ONT
217TH
HURST YAMAHA

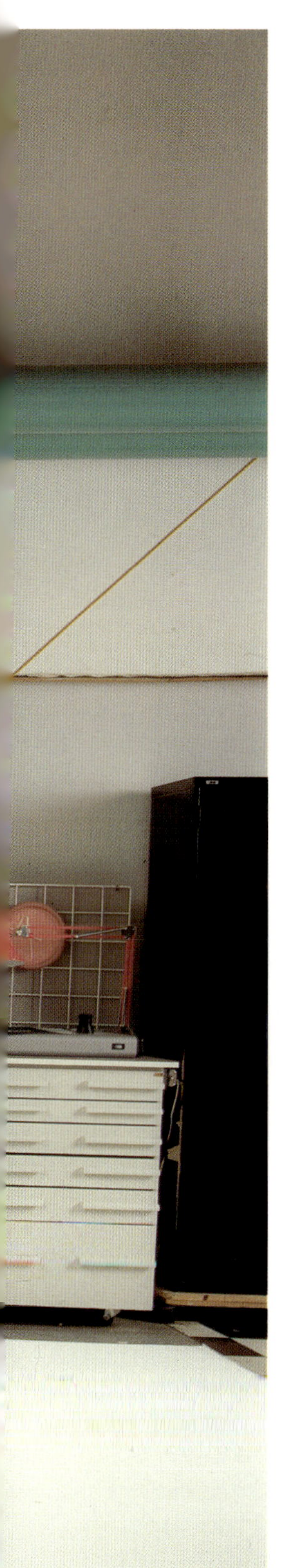

This large studio area, used primarily by Grosjean and McLeod, is self-contained, but also offers access to Simhoni's studio next door. Though smaller, measuring 25 × 40 feet, his is equipped in much the same way, has a kitchen and balcony area, and the same amenities. A balcony-level door leads into his office.

McLeod and Grosjean's studio faces a luxurious bathroom done in gray marble. This is both the visitors' facility and a dressing room for models. Behind this room is the smallest of the four studios. It measures 20 × 20 feet and, unlike the other spaces, contains neither a kitchen nor a client/balcony area. It is fully equipped with all the necessary photographic equipment, however, and is wired for maximum amperage. Simhoni explains that it is the "extra" space and is not assigned to any individual shooter.

Across the hall, a series of three small rooms is assigned to other studio business. The room closest to Simhoni's studio contains props and backgrounds. Next to this space is the largest of Westside's two darkrooms, and immediately after this room is the studio's largest prop room.

A narrow hallway next to the prop room leads to Calcagno's studio, which is 20 × 40 feet. It mirrors Simhoni's studio on the ground level, but does not have a balcony area. Facing this studio is another prop room, as well as the second of the studio's two darkrooms.

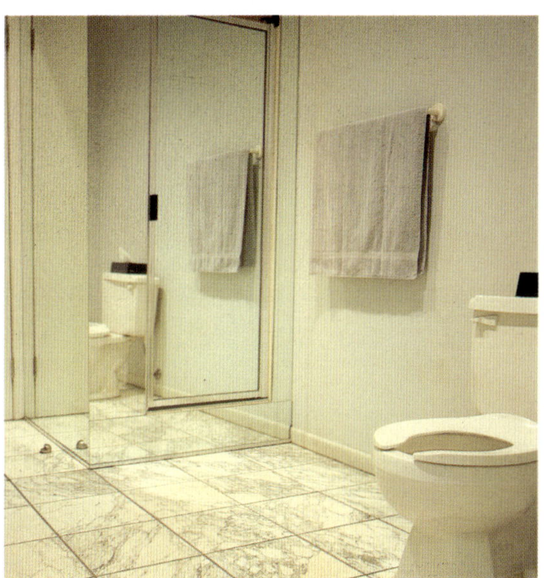

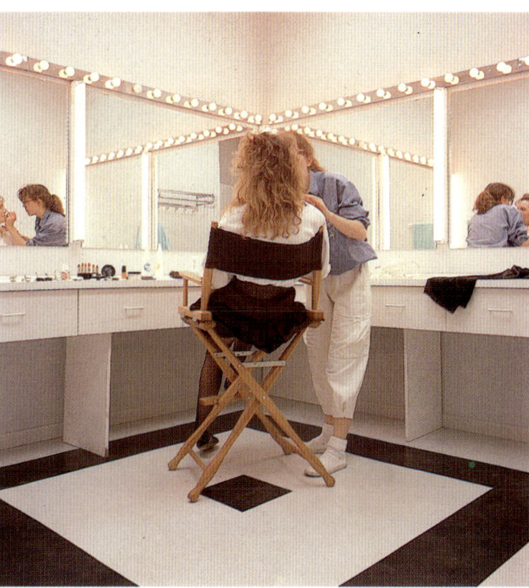

A luxurious bathroom and the studio's dressing room add ambience to Westside's already distinctive interior.

The larger shooting stages within the studio can accommodate oversized subjects.

The mezzanine is located above all of these various areas. At the front end of the mezzanine are the office cubicles used by Sandi Strauss, the general manager, and the studio's two reps, who are in charge of the portfolios of all five photographers. Simhoni and McLeod's offices are also accessible from here. The other end of the mezzanine recently has been given over to a design group. However, the rapid growth of Westside's billings, as well as the boom in video have caused the partnership to rethink the use of this space. Future plans call for a video production studio to be situated here.

Behind the main studio area is a large garage used mainly for storage, but, when all the studios are in use, this space can double as a shooting bay.

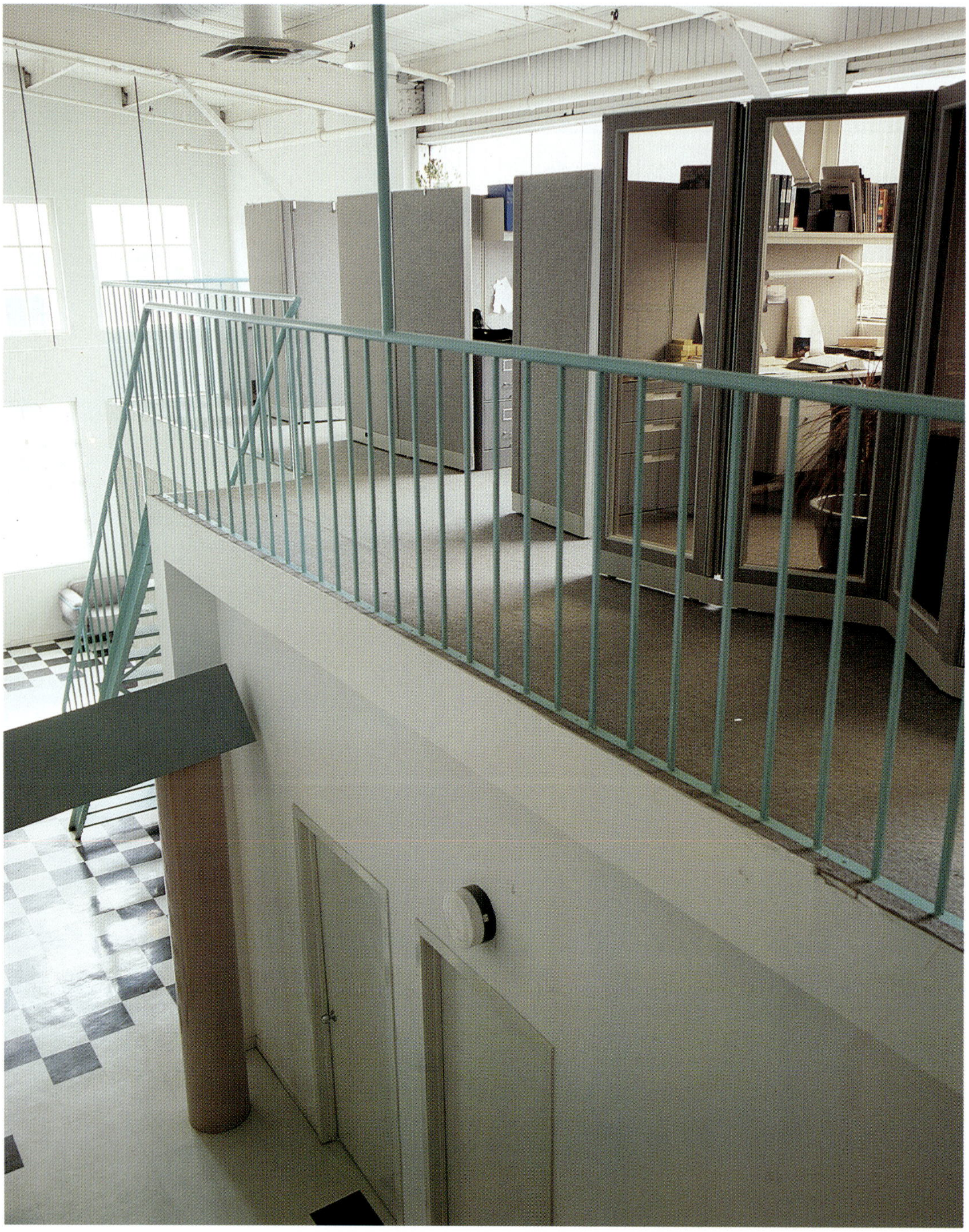

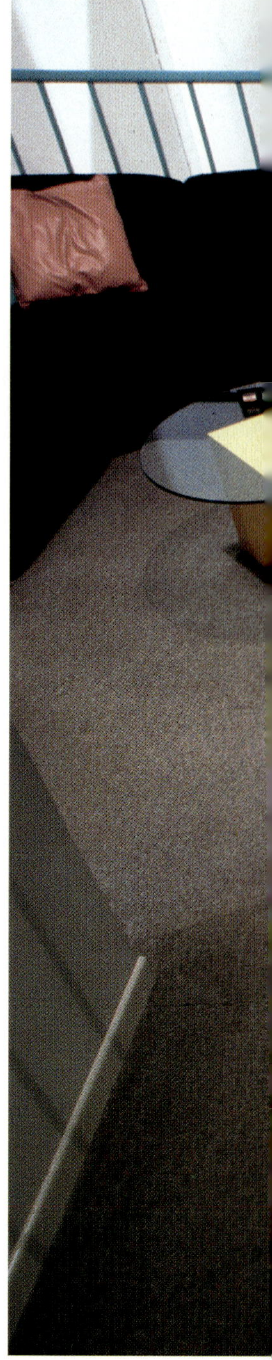

The studio's offices are located on the mezzanine, as is a small reception area from which clients and visitors can watch a shoot.

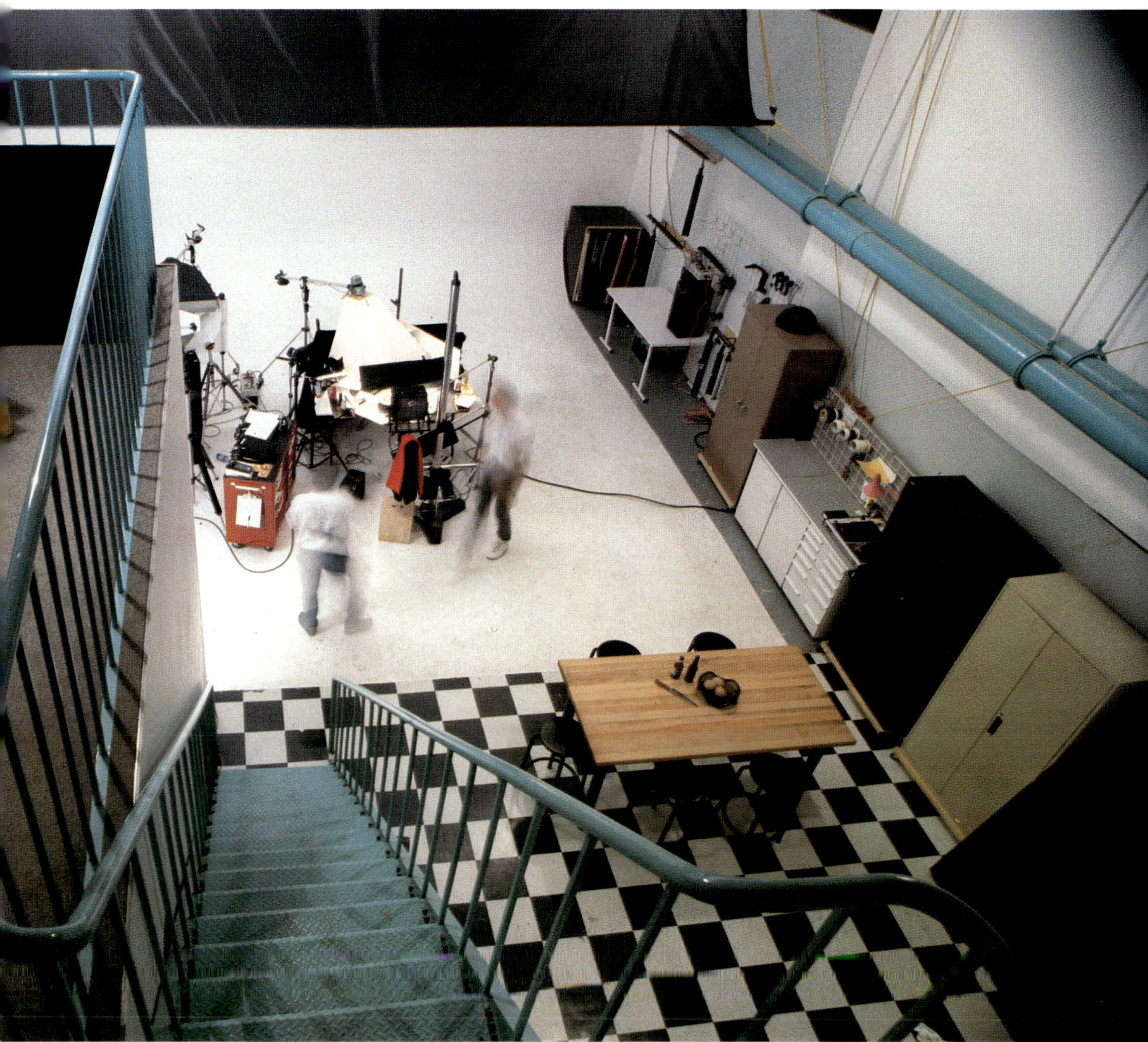

SPECIAL FEATURES

"Our initial design thinking was geared toward keeping clients comfortable for long periods," says Simhoni. "That, to us, meant open space. But, at the same time, the photographers wanted a lot of privacy for working. Therefore, the doors have locks as well as lights above each door to indicate when someone is shooting." The building has four separate shooting spaces of varying sizes, all located on the first floor. The largest studio, which measures 25 × 50 feet, is at the far end of the hall. Like the other three shooting areas, it is wired for 300 amps of power. Each of the spaces is equipped with a cyclorama at its rear wall, bank lights on movable stands, as well as large-format cameras, polecats, strobes, spotlights, and innumerable rolls of seamless paper. Studio tools and necessities, such as gaffer tape, wiring, and clamps, are neatly hung on a pegboard, along one wall.

A metal staircase to the left of the kitchen leads to a balcony that also overlooks the shooting bay. Overstuffed couches, chairs, a lamp, and a pinball machine—described by Simhoni as client amenities—are this area's only furnishings. In this way, clients can watch a shoot or retreat from it, as they wish. A door—usually kept closed—leads off the balcony and into McLeod's office.

Once the studio was complete, McLeod and Simhoni hired Grosjean and Desjardins, both former assistants of Simhoni. The business terms then, as now, were simple. Each photographer contributes a "photo fee" toward the operation of the studio, a payment that amounts to between 30 percent and 70 percent of their billings. In return, each photographer is paid on a weekly basis, even if he did not bill that week. The studio agrees to maintain existing equipment and augment hardware as it sees fit. The studio also takes care of cleaning each individual shooting area, stocking it with food, and heating and air conditioning each space. The studio also supplies accounting and bookkeeping services, as well as propping and styling for every job.

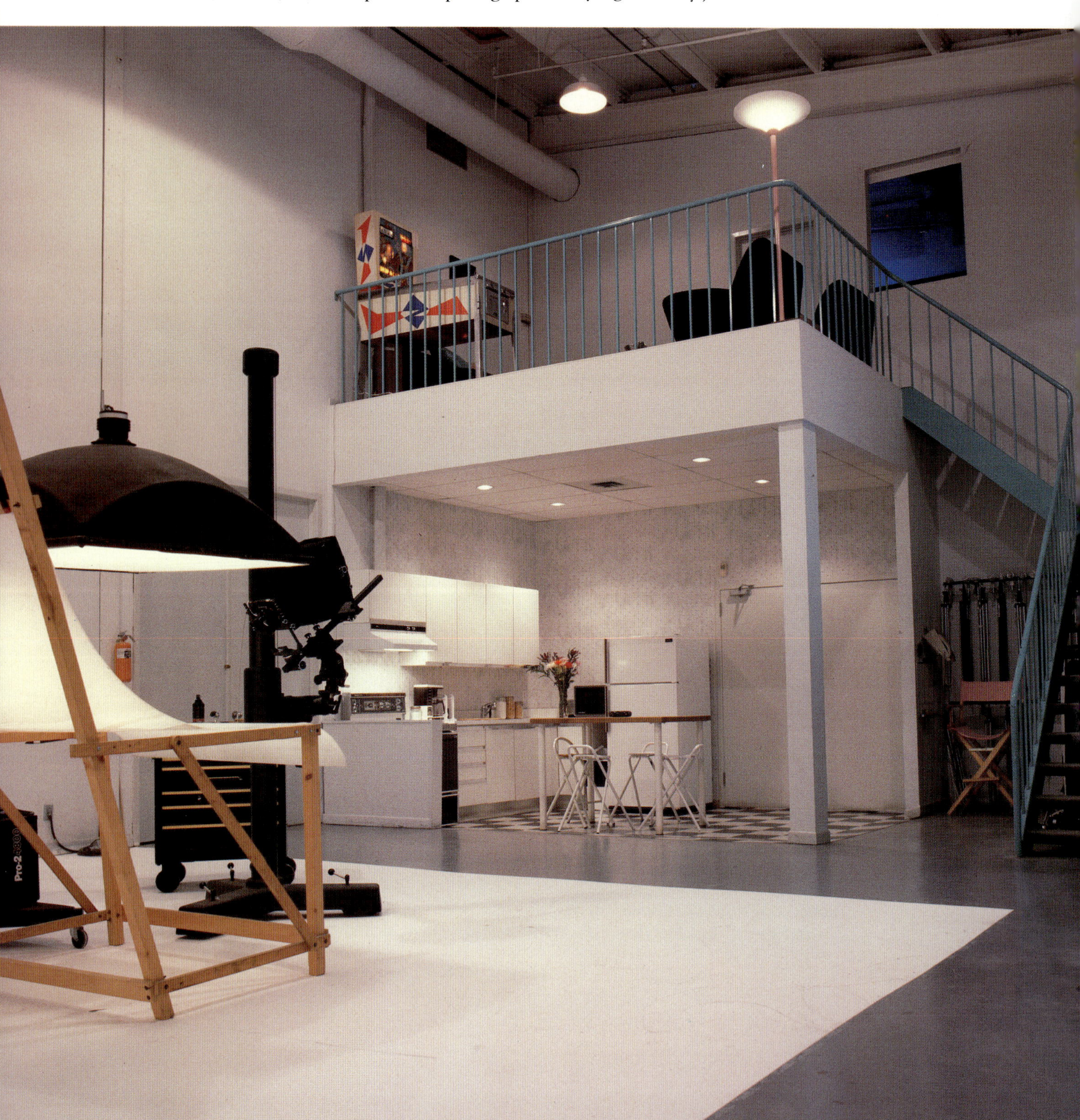

Yet for all the services the studio provides, says Strauss, "It's not like Bill and George dictate policy. Everyone has input," she explains. "The idea is not to have any problems except for picture-taking. Therefore, no individual photographer is burdened with billing, payouts, or purchasing."

The system seems to work quite well. In the almost three years since Westside began, not one associate has left. Perhaps that's because each photographer has a specialty of his own, and, though a few individuals may overlap within certain areas, each shooter was hired to complement the talents and abilities of existing staff members. In addition, the philosophy of Simhoni and McLeod allows for a great deal of creative freedom. "We don't want Westside to be known as an entity," says Simhoni. "Rather, we prefer to promote the individual photographer." Besides his own individuality, each shooter has the creative feedback of his peers. "We also have the companionship of people trying to do good work," Simhoni notes. "There's friendly competition, as well as advice."

But it's the partnership's lack of a billing quota that truly makes Westside an amiable place to work. Westside currently employs fifteen people: five photographers, five assistants (one per photographer), a studio manager, a receptionist, two reps, and one prop girl. As Simhoni explains, "We feel that good work is more important than money. But, of course, good work eventually generates larger billing." And, of course, a good working atmosphere generates all of the above.

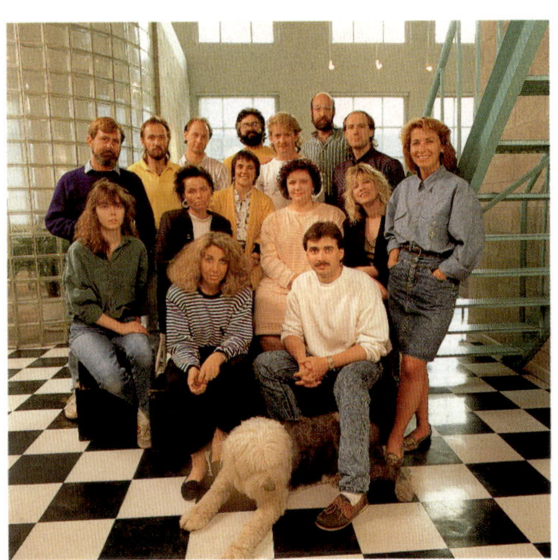

"We don't want Westside to be known as an entity. Rather, we prefer to promote the individual photographer."

CONSTRUCTING A VERSATILE STUDIO

One of the most overlooked specialties in photography is catalog work. Although its practitioners rarely work out of highly designed studios—often opting instead for cavernous warehouse spaces in industrial districts—the volume of work generated makes this area of expertise one of photography's most lucrative. **O**ne such enterprise, WFM Studio, which specializes in images of such items as furniture, flatware, jewelry, and electronics, is located in Chicago, only a few minutes from the city's bustling downtown loop. WFM (the initials stand for William F. Miller, the studio's owner) currently employs seven people. But the business had its roots in a much smaller undertaking. Started in 1972, the studio was then owned by Miller and his partner, Chuck Pirrello. The two did small photographic layout and design projects, such as toy catalogs. The careful, quality work that Pirrello and Miller produced began to draw bigger mail-order accounts, such as Alden's and Montgomery Ward. By 1982, the two had a thriving business; in that year, Pirrello sold his share to Miller, who began working with his son, Clark.

The studio's spacious shooting area accommodates the photographers' individual specialties and needs.

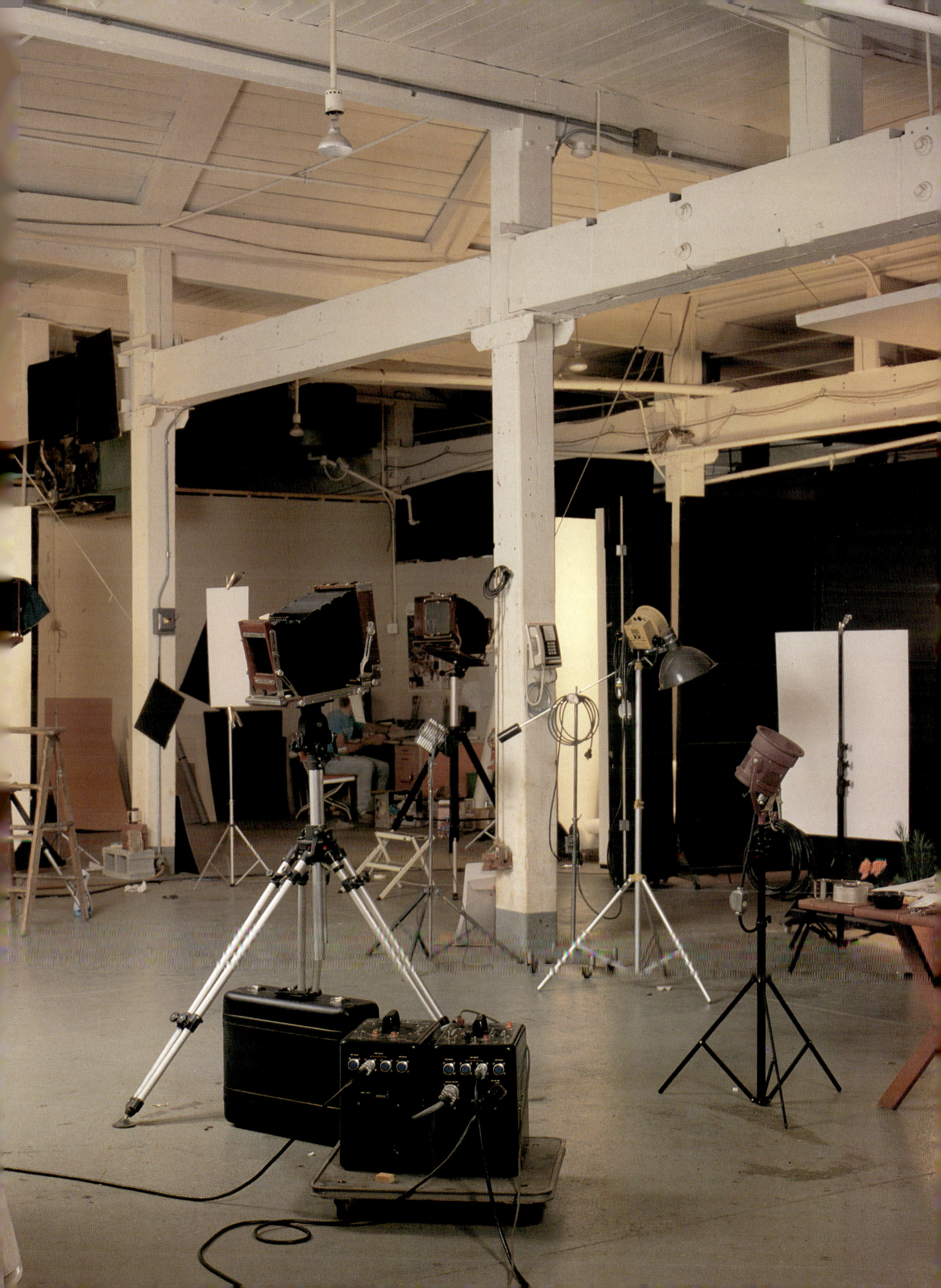

FACING STRUCTURAL PROBLEMS

The studio was located in Chicago's downtown loop on two floors of a pre-World War II building. The Millers had 12-foot-high ceilings, 10,000 square feet of space on the third floor, and 2,000 square feet of space on the second floor where merchandise was stored before and after a shoot. But the studio had one structural drawback: its wooden floors. The photographers shot mostly tungsten film and tended to rely on time exposures to achieve the clarity and sharpness their clients wanted. And the often unsteady wooden floors—which had a way of shaking at even the slightest step—were not anchoring the tripods and cameras properly. In addition, the floors could not support the weight of some of the larger furnishings and interiors that were increasingly becoming a major portion of the team's catalog work. In fact, the photographers often had to lease space in order to shoot bulkier sets.

With the acquisition of the large Spiegel account and the hiring of two more photographers, the Millers knew they needed a bigger, more stable space. "We also realized that we required more room for holding merchandise, more storage space, and a bigger shooting area," says Clark Miller. "We approached a real estate agent with very specific needs," he recalls, "and asked for a ground-level space with reinforced flooring."

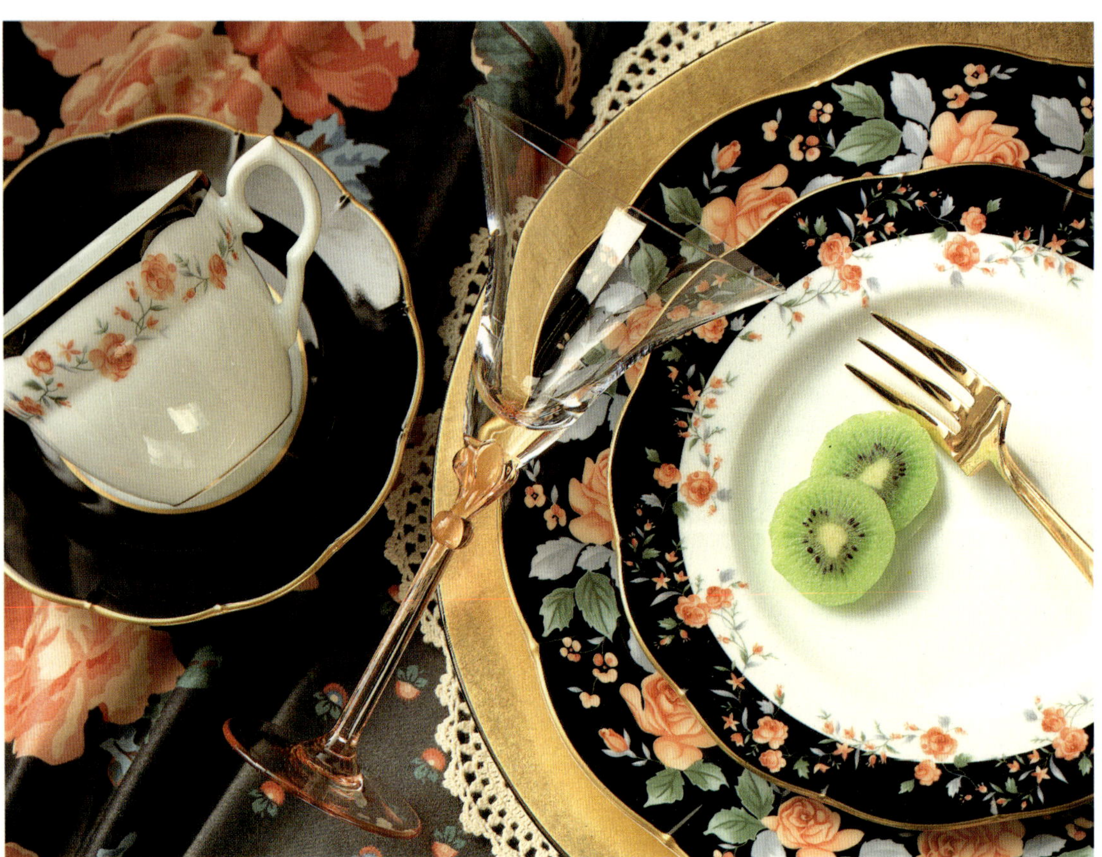

The photographers at WFM Studio are renowned for their high-quality catalog images.

PLANNING FOR CONVENIENCE AND COMFORT

The location the Millers eventually settled on has 15-foot ceilings and 16,000 square feet of space. The Millers came up with "fifteen different floor plans, which we showed to the staff at a meeting where everyone's needs were discussed." According to Clark, "It takes a lot of thought to put it all together."

Currently, visitors enter the studio through an unobtrusive doorway that leads into a large, clean, but not very fancy reception area. The conference room, in which "all business is conducted," is directly behind the reception desk. A lightbox, videocassette recorder, and television set are kept on the right side wall. The lighting in here is soft and warm, the floor is carpeted, and there are a small, well-stocked bar, couches, and a wooden table, all of which evoke a comfortable living room environment. The Millers keep all their transparency files in here, as well as stock photos, such as pre-shot screens that are stripped into product shots of television sets.

Across a small hallway and a bit to the right of the conference room is the senior Miller's office. Its most striking feature: the absence of an official desk. Instead, a large circular table occupies the central area. Behind the table is a Macintosh computer. In general, the copy for catalogs created by WFM is done on the computer by a freelance writer, then sent out to a typesetter, Clark explains. In addition, the company plans to traffic all merchandise brought into and taken out of the studio via the computer, so that even the smallest piece of jewelry can be easily located and accounted for.

Facing the entrance to the office is a large, walk-in safe. Camera equipment is stored here, as well as an assortment of props. There is also an entire shelf filled with magazines that often suggest styling ideas.

The production area contains flat files for storing layout boards, a series of lightboxes for viewing transparencies, and drafting tables on which mechanicals are designed and completed. Stat and copying machines are kept here as well. The entire right side wall is covered with homosote, a soft, cardboard-based surface that is cheaper than corkboard. Sketches of each page of every catalog [illegible] in-house are pinned up here. As each image is shot, it is marked off to indicate that it has been completed.

A workshop is situated in the far front corner of the studio. A large stock of tools is available to the photographers, who do most of the construction themselves. It is rare for an assistant to be hired, but on occasion the "merchandiser"—the person responsible for ordering, trafficking, and returning all items photographed—will double as an assistant/carpenter. A freestanding kitchen stands adjacent to the workshop. The photographers plan to purchase more modern equipment so that food photography can be added to the studio's roster. Currently, the kitchen has a sink, a stove, and two refrigerators. The older refrigerator is used to store flowers and film while the newer unit contains food and beverages.

The stylists' room is a short walk from the safe, down a narrow hallway. WFM currently has two full-time stylists on staff. Their job is to prop all the interiors created for furniture shoots. As such, this large, well-lit room is full of books, plants, and knickknacks—items commonly found in most homes. Shelves are used to store a motley assortment of paraphernalia, including pens, telephones, hats, Christmas decorations, baskets, planters, lamps, and door and window treatments. A sewing machine is also kept here, so that alterations on clothing, upholstery, and material backdrops can be quickly made. Sometimes accessories for various shoots are made from scratch, or items are repaired if they are damaged when they arrive. There are also a number of open racks for hanging merchandise and clothing.

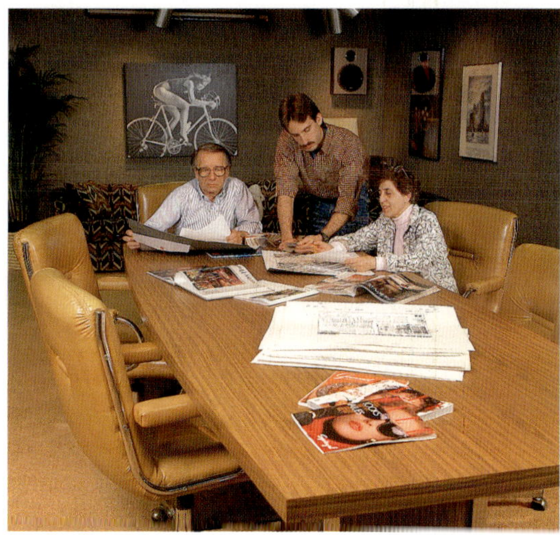

Clark and William Miller work with the studio secretary in the conference room.

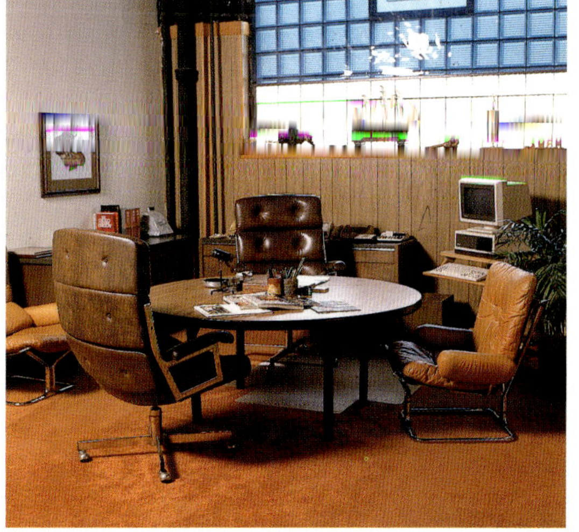

The senior Miller's office has no official desk.

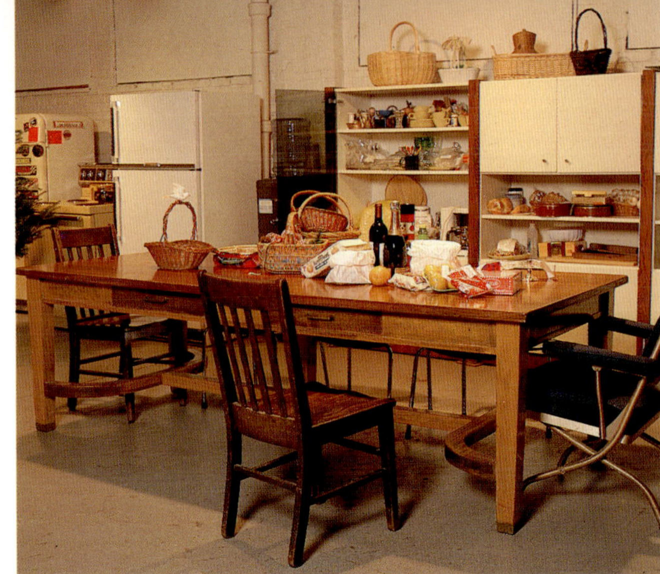

The studio's kitchen is located at the back of WFM's cavernous space.

The warehouse-like size of WFM allows entire rooms to be set up for shooting and then dismantled, while other work goes on undisturbed.

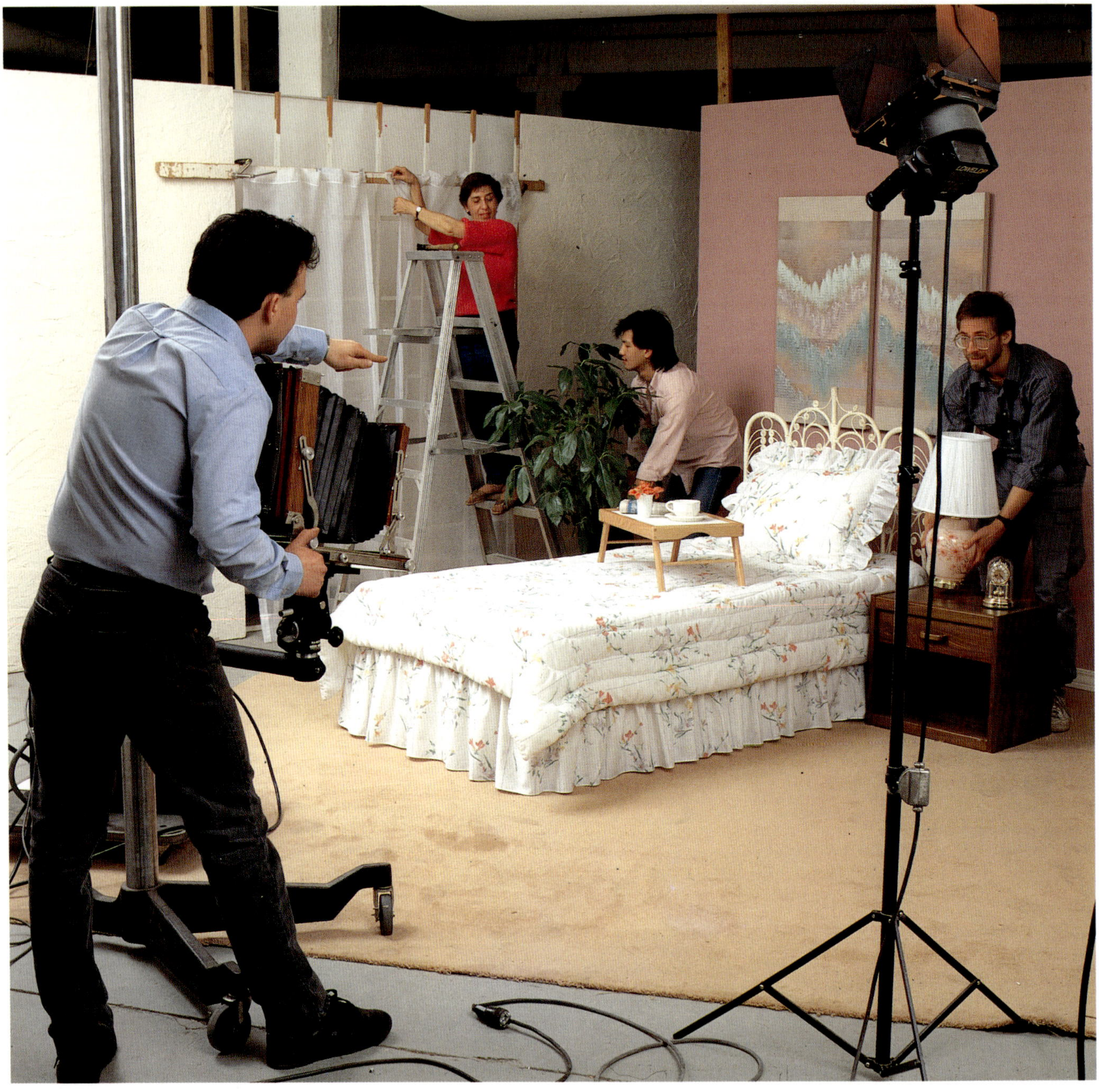

SPECIAL FEATURES

The shooting area is the largest section of the studio. It is divided into eight shooting bays at the front, and a kitchen. Miller estimates that at any time 13,000 square feet are available for shooting. Floating walls are put up here to distinguish each bay and are moved around depending on what is being shot. According to the photographer, most of the interiors shot here are built, painted, and decorated in-house. The entire assemblage stays up for at least a week, during which time lighting tests and preliminary Polaroids are taken. These images are given to the client, who can correct or approve the work done. Then the final 8 × 10 exposures are made. The flexible shooting bays allow other work to continue while this lengthy procedure goes on.

Another important part of the studio is the kitchen area, which leads toward the rear of the space. Most of this section is given over to storage, but two smaller shooting bays are also located here. A large door, big enough to admit cars and vans, offers studio access to vehicular subjects as well as to oversized furniture and props. A drain in the floor of this area absorbs moisture and dirt that might otherwise be brought deeper into the studio. An assortment of oversized backgrounds, such as Formica and glass, are kept here, as well as bricks, rocks, and firewood—items that are used to lend veracity to most interior scenes. Rolls of seamless, linoleum and other flooring, wallpaper, and patterns are stored here also.

One of the biggest assets of the building can also be found in this area: a mezzanine with a ramp and truck-level dock, so that big items can be wheeled right into the studio. Rows of shelving filled with sealed and resealed boxes sit waiting to be photographed or returned.

The two shooting bays situated back here are often rented out to freelancers, which generates a bit of extra income. On this particular day, one of the staff photographers is shooting watches on a tiny tabletop set that is dwarfed by the studio.

Off to one side of the bays is a series of doors. One opens to a smaller safe in which camera backs, lenses, and other photographic hardware are kept. Nearby is a dressing room. It is equipped with a shower, a sink and two bathroom bowls, as well as a makeup table and closet space. Although the Millers don't do much fashion work at the moment, the photographers hope to branch out into that specialty as well.

The unfinished feeling of the studio, with its cement block walls and floors and its exposed pipes, is an indication of its chameleon-like nature. By not designing every aspect of the space, the Millers have allowed themselves a lot of freedom to construct and reconstruct as business demands. "It takes a lot of effort to put it all together," says Clark, "and it's still evolving." The photographer is quiet for a moment, then grins and says, "But there's nothing wrong with rearranging the furniture, right?"

By not designing every aspect of the space, the Millers have allowed themselves a lot of freedom to construct and reconstruct as business demands.

PROFESSIONAL ADVICE

Without doubt, photographers' working environments are one of their most crucial assets. The specifics of space and ambience—the factors that are most visible to clients—should depend on the type of work that gets done within the studio as well as the available budget. Although these details are the most conspicuous, they don't begin to encompass the complete economic inventory. **W**hen photographers set up their first major studio—or, for that matter, redesign or relocate a working space—many factors will influence the final outcome. The type of neighborhood, proximity to services, interior design, amount of working and storage space, and interior amenities are all primary considerations. But, the photographers whose studios are featured in this book, as well as the architects and designers who worked with them, all stress one fact: The most important phase of a studio's design is the time before any physical work begins, the time taken to evaluate both present and future studio needs.

No money should be spent, nor work commence, before photographers understand the components of their business; this will indicate the minimal structural, space, and hardware needs of the planned studio. These specifications will also serve as a primary—and very necessary—guideline for the architect or designer hired to do the job.

Even if a photographer chooses to do this work alone, as did Chris Callis, David Langley, and Robert Wigington, this evaluation is useful as a design outline. When carefully executed and followed, it should produce an efficient design, since random decisions will be eliminated and even the tiniest details will be taken into account.

Perhaps Michael Prodanou of Prodanou Associates in Boston, the architect responsible for Clint Clemens's studio, puts it most succinctly. "Know your operation, how it works now and what you plan to be in a few years. Then, when you've got that all figured out, don't rush it. Be prepared to bash out all the details. It takes a lot of time. But," cautions Prodanou, "it's the cheapest time you'll spend because physical changes in a partially or completely constructed space are far more expensive than corrections on paper."

UNDERSTANDING YOUR SPECIALTY

Obviously, if you are just starting out in the business, you might not have a clear idea of the type of work you will be doing. Still, most individuals begin with some sense—however vague—of where their photographic strengths are, and where, professionally, they plan to be in the future. Space needs, as well as necessary amenities, depend entirely on what you intend to shoot.

To begin with, it is crucial to establish for yourself exactly what it is that will be shot inside the intended studio. In this way, you can determine optimum size. After all, tabletop or fashion photographers do not need the space or sound structure required by photographers with automotive accounts.

Although still-life shooters don't have to be confined to cramped, unpleasant quarters, nor fashion photographers relegated to a structurally unsound location, it is essential to remember that a variation of the old adage is true: Bigger—and fancier—isn't necessarily better.

Your subject matter will dictate the structural criteria of your studio. As a preliminary guide, consider these options:

- Will the items you shoot be large or small, or ponderous or of no significant weight?
- Will the items you shoot be hand-carried, or will they have to be brought into the studio via a vehicle, an oversized elevator, or a pulley system?
- Will you be dependent on a staff, or will you be operating independently, with periodic freelance help?
- Will you be working alone or sharing quarters with another photographer? Will you both work at the same time? How much privacy do you each need?
- Do you intend to work more than one job at the same time?
- Will clients be spending a great deal of time in your studio, and will you need to be prepared to "entertain" visitors?
- Will you be doing any amount of "beauty" work, so that dressing rooms, makeup facilities, and styling resources will be necessary?
- Will your specialty require, for example, a kitchen, a carpentry shop, an above-average amount of electricity, an extensive darkroom, a merchandise room, or a garage?
- Will location be a primary factor in the success of your studio? In other words, do you need to be in a "photo district" or a high-rent area?
- Do you plan to live, as well as work, in your studio?
- Will you need an elaborate security system to protect such expensive items as jewelry or furs?

Clearly, this is not a complete list. It is simply intended to get you to start thinking about the specific details of your particular business.

DETERMINING A BUDGET

Certainly, you should not undertake the entire enterprise of establishing a studio without a realistic idea of your budget. Once you have figured out spatial needs, you should decide whether to rent or buy the space in which you will be working. Although purchasing a building—and anticipating appreciation and tax advantages—is clearly the more attractive option, a rental may be the sounder proposition for you if you have a fledgling business. This is particularly true if you can obtain a long term lease and the monthly rent is attractive. In this way, you might be able to save enough money after your monthly expenses for a future down payment on a property, should your business prosper.

Naturally, different locations will have different inherent costs. A building or loft space in New York City will most certainly be more expensive than the same type of property in Kansas City. In addition, within individual cities, less stylish neighborhoods might offer better opportunities.

Finally, for both renters and buyers, alternative spaces can be both cheaper and more creative. Today, many photographers work out of spaces that are by no means traditional. Clint Clemens's converted carriage house and Eric Meola's renovated truck garage are only two examples. Other options include abandoned churches that were purchased at rock-bottom prices and renovated. One photographer works out of a redesigned movie theater. In many cases, these locations are on the fringes of rundown neighborhoods that are about to be rediscovered and gentrified.

You have to carefully consider what your priorities are. Jay Silverman in Los Angeles, Eric Meola in New York, Clint Clemens in Boston, and Craig Stewart in Houston all had significant starting budgets. All were able to purchase the buildings they now operate in, and, when necessary, all could afford major structural overhauls. Each photographer had the additional luxury of hiring a designer and/or architect to guide and assist him throughout the project. Each shooter could afford to spend money on such design details as electronic windows, compressors, state-of-the-art climate-control units, and, in many cases, luxurious design details such as flooring and furniture.

On the other hand, when Chris Callis first went in search of his current studio space, he had very little money available. So he started out by renting a space he knew he could afford. Then, whenever the needed cash became available, he added to his existing "inventory." During slack periods, Callis built equipment and furniture for his studio. He saved untold amounts of money by doing most of the construction himself, or, in rare cases, by buying items secondhand. Callis's studio may not feature the ultimate in technological gadgetry, and the construction may have taken quite a bit of time, but the results suited him and his budget perfectly.

Although many of the photographers questioned would not provide specific figures (and keep in mind that figures quoted often reflect costs incurred up to ten years ago), prices range from a low of about $50,000 for Callis's studio to highs of approximately $350,000 for Silverman's studio and almost $450,000 for Stewart's.

Another factor you should take into account is living arrangements. Both Callis and Meola live in their studios. Here, too, the differences are quite striking. Callis's kitchen doubles as the studio facility. The photographer, who occupies one floor within a larger loft building, effectively lives in one room, his bedroom. Meola, on the other hand, completely occupies an entire three-story structure. His work environment accounts for two stories, and he and his wife live on the top floor.

Generally, budgetary considerations are not so cut and dried. More often, a budget will allow for only certain amenities. Decide what is most important to you now; a growth in your business volume will allow you to improve or add on later.

If you are just starting out, a number of hidden costs, though unseen initially, will seriously affect the final budget. Before allotting a specific amount for rental or purchase of space and the attendant design, think about essentials:

- Cost of basic equipment—those items without which you can't work
- Fire and burglar alarms that will protect your investments
- Insurance premiums, including health, liability, fire, and property insurance
- Lawyer fees
- Renovation costs if you are buying property
- Personalizations costs if you are renting space—walls might have to be put up or demolished, shelves and closets might have to be removed or inserted, and electrical wiring might need to be improved in order to provide the amount of wattage required
- Higher monthly electric bills (a result of the rewiring) and higher monthly telephone bills
- Office supplies, such as stationery and invoice forms
- Promotional expenses, a laminated portfolio (that can be left with agencies and art directors), and postage costs—all of which are necessary to make potential clients aware of you and to make your business a success
- Staff salaries—for a part-time bookkeeper and several freelance assistants initially, but a full complement of office and studio help as your work load increases

Perhaps Clint Clemens's advice is most telling: "An exceptional studio is certainly a fine thing, but for the smaller business or the beginning photographer, you are much better off renting studio space. Unless you are really good, a studio is nothing but a large overhead. The cost, including salaries, maintenance, insurance, heating, and electricity, can be extraordinarily stiff."

CHOOSING A LOCATION

Although most of the photographers interviewed found the buildings they now work in through real estate agents, in some instances the events leading up to the discovery were more fortuitous. J. Barry O'Rourke and Robert Kligge were renting a studio from a landlord whose reputation they trusted. When they heard that he was involved in a new renovation project, they investigated the site and leased their new studio from him. David Langley just happened to stumble on the empty building that is now his studio. He simply noticed the blank windows and dark interior. Very often the most extraordinary spaces have been found under similar circumstances.

Once you have decided on a location, investigate the services available to you. Will models and clients hesitate to come to see you, either because of distance or because a neighborhood appears to be unstable or downright dangerous? Will messengers be reluctant or unable to make prompt deliveries to your address? Will you be able to obtain essential photographic services—including rapid processing, propping, and equipment—easily?

CONSIDERING NEIGHBORHOOD OPTIONS

For some photographers a residential neighborhood is ideal—and relatively crime-free. Though Robert Wigington's studio is located close to Toronto's downtown area, it is on a quiet, tree-lined street in that city's heavily residential South Annex. His operation is small enough so that it is contained on one floor of a two-story house. The traffic into and out of the studio is slight and does not disturb his neighbors. Significantly, Wigington does not require a building that features structural elements generally found in commercial spaces—extensive shooting space or heavily reinforced flooring. Aside from suitable studio equipment and supplies, he needs only access to houseware suppliers and greengrocers. (If you opt for a residential neighborhood, you should check local zoning laws before signing a lease or purchasing a building.)

If your subjects are oversized and/or overweight, you will have no choice but to look for space in commercial or industrial neighborhoods. Defunct factories, warehouses, or garages will be the only accommodations with reinforced flooring as well as I-beam (colonnade) configurations that can support a building while maximizing the space. David Langley, Clint Clemens, Eric Meola, William and Clark Miller of WFM Studio, and George Simhoni and William McLeod of Westside Studio all decided on this solution. Interestingly, Clemens originally chose a more residential Boston neighborhood. But, says his architect Michael Prodanou, "He needed width in which to move his cameras, and height for overhead shots. It became increasingly clear to us that a commercial space was our only real choice."

In general, commercial space is a reasonable solution; however, some industrial neighborhoods offer few basic amenities, such as groceries and delis, resources needed by staff members.

If you are interested in exploring an industrial neighborhood, you should check local zoning laws and city ordinances before settling on a space. Eric Meola ran into a zoning problem after work on his studio had already begun. The project went through a number of delays and legal complications until the city, the neighborhood's other commercial tenants, and Meola were all satisfied.

Many photographers may prefer to be located within a "photo district." Obviously, this is not an alternative in cities that can't support an extensive photographic community, but, wherever possible, this option tends to provide the most extensive support services. Suppliers and processors are within easy reach, as are prop houses and other shooters.

These photographic enclaves often will develop because loft space abounds in one particular locale. Pioneer artists and photographers discover a neighborhood, move in when the area is still considered undesirable, and then create the momentum for gentrification. Eventually, the area becomes more chic, and rents skyrocket. For photographers who work here, however, the ambience and cachet can be quite beneficial.

OWNING OR LEASING

Your budget will undoubtedly be the primary motivating factor when you decide whether to buy or lease. But, in many cases, benefits can be derived from either option.

The team that put together Toronto's Westside Studio got a long-term lease and extensive space modifications because the landlord realized that a high-tech photographer's studio could easily revitalize a failing neighborhood and bring in a better class of tenant, who could be charged higher rents. On the other hand, Chris Callis was able to secure a long-term lease in a New York City neighborhood that was considered to be very *outre*. Because Callis's landlord never imagined that the locale would improve, he was happy to have found any tenant at all for the space.

One of the better reasons to purchase a studio is the investment boon of property ownership. Perhaps the best example of a successful investment is the Boston studio that Clint Clemens owns. When he first viewed the building he now owns on Newbury Street, the property and the neighborhood were both on the decline. But the renaissance of the city and its artists' neighborhoods have made his building, and the site it sits on, extremely valuable.

Of course, not everyone can claim such spectacular gains. Eric Meola moved into one of Manhattan's less desirable neighborhoods. Since he has been there, it has turned around significantly. Nevertheless, the neighborhood is still in flux. Jay

Silverman has also seen his area of Los Angeles change. Trendy restaurants have begun to open nearby; this is always a sure sign that gentrification—with its rising property values—is taking place.

Some owners have other reasons for purchasing property. Robert Wigington supplements his photographic income by renting out the ground floor of his studio. For others, such as the Millers of Chicago's WFM Studio, the security connected with ownership is the best reward. Sometimes the terms of ownership are just too good to pass up. David Langley was able to purchase his studio by obtaining financing from its previous owners. They were eager to sell to someone who would be as sentimentally attached to the building as they were. Although this is not a common occurrence and most photographers will never find such an emotional seller, these diverse examples prove that landlords can and do have surprises on their agendas.

CALCULATING SPACE REQUIREMENTS

To reiterate, here are some questions about space that you should consider:

- Will you need a big shooting stage?
- Will you need a reinforced floor?
- Will you need the accessibility of a ground-floor space, or will you be able to operate on a higher floor?
- Will you run a few jobs at once?
- Will you be sharing the space with other photographers? Will you all work at once, or will you alternate hours?
- Will your studio require a large staff in order to operate efficiently? Will staff members need individual offices or cubicles?
- Will you need additional rooms for outside talent, such as models, stylists, prop people, and carpenters?
- Do you intend to live and work in the same place?
- Will you depend on an elaborate darkroom setup, or will you send most of your material out for processing?

Whatever your answers, you should be aware enough of your needs so that you don't buy or rent more or less space than you actually need. Too much space will only increase your overhead—taking funds away from areas of real need—and force you to carry the cost of extra, unused space. Too little space is just as unprofitable. A cramped operation hampers both photographers and their staffs. In addition, clients tend to regard an uncomfortable layout as an example of a greater inefficiency within the business.

RECOGNIZING YOUR POTENTIAL

If everything is proceeding smoothly, at this point it is up to you to decide on the amount of technology necessary for your studio. A top-of-the-line lightbox with seemingly infinite directional permutations and an ultrasensitive remote control is wonderful, but the costs of both purchase and installation might be overly ambitious for your first studio. You can often use secondhand equipment with great success until profits warrant a more extravagant, high-tech purchase. It is far more important for you to have on hand the cameras, electronic flash units, lights, and accessories that will allow you to do the job well—no matter what shape they are in—than to have only a partial inventory of state-of-the-art equipment.

You should use this same consideration when determining the overall design of a space. Stylish furniture and attractive decor are certainly necessities, but a clean, well-run studio that is merely comfortable says more about the photographer who works within it than does a lavishly appointed, chaotic situation.

Client and model amenities are also necessary, but they don't have to be extravagant. If your plans call for a small space, having clean facilities, basic office supplies, and a pleasant—though not necessarily large—area from which to view the shoot is always welcome. In the same vein, the studio need not have an opulent kitchen and extravagantly catered meals. Always remember that the photographic result is what counts most here, not the environment in which the images are made.

FINDING AN ARCHITECT OR DESIGNER

First and foremost, you should consider only those individuals whose taste appeals to you. Don't hire someone with intentions that only approximate your own. Design philosophies vary, and it's very difficult to change a trained professional's inclinations.

Another important point is finding someone whom you can trust. You should feel comfortable when working with the individual because the client–designer relationship is, of necessity, a long one. Make sure that the designer is willing to expend as much energy on the project as you are.

As Ralph Gillis, the New York City-based architect who designed and renovated Eric Meola's award-winning studio, says, "Don't be concerned if the architect or designer you are interested in has never done a photographer's studio before. The most important consideration is: Is the individual interested in finding out what's unique about a particular business? They should be willing to put their preconceptions aside in order to listen to the client's requirements."

When Gillis and Meola first began working together, the architect "gathered a lot of information about the business before any plans were even considered." Gillis explains: "I questioned Eric about what was wrong with his old studio and what he'd like out of the new one. We evaluated Eric's studio and home lifestyle. Once we pinpointed those issues, we knew how to proceed."

Michael Prodanou, whose firm renovated Clint Clemens's Boston studio, agrees. "The rapport between architect or designer and client is immensely important," he says. "We got to know Clint and his wife well. We talked a lot about their needs before we got involved."

Jay Silverman and Michel Tcherevkoff circumvented this portion of the design process by working with individuals with whom they were friendly. Silverman, who is located in Los Angeles, hired Brad Donenfeld, a Philadelphia-based environmental designer and graphic artist, as his studio designer. "Jay and I have collaborated throughout our careers," says Donenfeld. "I had once been a client of Jay's, and over the past twelve years, we've often worked together. Therefore," notes the designer, "I had an intimate knowledge of what his needs were. In addition, I could tell him what his client needs were."

Yet, for all his familiarity with Silverman and his work, Donenfeld still sat down and talked to his client. "I had Jay make a list of what he needed: darkroom, finishing room, changing room," explains the designer. "We also looked at how his business was changing and what his business projections were. It was important to see how he wanted to position himself as a photographer."

Similarly, Tcherevkoff worked with New York City-based architect Michael Wolfe, a social acquaintance who already had a good sense of the photographer's style and design orientation. He was quick to discern the photographer's working needs as well. According to Tcherevkoff, "He took my needs and technically interpreted them."

Never forget, though, that the more specific you are—and the more aware of your business you become—the better your architect or designer's results will be. George Tracy, half of the husband-and-wife architectural and design team that coordinated the work on Craig Stewart's Houston studio, credits the success of that project to "Craig's ability to be unspecific about his design requirements while being extremely specific about his studio needs." And, says Tracy, "He gave us program requirements down to the square footage he desired." Of course, the Tracys were eager for Stewart's input. "Initially, we sat him down and asked him what he wanted to accomplish." Michael Prodanou remembers that "Clint knew exactly what he would be taking photographs of, and he'd also mapped out his anticipations for the future."

Finally, be sure that the individual you are planning to work with will be able to see the job to its completion, which could mean an extensive time investment on his or her part. "You need a lot of time to plan and construct a really good studio," warns Michael Prodanou.

Every project documented here took a minimum of six months. In some cases, such as that of Eric Meola's studio, just locating a suitable building took almost two years, even with the aid of architect Ralph Gillis.

Because of the many variables involved in planning, finding, designing, constructing, or renovating a studio, each project will have its own specifics. These involve location (neighborhood and city), and construction and labor costs through the duration of the project.

WORKING INDEPENDENTLY

Don't be discouraged if your budget can't include a professional designer or architect. There are viable options. Working on your own may be more difficult and time-consuming, but be assured that the results can be just as gratifying.

Chris Callis designed and built his own space; as a result, he is now the owner of a unique studio, an indicator of the good taste and refined design sense of its owner. It is also a sign to all of Callis's clients that he will do a superb job no matter what his budget constraints.

David Langley did not have a large budget initially to pour into his New York City studio's design. Although his business is now thriving, the photographer prefers to keep his studio sparse; he feels that he works more efficiently in a big, raw environment. In this way, he never has to worry about scarring surfaces or ruining the floor or walls. William and Clark Miller of WFM Studio have the same philosophy about their Chicago space.

Some photographers who are more design-oriented find that their volume of business can't yet support a designer's fees. When faced with the problem of putting together his own studio, Toronto-based Robert Wigington looked carefully at other food photographers' studios. Armed with the design ideas he saw, he then interviewed those individuals who would be spending a great deal of time in the studio's kitchen: the food stylists. In this way, Wigington was able to ascertain a kitchen's design specifics exactly (see page 97 for a discussion of kitchen design).

WORKING WITH OR WITHOUT CONTRACTORS

As anyone who has ever been involved in renovation knows, dealing with contractors, though necessary, is sometimes tricky. The best reason to hire contractors is to free yourself of all the detailed work involved in construction or renovation. Professional contractors will obtain and traffic all necessary building supplies, as well as oversee the minute-by-minute work that is being done on your space. Unfortunately, in many cases, contractors' inattention to small details is often the cause of major delays and cost overruns. When the contractor involved in the design of J. Barry O'Rourke and Robert Kligge's New York City studio could not complete the job to the photographers' satisfaction, Kligge took over the task himself. Although this meant that he could not devote as much time to his photography, the studio was completed within months.

If, like Chris Callis and Robert Wigington, you handle the job yourself, a contractor might be an unnecessary consideration. Yet, even for small jobs, the rule of thumb is: Whenever another party—aside from the designer or architect, whom you should trust—is involved, extra vigilance can only be beneficial.

Clint Clemens and Michael Prodanou, Jay Silverman and Brad Donenfeld, and George Simhoni and William McLeod all say that frequent visits to the studio site were a crucial factor in the satisfactory completion of their projects. McLeod and Simhoni, as well as Silverman and Donenfeld, visited their respective sites every single day, and on some days—when a complex procedure was being carried out—they visited a few times during the course of the day. Often photographer and designer, or the photographic partners, visited at the same time. This solid, and very regular, presence generated undeniably positive results.

LIGHTING DESIGN AND POWER CONSIDERATIONS

According to Brian Heller, who designed Clint Clemens's custom light banks, "Putting together an in-studio lighting system is actually a collaboration of cost and need." Heller explains: "Sometimes a studio's budget will determine how big a unit, or how many banks, they can afford." But, the lighting designer says, "The size of the subject matter, such as the predominance of cars that Clint shoots, dictates the proportions, and therefore the cost, of the bank." Other factors that determine the cost of a light bank: the placement of the unit, either positioned on the floor or suspended from the ceiling; the type of light generated, such as strobe lighting; and the maximum amount of watt/seconds the unit can put out.

A studio's size also has to be factored into the equation. "A bank that is too big for the space will overilluminate the set," says Heller, "and a unit that is too small won't satisfactorily light the desired area." The maneuverability of floor units will also be affected by limited studio space. Also, the studio's ceiling should be able to support a suspended bank, or, if the unit is on the floor, it shouldn't be heavier than what the building can tolerate. A movable unit should also be rigid enough to survive a lot of activity.

Normal studio wiring should be sufficient to power a large strobe unit, says Heller, "because modern systems are all capacitor-driven, which means that they can store electricity." But, Heller cautions, "A good working studio needs at minimum a 200-amp service; larger, as one's budget permits." The cost of wiring a studio in this way can be high. When Heller reserviced his Providence, Rhode Island, studio (which houses his business, Atlantic Lighting and Grip), he spent $15,000. Nevertheless, rewiring in order to add to already existing amperage will not defray costs, he points out. "It doesn't matter what you've got," explains Heller. "Once you put in a new service, the electrician has to start from scratch." Costs will vary, depending on the age of the building, the floor you are on, the code requirements for your region, and the construction costs in your area. Before you consider rewiring, Heller suggests that you consult *Building Construction Cost Data*, a reference book published in 1985 by R.W. Means. Updated annually, it is broken down by region and building code data, and covers every type of building cost, including plumbing and electrical work.

Heller's company deals primarily with the movie industry, but he has worked with photographers, too. The following are his suggestions for still shooters:

- A 4 × 4-foot or 6 × 6-foot bank is generally all that a tabletop shooter will need.
- A studio's lighting should answer the problem of trying to simulate sunlight.
- Studio space should have running water and compressed air. A drain in the floor would be admirable.

Other photographers have come up with different solutions. For example, Craig Stewart, whose studio is wired for 525 amps, bought a state-of-the-art infrared controlled lighting system from Broncolor. The unit, one of just two in the United States, moves on a double rail grid, is suspended over the shooting cove, and covers the entire stage. Everything is controlled by a single hand unit. To augment his power outlets, Clint Clemens thought of a unique solution. He designed a movable light cart that can be wheeled anywhere within the studio and holds fourteen Norman 2000D power packs. It can generate up to 40,000 watt/seconds of power, and the units need only one 150-amp plug to service them.

THE LIGHT FACTOR

Whether you want an abundance of daylight or darkness near the shooting stage is more a matter of taste and habit than professional need. If you prefer to shoot under ambient-light conditions and regard studio lighting as the less desirable alternative, a studio with numerous windows or a skylight is the only solution. You should keep in mind that the direction a studio's windows face will affect the quality and amount of light received. There is no direct sunlight at all with northern exposures. Furthermore, eastern exposures get only morning light, western exposures get afternoon light, and southern exposures get light all day long. Although this might be a boon to the natural light enthusiast, it can heat up a studio space considerably. Michel Tcherevkoff's New York City studio faces south, for instance. "It's great in the winter," he says, "but in the summer, our air conditioning costs skyrocket."

If you are satisfied only if you can control the degree and intensity of the illumination your subject receives, a darker studio with hardly any direct sunlight is preferable. If, on the other hand, you don't want natural light on or near the shooting stage, you wouldn't want to work in a dark, cavelike setting. For you, then, an outer bank of windows with an interior shooting stage is a better choice.

Get to know your personal preferences, and choose a site accordingly.

THE FLOOR FACTOR

As stated earlier, subject weight and size will determine how necessary increased floor stability should be. At one end of the scale, for photographers with large [illegible] subjects, a poured concrete or reinforced floor is imperative. But you should remember that the cost of pouring and reinforcing a concrete floor can be prohibitive. Reconfiguring the columns in a space is even more expensive and time-consuming. These are not renovations to be undertaken without a great deal of consideration.

If you find yourself in need of a reinforced floor, you might also discover a need for drains in the floor, because large-scale objects often must be washed before they are to be photographed.

Oversized subjects are often quite hefty as well. Ground-floor entry might be important. If the subject matter is only moderately heavy or large and the studio is on something other than the ground floor, consider whether the freight elevator can support your subjects.

Even if these considerations do not come into play, an old building with unsteady flooring can still cause problems. Aged wooden planking will often become loose after years of use. The unsteadiness caused by traffic might seem imperceptible, but if long exposures and razor-sharp results are crucial to your work, the slightest in-studio movement during a shoot can drastically blur your subject. This does not mean that old buildings are not suitable studio locales; many have been soundly constructed and would fulfill your needs ideally. But it might be worthwhile, when you consider a noticeably rundown location, to think about bringing in an outside consultant for advice.

PLUMBING

No studio, no matter how sparse, should be without running water. Even if the studio is nothing more than a "bare bones" type of space, the restroom should be kept clean, with an ample supply of tissues and toilet paper. Poor maintenance makes a business look amateurish.

The amount of human traffic in and through a studio should be considered when plumbing needs are evaluated. A busy space, for example, should have more than one bathroom. And, if models are part of the daily business, makeup mirrors, changing areas, and showering facilities are vital. Without doubt, a fancy bathroom makes a good impression, but not if it is more opulent than the rest of the studio space. A clean, neat, and well-supplied room is far more important.

SECURITY NEEDS

The neighborhood the studio is in, as well as the amount of equipment you own and the type of subjects you shoot, all will determine how much security you need.

Some photographers are satisfied with a door that can be buzzed open and an intercom. Others, such as Clint Clemens and Jay Silverman, have had their entire studios wired against break-ins. Clemens's system can be activated at the door of the studio; the last person to leave simply flips a switch before locking the door.

Many shooters, such as Michel Tcherevkoff and William and Clark Miller, have small safes for storing their hardware. Even if you can't afford an elaborate system, you should still consider securing your most important assets: your equipment. A secondhand safe is a smart, economical alternative.

RECEPTION AREAS

For most photographers, a space, no matter how small, that shields them from unwanted visitors and keeps undesired guests out of the studio is a necessity. In general, photographers use reception areas to display examples of their best work. Some, such as Clint Clemens, have set up elaborate displays of their photographs; these exhibits give waiting visitors something to look at until they are received. Michel Tcherevkoff uses his reception room to display the many professional awards and citations he has accumulated over the years.

The presence of chairs in your reception area depends to some degree on whether you intend to keep people waiting. Tcherevkoff explains that he *prefers* to have people wait a few seconds so that they can study his display.

A reception area can also be part of your studio's security system, if you feel you need one. In many cases, the door leading into a studio's interior is kept locked and can only be opened by staffers.

Sometimes, though, such as in Chris Callis's studio, the space isn't big enough for a separate reception area. Instead, a counter with a receptionist is situated in an alcove opposite the entryway. Although the arriving visitors can see the shooting stage, they aren't immediately directed onto it.

CONFERENCE ROOMS

All photographers need a relaxed place where they and the client can sit and talk. Of the eleven photographers featured here, each has solved this problem in his own personal way.

Clint Clemens has built a carpeted balcony area that looks out over the shooting stage, with comfortable couches and chairs, as well as plants and a small bar, giving the area the feeling of a living room. Robert Wigington also sees clients in a living room setting. His conference area is at the back of the studio, and has couches, chairs, a cocktail table, and an abundance of plants.

Chris Callis's studio contains no specific conference room. Clients and visitors are entertained either at the counter in the kitchen, which gives the proceedings a homey feeling, or at the movable table and chair set that the photographer designed. This unit—consisting of four stools and a table—rests on wheels and can be rolled into any corner of Callis's space. Sitting here lends a relaxed, almost "funky" feeling to the discussion.

David Langley meets clients at his in-studio bar. The photographer purchased the complete interior of a pub that was going out of business. He transported all of the fixtures, including the taps, bar rails, overhead lights, counter, and mirrors, to his studio and then faithfully reproduced the setting. It's a whimsical alternative to a more formal conference room, and the elaborate, well-cared-for bar is a marked contrast to the rest of Langley's very raw space.

J. Barry O'Rourke and Robert Kligge see clients in their kitchen. This part of their studio is actually a large space off the shooting stages, set up against one wall, with counters and a large table in the middle of the space. The photographers discuss much of the studio's business here.

Eric Meola, Craig Stewart, and Michel Tcherevkoff take care of business in their offices. Meola's office is a formal space on the mezzanine level of his studio, where, besides the regular office supplies, he keeps a slide projector within easy reach so he can refer his clients to previous jobs. Tcherevkoff's office is less formal, yet all of his transparencies and business records are also within easy reach, as is a light table. A long banquette against one wall of the office takes care of seating. Stewart's office is located at the front of his space. It is completely enclosed, private, and, like the rest of his studio, elaborately designed.

Jay Silverman, William and Clark Miller, William MacLeod, and George Simhoni all have formal conference rooms. Standard items within these rooms include large formal tables that are able to seat at least eight people, video equipment, a television monitor, and, often, a bar or refrigerator for beverages.

Photographers' conference spaces have a great deal to do with personal taste and the type of business personality they want to project to current and potential clients. Neither a formal setting, nor a unique alternative are, in themselves, important. Like expensive design, a conference room is just icing on the professionals' cake.

OFFICES

For many photographers, a formal office is a luxury. For others, it serves as a private space into which they can withdraw. Whether you have a private office or not depends primarily on what your priorities are and how much traffic your studio gets.

For those photographers with larger staffs, extra offices to accommodate certain workers might be necessary. Although photographic assistants don't usually require their own offices, studio managers, bookkeepers, accountants, and representatives might need a quiet place to work, removed from the bustle of the shooting stage. Discuss the possibilities with your staff, if necessary. Jay Silverman points out that it's often a staff that makes or breaks a studio's professional reputation.

KITCHENS

Whether photographers choose to specialize in food photography of prefer instead to remain generalists and accept an assortment of assignments, some type of kitchen setup is necessary. The facilities don't have to be fancy, nor the space large. Nevertheless, photographers, staffers, art directors, and clients all agree that a suitable kitchen area is a necessity.

For photographers whose work has little to do with food, a full kitchen—with the requisite appliances—might be a luxury. For those just starting out, whose studio space is limited, counter space, a table, a small refrigerator, and running water are absolute musts. Although fancy catered meals are hardly necessary, attending to clients' gastronomic needs is an excellent business practice. With this equipment, you can supply beverages and serve takeout meals at any time. Larger studios with bigger budgets should have fuller kitchens.

Many photographers prefer to serve catered lunches and even dinners during extended shoots. Diane Iocolano, a New York City-based caterer who often works with Chris Callis, says, "If you are going through the expense of serving a catered meal, have your own dishes and silver, as opposed to paper plates and plastic utensils. In the same vein, it's always nicer to have platters rather than aluminum tins." And, Iocolano recommends, "If you do buy platters, make sure to have an assortment of sizes and pieces."

In general, a caterer always arrives at a photographer's studio with the meal fully cooked. As a result, notes Iocolano, "You don't need an extensive kitchen area. But a decent amount of counter space plus a table to set the food up on is imperative." Iocolano prefers to serve meals at room temperature. Consequently, she feels that "a stove is not necessary, although it's a very nice feature." There are times during the year though when hot food may be appropriate. "During the winter, people like to have hot soup," the caterer says. "Therefore, if you don't have a stove, at least buy a hot plate."

Iocolano adds that a refrigerator "with a shelf that isn't filled with film" should be available "for storing beverages." Finally, she notes, "If your studio has no kitchen, at least have a place off the shooting stage where a meal can be set up. Otherwise, it's hardly worth the catering expense."

If food photography is a significant part of your business, more equipment is required. "A lot of photographers can barely afford anything at the beginning," says Kate Bush, a Toronto-based food stylist. "They start out with a refrigerator, one counter, and a stove. Often the running water will be outside." Obviously, this is far from ideal. Olga Truchan, who also styles food in Toronto, notes, "The kitchen can't be too far from the set. It's important to be able to hear sounds from the set so you can give instructions or take directions from the photographer without leaving the food as it cooks."

Both Truchan and Bush stress the need for a separate kitchen space, however. To begin with, if the photographer and food stylist have to work in the same area, one will inevitably get in the other's way. More significant, though, says Bush, "If you have to stop or turn off the overhead lights so the photographer can check his strobe setup, it's bound to interfere with the cooking. After all, in preparing or decorating certain dishes, a few seconds can make all the difference." In addition, Truchan says, "good ventilation is imperative. Otherwise, you can ruin the air for both the photographer and the kitchen staff."

Both food stylists also emphasize the importance of counter space. Bush prefers a sink with its own counter, and a stove with counter space on either side. And, she notes, "Ten feet of working area is ideal." Truchan, however, says "Counter space is crucial. I'm partial to long, narrow galley kitchens. I find that they work better than a square setup with a work island in the middle." When working in a long, narrow kitchen, Truchan can organize all her equipment and afterward lay out all the cooked articles. A small work triangle, with a sink at one point, a stove at the next point, and a refrigerator at the third point is another preferred option. Still, whichever configuration she uses, Truchan says, counter height is paramount. "Too low is difficult on the back," she says.

But the two women agree that good lighting is essential. "Ideally, the kitchen light should match the amount of light used to illuminate the picture," advises Truchan. In this way, the stylist and photographer can ensure that food tones and textures will appear the same in the kitchen and on the set. "Natural light is infinitely preferable," says Bush. "The kitchen should be very bright. In fact, a window is glorious," she notes.

Bush prefers a gas range and "old stoves with an oven that actually works." Truchan looks for "a good working oven with stable and reliable temperature controls." Also, for those really interested in food photography, a freezer is necessary. Truchan stresses the need for one large refrigerator or two regular ones.

The best food stylists bring along many of the cooking utensils that are the tools of their trade. "I have a kit that contains everything I need for cutting, tying, twisting, browning, and burning," explains Bush. She also brings along boxes with bowls, pans, and pots because she is familiar with the speed at which her kitchenware cooks. "I do prefer, though, if the studio kitchen has knives, forks, spoons—both large and small—spatulas, whisks, a mixer, and a basic pastry container," says Bush. Certain appliances are obviously luxuries. "A microwave and food processor are taking it to the ultimate," notes Bush. "If either or both are there, it is useful, but certainly not necessary." One utensil no kitchen should be without, Bush points out, is "a giant garbage can. The best kind are on a platform with wheels, so the food stylists can move it along as they work."

There is one point that both stylists heartily agree on. "The client area should never be inside the kitchen," cautions Truchan. "People tend to leave dirty coffee cups around, and worse, nibble at the food that is being prepared for the shoot."

STORAGE

All photographers, no matter how small their business, need to be able to keep hardware, transparencies, company records, and studio supplies out of sight. Some shooters, such as Michel Tcherevkoff and Eric Meola, have had elaborate cabinetry installed into their studios for this purpose. Others have made entire rooms available at the back of their spaces for props, rolls of seamless, and other background materials. In specific cases, such as at WFM Studio, where William and Clark Miller specialize in catalog work, entire segments of the studio are devoted to trafficking and storing incoming and outgoing merchandise. If your space is small, carefully weed out extraneous items, and store only those items that are critical for a shoot.

SMALL SPACES

Michael Wolfe, the New York City-based architect who created Michel Tcherevkoff's studio, pinpoints the problem inherent in designing a small work area. "It is imperative to free up as much space as possible," he points out. The solution? "We stacked everything up. We doubled up on every inch of space around areas like the darkroom and office so that we could maximize the shooting space," Wolfe says.

Indeed, Tcherevkoff's office is actually a 16 × 13-foot loft space from which he can see the rest of the studio from three sides. The loft was built specifically to take advantage of the studio's 25-foot-high ceiling. The area underneath the office was given over entirely to storage, after a warren of closets and cabinets had been built there. The storage options range from small shelving, for cleaning supplies, to a two-ton safe for equipment. "We didn't care that storage was low," says Wolfe. "Michel preferred to have the psychological privacy of his own office, with visual command of what was going on."

Other storage needs have been answered just as cleverly. A long radiator that extended along the studio's southern wall and abutted into the shooting area has been subtly disguised by waist-high cabinetry. "We knew that the studio had no room for an equipment cart," notes Wolfe. "This gave Michel counter space on which to keep tools and equipment during a shoot. The cabinets also allow the photographer quick access to other materials while he is working."

To keep the long line of the shooting bays intact, Wolfe placed the studio's kitchen next to the office but away from the set. A work island in the middle of this space also contains cabinetry for storage. "This portion of the studio was designed as a multi-function space," says Wolfe. "It serves as a conference area if necessary, a staff meeting area, and a holding tank for clients. And," adds Wolfe, "clients like the idea of not being shut away in a separate room. From here, they can see the shoot without getting underfoot."

When asked to sum up the major design concerns of a small studio, Wolfe says, "Studio equipment should be as close to the shooting bay as possible. Time is often a crucial factor in a shoot, so everything should be accessible from the floor. And, of course, every inch of space should be utilized."

CYCLORAMAS

For those unfamiliar with the term, this is simply a curved white wall that generates no shadows. Many photographers depend on a cyclorama to provide an illusion of endless background.

The costs involved in constructing a cyclorama can be considerable, however. Eric Meola had his cyclorama suspended from his building's ceiling, so that it would not crack as the structure settled into the damp New York City soil.

The angle of the cyclorama's curve is crucial to its success. Clint Clemens used a piece of paper to ascertain the exact angle of his. By aiming a floodlight at the piece of paper and bending it until absolutely no shadows were visible, he determined the optimum curvature for his use.

David Langley, on the other hand, doesn't believe in elaborate measures. He uses pieces of white seamless paper, which he sets up before each shoot. When the job is finished, the paper is discarded, so that each new job requires a complete re-angling.

COLOR CHOICES

According to Maria Tracy, who designed the interior of Craig Stewart's Houston studio, "The most critical factor in a photographer's studio is his usage of light and how it affects the product he's shooting. Therefore, the colors that are closest to the shooting stage are the most crucial choices."

Stewart's studio is a striking mix of black, gray, and red. Tracy points out that the red details have been kept far away from the shooting bays because the strength of the color could reflect onto the subject and alter its natural tones. "I would recommend black paint on the ceiling to guard against reflectance," she says. "But the paint should have a matte surface." Many photographers prefer white studios because the neutral tones can't detract from their controlled lighting setups.

Tracy suggests that, regardless of color, photographers should carefully check the luminosity of the paint. This means that the pigment should not be too glossy, for it will cause light to bounce uncontrollably. "Some paints have luminosity factors as high as 50 to 75 percent," she notes.

Careful use of color can also enlarge a space and subtly direct traffic patterns. Tracy used the gray and black hues of Craig's studio in just such a manner. "As the planes of the recessed walls receded," she says, "we had them painted with darker shades of gray until they faded back to black."

Brad Donenfeld kept much of this in mind when he worked on Jay Silverman's space. "Since Jay's forte is dealing with people, we wanted the space to be just as interactive as the photographer," he says. Donenfeld installed "soft gray Berber carpeting and a similar-toned sofa" that conformed to the studio's curved walls. "This provided the area with a sense of intimacy and warmth," he says.

Clearly, color choices will mirror photographers' corporate sensibilities. Chris Callis's pastel-toned space reflects his own relaxed working style, while Stewart's bolder approach signals a more exotic image. Most photographers opt for warm, unobtrusive colors, and many simply stick to white, a safe and pragmatic alternative.

FINAL CONSIDERATIONS

Commercial studios, aside from having to be workable for photographers and their staffs, also have to make an impression on the art directors who spend time there. A good—and lasting—impression can go a long way toward renewed bookings.

Rich Croland, an art director at BBD&O in New York City, has worked on such national accounts as HBO and Polaroid. He says, "It's best to keep the client out of the studio and only show him the finished product." But for the art director who represents the client and can often spend days at a shoot, you should have basic supplies available. "Lack of art supplies is extremely frustrating," Croland says. "Pads, pens, and a little area in which to revise layouts should be handy. Privacy for phone calling or talking to the client should also be available," he notes.

What does Croland prefer to have on hand for art directors? "I'd like them to be near any supplies they need, such as bulbs or tools. I hate to see a photographer waste costly time by leaving the set in search of mundane supplies." On the issue of having a conference room, Croland has his own opinions. "It impresses clients if you have one, but a meeting area with a table and chairs is sufficient," he says. "In fact, this space can also be used for presentations or for lunch."

Sometimes an established or high-tech studio will have amenities specifically for art directors. Westside Studio in Toronto has pinball machines and a private sitting area, and Langley allows art directors free reign at his bar. Croland recalls a studio that had "a library with books. It was very nice because the shoot was so tedious. Another space had a pool table," he recalls. "It's cool, certainly, but definitely not necessary." Parry Merkley, whose campaign for American Express recently netted his ad agency, Ogilvy & Mather, a large number of awards, recalls a studio that was supplied with a jacuzzi. But, he says, "It makes me uncomfortable when a studio is too slick." His criteria are as basic as Croland's. "All I'm really looking for is a private place to receive calls, or a studio manager who can take my calls," he says. An amenity is fine, Merkley notes, "if it's something the photographer and his staff uses as well. But if it's acquired just to impress the art director, I say, 'Pay more attention to your work.' "

A highly stylized studio, though impressive, is not of utmost importance. The photographers whose studios are featured here are successful, not because of the uniqueness of their spaces, but because the work they produce is creative and professional. However, Clint Clemens cautions, "An exceptional studio is certainly a fine thing, but for the smaller business or the beginning photographer, you are much better off renting studio space," he says. "Unless you are really good, a studio is nothing but a large overhead. The cost, including staff salaries, maintenance, insurance, heating, and electricity, can be extraordinarily stiff." Merkley goes a bit further. "When I hire someone, I know why I'm using them," he notes. "The work is what should impress, not the dazzling studio." Eric Meola concurs. "What it all comes down to is the making of photographs," he explains, "not work spaces. A great studio doesn't always guarantee terrific pictures."

INDEX